Trauma and Post-traumatic
Stress Disorder

Titles in the *Stress Counselling* Series

STRESS COUNSELLING SERIES

TRAUMA AND POST-TRAUMATIC STRESS DISORDER

Edited by
Michael J. Scott and Stephen Palmer

CASSELL

Cassell

Wellington House
125 Strand
London WC2R 0BB

370 Lexington Avenue
New York
NY 10017-6550

Collection first published 2000

British Library Cataloguing-in-Publication Data
A catalogue record for this book is available from the British Library.

ISBN 0–304–70543–8 (hardback)
0–304–70544–6 (paperback)

Typeset by Rowland Phototypesetting Ltd,
Bury St Edmunds, Suffolk
Printed and bound in Great Britain by
Redwood Books, Trowbridge, Wiltshire

To Geraldine for her patience. (MS)

To my clients and the millions of others who have
suffered from traumatic stress. (SP)

Contents

Note on the Editors

Michael Scott PhD is a chartered counselling psychologist and an Honorary Research Fellow in the Department of Psychology, University of Manchester. He is a consultant to ICI, Merseyside Police and a number of other large organizations and works part-time in the National Health Service. He is the author of six books including *Counselling for Post Traumatic Stress Disorder* (with Stephen Stradling, 2nd edition, Sage) and numerous papers including 'Compliance with exposure treatment', in the *Journal of Traumatic Stress*, and 'PTSD without the trauma', in the *British Journal of Clinical Psychology* and book chapters including 'Stress compensation', in *Industrial Diseases Litigation* (Sweet and Maxwell).

Stephen Palmer PhD is a chartered psychologist (counselling and health), a UKCP-registered cognitive-behavioural psychotherapist and a Diplomate of the American Academy of Experts in Traumatic Stress. He is Director of the Centre for Stress Management and the Centre for Multimodal Therapy in London, an Honorary Visiting Professor at City University, and Honorary Senior Research Fellow at the University of Manchester. He is a Fellow of the British Association for Counselling and the Royal Society of Arts. He is currently President of the Institute of Health Promotion and Education and Vice-President of the International Stress Management Association UK. He has written and edited sixteen books including *Integrative Stress Counselling* (with Pat Milner, Cassell) and edits three book series including *Stress Counselling* (Cassell).

Series Foreword

The main aim of this series is to focus on different approaches to stress counselling and management. It is intended that the books will link theory and research to the practice of stress counselling and stress management. Leading counselling, clinical, health and occupational psychologists, biologists, counsellors and psychotherapists will report on their work, focusing on individual, group and organizational interventions.

The books will interest both undergraduate and postgraduate students as well as experienced practitioners in the helping professions, in particular those who work in the fields of counselling, psychology, psychotherapy, sociology and mental and occupational health.

This book, *Trauma and Post-traumatic Stress Disorder*, is the fourth book in the *Stress Counselling* series. It focuses specifically on traumatic stress and provides information on assessment and treatment as well as on 'helping the helpers'. It includes chapters written by well-known researchers and practitioners working in the field of trauma such as Donald Meichenbaum and Michael Scott. Each chapter includes four suggested discussion issues to help initiate further reflection (see Appendix). Trainers and lecturers may also find suitable essay subjects in some of the discussion issues.

Stephen Palmer
Centre for Stress Management, London

Acknowledgements

Chapter 1 by Matthew J. Friedman was first published in *Community Mental Health Journal*, **32**(2): 173–89 (April 1996), and is published with permission.

Chapter 2 by Michael J. Scott is based upon an early draft of the introductory chapter of the second edition of *Counselling for Post-traumatic Stress Disorder* (in press), reproduced with permission of Sage Publications. In addition Weiss's elaboration of the seventeen PTSD symptoms is reproduced with permission of Guilford Press.

Chapter 3 by Michael J. Scott was first published in *Counselling for Post-traumatic Stress Disorder*, (1992), pp. 185–7, reproduced with permission of Sage Publications.

Chapter 4 by Michael J. Scott was first published in *Counselling Psychology Quarterly* (1997), **10**, 125–37, reproduced with permission of the Editor.

Chapter 5 by Michael F. Hoyt was first published in *Constructive Therapies*, Vol. 2 (1996), pp. 124–47, reproduced with permission from Guilford Press.

Chapter 6 by Michael J. Scott and Stephen G. Stradling was first published in *Brief Group Counselling – Integrating Individual and Group Cognitive-Behavioural Approaches* (1998), pp. 101–37, reproduced with permission from John Wiley & Sons.

Chapter 7 by Donald Meichenbaum was first published in *Treating Post-traumatic Stress Disorder* (1994), pp. 448–51, reproduced by permission of John Wiley & Sons.

Chapter 8 by Donald Meichenbaum was first published in *Treating Post-traumatic Stress Disorder* (1994), pp. 330–9, reproduced by permission of John Wiley & Sons.

Chapter 9 by Donald Meichenbaum was first published in *Treating Post-traumatic Stress Disorder* (1994), pp. 536–9, reproduced by permission of John Wiley & Sons.

Chapter 10 by Donald Meichenbaum was first published in *Treating Post-traumatic Stress Disorder* (1994), pp. 278–81, reproduced by permission of John Wiley & Sons.

Chapter 11 by Frank M. Ochberg was first published in the *Journal of Traumatic Stress* **9**, 473–80 (1996), and reproduced with permission of Professor Ochberg.

Chapter 13 by Gerald M. Rosen, Jeffrey M. Lohr, Richard J. McNally and James D. Herbert was first published in *Behavioural and Cognitive Psychotherapy*, **26**, 99–101 (1998), and reproduced with permission of Gerald M. Rosen.

The editors and publisher would like to thank the various authors and publishers for granting permission to reproduce the above material.

Every effort has been made to trace all copyright holders, but if any parties have been inadvertently overlooked, we shall be pleased to include an acknowledgement at the next opportunity.

Introduction

Michael J. Scott and Stephen Palmer

Much of human distress is a reaction to extreme stress. It is commonplace that traumas such as divorce or loss of job can usher in depression. But not everyone experiencing such events becomes depressed. There is, then, something about the fit between the event and the person that leads to depression. In a similar way there is another class of more extreme events, which, depending on particular features of the individual, can lead to Post-traumatic Stress Disorder (PTSD). Many of the soldiers returning from the trenches of the First World War were described as 'shell-shocked' and would now be described as suffering from PTSD, in that they suffered intrusive recollections of the events, perhaps in the form of nightmares, avoided anything reminiscent of battle, such as conflicts, and suffered disordered arousal symptoms such as heightened vigilance, sleep disturbance and irritability. PTSD is characterized by the three symptom clusters of intrusion, avoidance and disordered arousal. In the United Kingdom there are probably many more cases of PTSD from car accidents than from combat or disasters such as those that grab the newspaper headlines. It was not until the 1980s version of the *Diagnostic and Statistical Manual* published by the American Psychiatric Association that PTSD first entered the diagnostic nomenclature. This was a landmark development in that it implied that those debilitated by trauma were not simply 'weak' but that the nature of the event had been taken seriously into account. However, it left unanswered the question of why some were debilitated and others unaffected. According to Kessler *et al*. (1995) 75% of the population have experienced an extreme trauma but only 7.5% have suffered PTSD.

Since 1980 the only clear vulnerability factor for PTSD to emerge is that those who have a previous psychiatric history are more likely to suffer from PTSD in the wake of a trauma and further recovery is more problematic for this sub-population. But this does not help a great deal, as most of those with PTSD do not have any previous psychiatric history. It has also become apparent that traumas where there is no personal intent to harm produce less severe PTSD than events such as assaults where personal agency is involved. The recovery of clients with PTSD is affected by the degree of support that they receive, and in this connection they are similar to depressed clients. It is also the case that the more severely traumatized the client is, the less likely he or she is to recover from PTSD. Most of those that do have PTSD have recovered by six to nine months post trauma, and relatively few recover in the succeeding 9 to 24 months and proportionately very few after that. There is then a window of opportunity of natural recovery that is probably no greater than two years. A significant minority of those suffering from PTSD, about 33% according to Kessler *et al.* (1995), continue to be debilitated in the long term.

It is possible to summarize somewhat crudely our current knowledge of Post Traumatic Stress Disorder using the mathematical concept of multiple regression, in which if one wanted to predict the client's severity of post-traumatic stress symptoms (the dependent variable), the following independent variables would partially predict the score:

- current severity of PTSD symptoms 15%
- severity of physical injury 5%
- previous psychiatric history 5%
- time that has elapsed since trauma 10%
- social support 7%.

This means that in our present state of knowledge it is only possible to account for about 45% of subsequent distress. Though one could quibble about the precise percentages accounted for by each of the independent variables, the exercise does illustrate that our understanding of PTSD is incomplete. It is not therefore surprising that Kessler *et al.* (1995) found that whether PTSD clients had treatment or not made only a slight difference to outcome, speeding up the recovery process. Thus if one were to include a further independent variable, routine treatment, into a multiple regression this might explain a further 10% to 20%, explaining 55% to 65% of the variance in total.

But the hard-pressed mental health professional does not have the luxury of waiting until there is a full understanding of the condition before offering help. There is a call to action, and what follows in this volume is a guide to best practice. At the same time the editors have striven to alert the reader to the types of consideration, which would protect them from dogmatism about the particular cognitive-behavioural approaches outlined and enable them to be critically alert to new developments.

In Chapter 1 Matthew J. Friedman, Professor of Psychiatry and Pharmacology, Dartmouth Medical School, provides a succinct and cogent overview of the field of PTSD. Friedman suggests that whilst PTSD is easy to diagnose if the client discloses the extreme trauma, clients are often not asked about traumas in their lives and may be reluctant to discuss them because of emotional pain involved. He then goes on to discuss the various psychological and pharmacological treatments for the condition, suggesting that while no particular drug has emerged as the definitive treatment for the condition, medication is clearly useful for symptom relief, making it possible for clients to participate in therapy. Friedman then highlights three sets of circumstances in which counsellors working with traumatized clients can become traumatized themselves. Finally he looks at four controversies in the trauma field: advocacy, eye movement desensitization reprocessing, the false memory syndrome and complex PTSD. In Box 1.1 at the end of his chapter he reproduces the DSM-IV criteria for

PTSD (American Psychiatric Association, 1994). The criteria are not self-explanatory and in Chapter 2 Scott presents an understanding of the PTSD symptoms that has been distilled by Daniel Weiss, at the Department of Psychiatry, University of California, and used as a basis for conducting a structured clinical interview. This is followed by a review of the most popularly used PTSD self-report measures, and finally Scott presents a synthesis of biological and psychological models of PTSD which informs his counselling of the trauma victim.

Following disasters in the public domain counsellors are likely to be pressed into service within a month of the incident, that is, before the time at which the diagnostic label PTSD can be applied, and they typically respond with various forms of debriefing. In Chapter 3 Scott describes guidelines for crisis counselling which encourage counsellors to go at the client's pace, without pressure to disclose information, thereby minimizing the risk of deleterious influence. Although there is agreement across psychotherapeutic schools that properly processing the trauma is necessary for psychological adaptation, many of those that survived the Holocaust never talked about their ordeal.

In Chapter 4 Scott suggests that as most of those that suffer from PTSD recover there is perhaps a natural mechanism for shifting from a primarily perceptual focus on the trauma to a more conceptual view coupled with a contextualizing of the incident within the overall life experience. He explains how clients can be taught to re-evaluate the trauma and its significance. The focus in this chapter is on the relatively discrete thoughts of clients during the incident, and how these fit in with the data of their previous experiences. As such it exemplifies the rational-scientific style of cognitive-behavioural therapy.

It is perhaps more probable that our ancestors coped with extreme traumas by constructing stories around them, and in Chapter 5 Donald Meichenbaum, Emeritus Professor of Psychology, University of Waterloo, Canada, in conversation with Michael Hoyt explains how a more macro cognitive-behavioural approach of story construction and reconstruction can be profitably used with PTSD clients.

Chapter 6 by Scott represents something of a hybrid of the two previous chapters in that the group cognitive-behavioural programme for PTSD is described, in which participants have the opportunity to tell and reframe their trauma narrative whilst at the same time learning cognitive-behavioural skills that they can apply themselves. He argues that not only is a group approach beneficial from a therapeutic point of view but it also makes best use of counsellor resources, though as with most group interventions for emotional disorders (see Scott and Stradling, 1998) it is necessary to use some individual sessions judiciously.

In Chapter 7 Donald Meichenbaum looks at a variety of therapeutic tools as 'healing' metaphors. PTSD may represent a circumscribed definition of the difficulties of adult survivors of abuse, and a broader notion of Disorders of Extreme Stress (DES) has been canvassed with a special emphasis on the interpersonal and loss-of-identity issues of this group. In Chapter 8 Donald Meichenbaum addresses the needs of those with PTSD and DES. Children may have difficulty in translating their upsetting experiences into language, and in Chapter 9 Donald Meichenbaum highlights another form: expression through art. Counsellors working with traumatized clients are particularly walking a tightrope between a lack of empathy, in order to protect themselves, and overinvolvement. In Chapter 10 Donald Meichenbaum flags up the warning signs and steps that can be taken to ensure that the counsellor does not fall off the 'rope'.

Probably the greatest single therapeutic difficulty in counselling PTSD clients, irrespective of theoretical orientation, is that the effect of the counsellor's strategy is that the client 're-lives' the trauma and they are therefore on a collision course because the client has been devoting almost all his or her energies to blanking out the memory – cognitive avoidance. In Chapter 11 Professor Frank Ochberg, of the Department of Psychiatry, University of Michigan, helps to troubleshoot this major sticking point in counselling clients with PTSD – cognitive avoidance. With his 'counting method' he introduces a useful way around this impasse, and in so doing he suggests that the counsellor's role is to 'visit' the trauma with the client.

In the penultimate chapter Scott describes his 'journeying with the victims' of the Hillsborough disaster and suggests that no treatment protocol can insulate the counsellor from the complexity of the client's misery. He describes how in the immediate aftermath of the disaster he met people with very wide-ranging responses. For some the incident re-directed their life in a positive way, but for most it was a struggle to adapt and some are still struggling ten years later. Those with chronic PTSD see themselves as damaged, 'not the same person', and in some instances have been re-traumatized by the judicial system. He argues that no thought was given to long-term (post eighteen months) help. In Chapter 13 Rosen, Lohr, McNally and Herbert, from the University of Washington, sound a note of caution for counsellors not to be taken in by the advertising of psychotherapeutic products for PTSD, and argue that some much-publicized approaches have little or no evidence to support their efficacy.

REFERENCES

American Psychiatric Association (1994) *Diagnostic and Statistical Manual of Mental Disorders* (fourth edition). Washington, DC: American Psychiatric Association.

Kessler, M.J. *et al.* (1995) Post-traumatic stress disorder in the National Comorbity Survey, *Archives of General Psychiatry*, 52, 1048–60.

Scott, M.J. and Stradling, S.G. (1998) *Brief Group Counselling*. London: John Wiley and Sons.

CHAPTER 1

PTSD Diagnosis and Treatment for Mental Health Clinicians

Matthew J. Friedman

This chapter focuses on four issues: PTSD assessment, treatment approaches, therapist issues, and current controversies. Important assessment issues include the trauma history, co-morbid disorders, and chronicity of PTSD. Effective intervention for acute trauma usually requires a variant of critical incident stress debriefing. Available treatments for chronic PTSD include group, cognitive-behavioural, psychodynamic, and pharmacological therapy. Therapist self-care is essential when working with PTSD patients since this work may be functionally disruptive and psychologically destabilizing. Current controversies include advocacy v therapeutic neutrality, eye movement desensitization and reprocessing (EMDR), the so-called false memory syndrome, and the legitimacy of complex PTSD as a unique diagnostic entity.

PTSD is an easy diagnosis to make when the patient tells you that she or he has been badly traumatized and believes that such exposure has precipitated current psychological problems. Thanks to a massive psycho-educational programme provided by the print and electronic media, the public has become familiar with the concept of PTSD and recognizes that it can be caused by war trauma, domestic violence, sexual assault, industrial accidents and natural disasters. Media coverage of major recent events such as the Persian Gulf War, Hurricane Andrew, cases of child abuse and the genocide in Bosnia have often underscored the psychological impact of such events, thereby contributing to the growing sophistication of a public that knew little about PTSD until the late 1980s. Furthermore, PTSD is an attractive explanatory model for many people because it places responsibility for their suffering on factors outside themselves, factors over which they often had neither responsibility nor control.

Clinicians have also found the PTSD construct attractive and useful. It provides an explanatory model that is easy to address therapeutically and that promotes empathic patience, even with the most difficult and demanding clientele. Although the growing acceptance of trauma-focused assessment and treatment strategies has created clinical options that were not exercised as recently as ten years ago, such options have also generated a number of potential problems. In this article I will address four issues: PTSD detection and diagnosis; treatment approaches; therapist issues; and current controversies.

MAKING THE DIAGNOSIS

The switch from DSM-III-R (American Psychiatric Association, 1987) to DSM-IV (American Psychiatric Association, 1994) will bring few changes in the diagnostic criteria for PTSD. As shown in Box 1.1, the stressor criterion (A1) will no longer characterize trauma as outside the range of normal human experience since we have been forced to recognize that exposure to catastrophic stress is an unwelcome but not unusual aspect of the human condition. Furthermore, the stressor criterion (A2) now requires that in addition to exposure, the patient needs also to have an intense emotional reaction to the traumatic event such as panic, terror, grief, or disgust. (In DSM-III (American Psychiatric Association, 1980) and DSM-III-R, Criterion A was restricted to exposure per se [A1] and did not address the subjective response [A2].) Otherwise, the B, C and D symptoms have remained the same with the exception of a slight rearrangement such that D6 in DSM-III-R has become B5 in DSM-IV.

PTSD patients are stuck in time and are continually re-exposed to the traumatic event through daytime recollections that persistently interrupt ongoing thoughts, actions or feelings. They are assaulted by terrifying nightmares that awaken them and make them afraid to go back to sleep. They cannot tolerate any reminders of the trauma since these often trigger intense fear, anxiety, guilt, rage or disgust. In some cases, they suffer PTSD flashbacks, psychotic episodes in which reality dissolves and they are plunged back into the apparent reality of a traumatic event that has haunted them for years or decades. During such episodes they find themselves fighting off rapists, being attacked by enemies, or fleeing from explosions with the same intense feelings they experienced during the initial trauma. Such intrusive recollections (Criterion B) can persist for over 50 years (Schnurr, 1992) and may get worse, rather than better, with time (Archibald and Tuddenham, 1965).

PTSD patients develop avoidant/numbing symptoms (Criterion C) to ward off the intolerable emotions and memories recurrently stirred up by these intrusive recollections. Sometimes they develop dissociative or amnestic symptoms which buffer them from painful feelings and recollections. They also adopt obsessional defences and other behavioural strategies such as drug and alcohol abuse, eating disorders, sexual acting out and workaholism, to ward off intrusive recollections.

Finally, PTSD patients suffer from autonomic hyperarousal (Criterion D). Such symptoms include insomnia, irritability that may progress to rage, agitation and jumpiness manifested by an exaggerated startle response, and hypervigilance that may become indistinguishable from frank paranoia. PTSD patients are always on guard, dedicated to avoiding ever being re-exposed to the terrifying circumstances that changed their lives for ever. It is difficult for them to trust other people or the environment. The need for safety and protection may outweigh all other considerations including intimacy, socialization and other pleasurable pursuits.

In other words, the clinician attempting to engage the PTSD patient in treatment is asking the patient to take a tremendous risk. He or she is asking the patient to give up all the protective behaviours and psychological strategies that have emerged to ward off intrusive recollections and hyperarousal symptoms. Therefore, the therapist must recognize that assessment and treatment are potentially destabilizing. Therapy can only succeed in an environment of sensitivity, trust and safety (Herman, 1992). Therapists must recognize that it may take a long time for patients to shed the many layers of protective symptoms that have evolved over countless years since the trauma. It is important for the therapist to let the patient know as soon as possible that he or she recognizes that the prospect of therapy is frightening and painful. It is also important that therapists suppress their own need to get a trauma history as soon as possible and set a pace that the patient can tolerate. In my own work, I always tell patients to signal me when our trauma-focused therapy has become too upsetting. I promise to back off whenever they signal me that therapy has become too distressing. And I always keep my promise. In this way, I fortify the atmosphere of trust and safety and preserve the forward momentum of therapy despite a momentary pause or two.

Some patients may be so relieved that they finally have an opportunity to discuss long-suppressed, painful and possibly shameful past events, that they cannot wait to review such material with a therapist. A second group may be equally motivated but may appear resistant because of fears that therapy will stir up intolerable feelings. They require the safety mentioned earlier. A third group may have sought treatment for depression, anxiety, chemical dependency, eating disorders, somatic complaints or adjustment disorders rather than for PTSD. Indeed, among cohorts of treatment-seeking PTSD patients, up to 80% have at least one additional psychiatric diagnosis including affective disorders (26–65%), anxiety disorders (30–60%), alcoholism or drug abuse (60–80%), or personality disorders (40–60%) (Friedman, 1990; Jordan et al., 1991; Kulka et al., 1990). For such patients, PTSD sometimes emerges as a diagnostic possibility only after the clinician has obtained a careful trauma history as part of a comprehensive assessment. Finally, there is a group of difficult patients who present because of disruptive or self-destructive behaviours and who initially appear to suffer primarily from a personality disorder. Patients in this latter category may be adult survivors of protracted childhood sexual abuse whose trauma history may be obscured by DSM-III-R labels such as borderline personality disorder (BPD), multiple personality disorder (MPD), and somatoform disorder. In addition to PTSD symptoms, they often present with problems of affect regulation, impulsive behaviour, dissociative symptoms, problems of trust, inappropriate sexual behaviour, and a wide variety of somatic complaints (Herman, 1992). These latter problems may demand the lion's share of therapy. Treatment of these patients may be further complicated by fragmented thought processes, incomplete memories and dissociative symptoms.

The trauma history is essential. Given high rates of co-morbidity mentioned earlier, and given a significant amount of overlap between symptoms seen in PTSD, depression and other anxiety disorders, the trauma history is the major vehicle through which PTSD can be diagnosed and distinguished from other major mental disorders. There are many anecdotes about severely traumatized patients whose therapists never bothered to ask about childhood or adult trauma. They followed their therapists' leads and spent countless hours reviewing Oedipal conflicts, family dynamics, or here-and-now interpersonal conflicts. Belated discovery of the centrality of sexual abuse, combat stress or domestic violence provided the key to understanding their current symptoms and became a productive focus for therapy.

It is usually not difficult to obtain a trauma history. Patients are generally forth-coming and frequently pleased to finally have an opportunity to tell their trauma story to someone who appears sufficiently knowledgeable and sensitive to ask about it. For all the reasons mentioned earlier, however, telling the trauma story can be difficult. The first trauma story to emerge is often only the tip of the iceberg. More distressing material will come later after the therapist has established trust and safety and has shown that he or she has the courage, wisdom and empathy to listen to such material and sufficient positive regard for the patient to encourage further disclosure. Therapists can signal patients through their questions and responses that they under-stand the behavioural and emotional impact of a rape, natural disaster or war. Such signals are readily perceived by patients who usually respond positively now that they have been reassured that it will be safe and productive to tell the full trauma story to this therapist at this time.

As with other medical and psychiatric disorders, PTSD patients may exhibit a wide spectrum of impairment. At one extreme, affected individuals may exhibit a high level of interpersonal, social and vocational function. At the other extreme, some PTSD patients may be totally incapacitated by this disorder and may appear to have a chronic mental illness. Such patients may be misdiagnosed as having chronic schizophrenia and may be indistinguishable from such patients unless the clinician has undertaken a careful trauma history and diagnostic assessment. Two reports on psychotic female state hospital inpatients (van der Kolk, 1987; Craine et al., 1988) indicate that those with a history of childhood or adolescent sexual abuse were more likely than non-abused patients to have intrusive, avoidant/numbing and hyperarousal symptoms associated with the abuse. In fact, 66% of these previously abused and currently psychotic patients met criteria for PTSD although none had ever received that diagnosis. Furthermore, they could be distinguished from non-abused state hospital patients by the prominence of sexual and abusive themes in their thoughts and behaviour.

To summarize, detection of PTSD can be difficult because of patient fears that therapy will reactivate intolerable symptoms, because of the many co-morbid Axis I and Axis II DSM-III-R disorders that frequently accompany PTSD, and because some patients may be too fragmented, amnestic, dissociative and otherwise impaired to participate in therapy. Assessment can only succeed in a safe therapeutic environ-ment that promotes a comprehensive review of each patient's trauma history at a pace and intensity that is tolerable.

TREATMENT

Many therapeutic approaches have been advocated for PTSD. The reader is referred to a number of comprehensive reviews of the most prominent treatments for PTSD including psychodynamic therapy (Marmar et al., 1993), cognitive-behavioural therapy (Foa et al., 1995), pharmacotherapy (Friedman and Southwick, 1995), group, family, couples, and inpatient treatment (Williams and Sommer, 1994), and treatment for patients dually diagnosed with PTSD and alcoholism/substance abuse (Kofoed *et al.*, 1993). Therapists working with patients who have survived a variety of traumatic events (war, natural disasters, etc.) generally agree that therapy can be divided into three phases:

1. establishing trust, safety, and 'earning the right to gain access' to carefully guarded traumatic material (Lindy, 1993; p. 806);
2. trauma-focused therapy: exploring traumatic material in depth, titrating intrusive recollections with avoidant/numbing symptoms (Horowitz, 1986); and
3. helping the patient disconnect from the trauma and reconnect with family, friends and society.

It should be noted that patients who reach the third phase have integrated post-traumatic events and are ready to concentrate, almost exclusively, on here-and-now issues concerning marriage, family and other current issues (Herman, 1992; Lindy, 1993; Scurfield, 1993).

Marmar *et al.* (1995; 1993) have suggested that there are five identifiable post-traumatic syndromes, each requiring a different treatment approach: normal stress response; acute catastrophic stress reaction; uncomplicated PTSD; PTSD co-morbid with other disorders; and post-traumatic personality.

The *normal stress response* occurs when healthy adults who have been exposed to a single discrete traumatic event in adulthood experience intense intrusive recollections, numbing, denial, feelings of unreality, and arousal. Such individuals usually achieve complete recovery following individual or group debriefing (Armstrong *et al.*, 1991) derived from critical incident stress debriefing, CISD, models initially developed by Mitchell (1983) and Raphael (1986). Often a single two-hour group debriefing experience is all that is needed. Such sessions begin by describing the traumatic event. They then progress to exploration of survivors' emotional responses to the event. Next, there is an open discussion of symptoms which have been precipitated by the trauma. Finally, there is a resolution in which survivors' responses are normalized and adaptive coping strategies are identified.

Acute catastrophic stress reaction is characterized by panic reactions, cognitive disorganization, disorientation, dissociation, severe insomnia, tics and other movement disorders, paranoid reactions, and incapacity to manage even basic self care, work and interpersonal functions (Marmar, 1991). Treatment includes immediate support, removal from the scene of the trauma, use of anxiolytic medication for immediate relief of anxiety and insomnia, and brief supportive aggressive dynamic psychotherapy provided in the context of crisis intervention.

Uncomplicated PTSD may respond to group, psychodynamic, cognitive-behavioural, pharmacological or combination approaches. During the past ten years we have come to appreciate the powerful therapeutic potential of positive peer group treatment as practised in Vet Centers for military veterans and in rape crisis centres for sexual assault and domestic violence victims. It can be argued that the peer-group setting provides an ideal therapeutic setting for trauma survivors because their post-traumatic emotions, memories and behaviours are validated, normalized, understood and de-stigmatized. They are able to risk sharing traumatic material in the safety, cohesion and empathy of fellow trauma survivors. It is often much easier to accept confrontation from a fellow sufferer who has impeccable credentials as a trauma survivor than from a professional therapist who never went through those experiences first-hand. As group members achieve greater understanding and resolution over traumatic themes, they are remoralized. As they climb out of the pit of trauma-related shame, guilt, rage, fear, doubt and self-condemnation, they prepare themselves to focus on the present rather than the past (Herman, 1992; Scurfield, 1993).

Brief psychodynamic psychotherapy focuses on the traumatic event itself. Through the retelling of the traumatic event to a calm, empathetic, compassionate and non-judgemental therapist, the patient achieves a greater sense of self-cohesion, develops more adaptive defences and coping strategies, and more successfully modulates intense emotions that emerge during therapy (Marmar *et al.*, 1995). The therapist needs constantly to address the linkage between post-traumatic and current life stress. He or she needs to help the patient identify current life situations that set off traumatic memories and exacerbate PTSD symptoms.

There are two cognitive-behavioural approaches, exposure therapy and cognitive-behavioural therapy. Exposure therapy includes systematic desensitization on the one hand and imaginal and *in vivo* techniques such as flooding, on the other. In general, flooding has been much more effective than systematic desensitization. The second approach, cognitive-behavioural therapy, includes a variety of anxiety management training strategies for reducing anxiety such as relaxation training, stress inoculation training, cognitive restructuring, breathing retraining, biofeedback, social skills training, and distraction techniques (see Hyer, 1994 and Foa *et al.*, 1995 for references). Foa and associates (Foa *et al.*, 1991; Rothbaum *et al.*, 1992) have shown flooding and anxiety management training (stress inoculation therapy) are both effective for rape victims with PTSD. They have also speculated that a combination of both treatments might be more effective than either treatment alone.

Given our expanding understanding of the many neurobiological abnormalities associated with PTSD (see Friedman, 1991; Southwick *et al.*, 1992; Murburg, 1994; Friedman, Charney and Deutch, 1995), pharmacotherapy appears to have a place in PTSD treatment. From a practical perspective, there is no question that drugs can provide some symptomatic relief of anxiety, depression and insomnia, whether or not they ameliorate core PTSD intrusive and avoidant/numbing symptoms. In most but not all trials, improvement has been achieved with imipramine, amitriptyline, phenelzine, fluoxetine, and propranolol. A quantitative analysis by Southwick *et al.* (1992) suggested that tricyclic antidepressants and monoamine oxidase inhibitors are generally efficacious in PTSD patients, especially with regard to intrusion and avoidant symptoms, although fluoxetine, amitriptyline and possibly valproate have shown efficacy against avoidant symptoms (Fesler, 1991; Davidson *et al.*, 1990; van der Kolk *et al.*, 1994). At this time no particular drug has emerged as a definitive treatment for PTSD although medication is clearly useful for symptom relief thereby making it possible for patients to participate in group, psychodynamic, cognitive-behavioural or other forms of psychotherapy.

PTSD co-morbid with other DSM-III-R Axis I disorder is actually much more common than uncomplicated PTSD. As noted earlier, PTSD is usually associated with at least one other major psychiatric disorder such as depression, alcohol/substance abuse, panic disorder, and other anxiety disorders (Friedman, 1990; Jordan *et al.*, 1991; Breslau *et al.*, 1991; Kofoed *et al.*, 1993). Sometimes the co-morbid disorder is the presenting complaint that requires immediate attention. At other times, the PTSD appears to be the major problem. In general, the best results are achieved when both PTSD and the co-morbid disorder(s) are treated concurrently rather than one after the other. This is especially true for PTSD and alcohol/ substance abuse (Abueg and Fairbank, 1991; Kofoed *et al.*, 1993). Treatment previously described for uncomplicated PTSD should also be used for these patients.

Post-traumatic personality disorder is found among individuals who have been exposed to prolonged traumatic circumstances, especially during childhood, such as childhood sexual abuse. These individuals often meet DSM-III-R criteria for diagnoses such as borderline personality disorder, somatoform disorder and multiple personality disorder. Such patients exhibit behavioural difficulties (such as impulsivity, aggression, sexual acting out, eating disorders, alcohol/drug abuse and self-destructive actions), emotional difficulties (such as affect lability, rage, depression, panic) and cognitive difficulties (such as fragmented thoughts, dissociation and amnesia). Treatment generally focuses on behavioural and affect management in a here-and-now context with emphasis on family function, vocational rehabilitation, social skills training, and alcohol/drug rehabilitation. Long-term individual and group treatments have been described for such patients by Herman (1992), Koller *et al.* (1992), and Scurfield (1993). Trauma-focused treatment should only be initiated after long therapeutic preparation. Inpatient treatment may be needed to provide adequate safety and safeguards before undertaking therapeutic exploration of traumatic themes. The three phases of treatment, described earlier, apply to these patients as well as those with uncomplicated PTSD, but treatment may take much longer, may progress at a much slower rate, and may be fraught with much more complexity than with other traumatized patients.

THERAPIST ISSUES

Trauma work is difficult. Traumatized patients have suffered greatly and the therapeutic process often opens old wounds with alarming intensity. It is difficult, if not impossible, to maintain a stance of therapeutic neutrality when a patient tells you how he or she was brutally abused as a child, tortured by political enemies, or was forced to watch loved ones be murdered. Such narratives generate powerful emotions in therapist as well as patient. Therapists sometimes find themselves having intrusive thoughts or nightmares about the events recounted by their patients. Therapists may experience guilt that they were personally spared from such horrors. They may feel profoundly powerless because they could not protect patients from previous trauma and present distress. Such feelings can produce a number of inappropriate responses that interfere with therapy and disturb the therapist on a personal level. Herman (1992) notes that powerful emotions generated during therapy may prompt the therapist to engage in rescue attempts, boundary violations, or attempts to control the patient. Therapists may also activate a number of avoidant/numbing coping strategies such as doubting, denial, avoidance, disavowal, isolation, intellectualization, constricted affect, dissociation, minimization or avoidance of traumatic material (Danieli, 1988; Herman, 1992; Lindy, 1988). McCann and Pearlman (1990) have called this phenomenon 'vicarious traumatization', while Figley (1995) has called such secondary traumatization 'compassion fatigue'.

In my opinion, it is useful to separate out three different, but not mutually exclusive, circumstances in which therapists working with traumatized clientele may become distressed, immobilized and symptomatic. First, therapists who have never been traumatized themselves may become overwhelmed by the material generated during the course of treatment with PTSD patients. They may experience (secondary) traumatic nightmares, guilt, feelings of powerlessness, rescue fantasies, or avoidant/numbing behaviour as described above. This can set up a vicious cycle in which the more symptomatic, maladaptive and ineffective therapists become, the more they plunge themselves into their work. When this occurs they are less likely to recognize that they have a serious problem and, unfortunately, are less likely to seek supervision or assistance from colleagues. Second, therapists experience a bona fide countertransference reaction in which the patient's material triggers intrusive recollections of traumatic experiences that happened to them in the past. Since exposure to trauma is not a rare event and since mental health professionals have no more immunity from such exposure than anyone else, such countertransference reactions should be expected to arise often enough to warrant careful monitoring by therapists and supervisors alike. Third, therapists are themselves exposed to the same kind of traumatic experiences for which they attempt to assist others. An example would be offering treatment to survivors of a natural disaster to which the therapist him- or herself has also been exposed. Under such circumstances, the therapist must seek debriefing or treatment for his or her own post-traumatic symptoms before he or she can expect to assist others.

It is not enough for therapists to recognize these occupational hazards. They must make a conscious, sustained and systematic effort to prevent such secondary traumatization through self-care activities. Such measures include developing a supportive environment, monitoring case loads in terms of size and number of trauma cases, making boundaries between personal and professional activities, having regular supervision, and establishing an institutional structure that will address this problem (Courtois, 1988; Gusman et al., 1991). For example, Yassen (1993) has recommended time-limited group treatment for therapists and human service professionals who work with victims of sexual abuse and who themselves have previously been exposed to sexual trauma.

CONTROVERSIAL ISSUES

Although the PTSD diagnosis, itself, was controversial when it first appeared in 1980, that is no longer the case. However, there are currently four controversies in the trauma field that are worth noting: advocacy, eye-movement desensitization and reprocessing (EMDR), the false memory syndrome, and complex PTSD.

Many trauma patients have been victimized by an overpowering aggressor such as a rapist or terrorist. Most therapists are privately outraged by the violence that has been perpetrated on their clientele. Under such circumstances it can be exceedingly difficult to balance one's stance as a neutral professional with one's humanistic values concerning justice and abusive power. Some argue that advocacy is an essential component of the therapist role when your clientele are victims, while others insist that one must always maintain therapeutic neutrality despite one's personal beliefs.

It is crucial for each clinician to acknowledge this issue and to strive to achieve the proper balance for him- or herself.

EMDR is a controversial therapy developed by Shapiro (1989) in which the patient is instructed to imagine a painful traumatic memory while visually focusing on the rapid movement of the therapist's finger. Shapiro believes that such saccadic eye movements reprogramme brain function so that the emotional impact of the trauma can finally be integrated. She and her followers are convinced that patients can achieve resolution of previously disruptive trauma-related emotions through this procedure. Others have suggested that EMDR is really an exposure therapy in disguise and that eye movements may be irrelevant (Foa *et al.*, 1995; Pitman *et al.*, 1993). Well-controlled empirical support for EMDR is lacking, the few completed controlled studies have been equivocal, and methodological questions have been raised (Boudewyns *et al.*, 1993; Foa *et al.*, 1995; Pitman *et al.*, 1993). What is remarkable, however, is that a number of seasoned PTSD clinicians are convinced that EMDR is the most effective available treatment for PTSD despite the fact that many others are highly sceptical of this approach.

Therapists working with adults who had been sexually assaulted as children have reported that such patients have sometimes had no memories of these childhood assaults at the start of treatment. During the course of therapy, however, such repressed traumatic memories reportedly emerge so that patients regain access to discrete recollections of childhood events such as father–daughter incest (Herman and Schatzow, 1987). Patients who claim to have regained traumatic memories of this nature have confronted parents whom they now regard as perpetrators of childhood sexual trauma. In some cases they have taken parents to court for these alleged abuses. Sometimes the accused parents vehemently deny that such events ever occurred and maintain that these 'traumatic memories' are really emblematic of a 'false memory syndrome' that has been manufactured in the course of therapy. Loftus (1993) has written extensively about the problem of authenticating such rediscovered previously repressed memories. Williams (1994), on the other hand, has shown that women who were sexually assaulted during childhood (documented by recorded visits to hospital emergency rooms), are sometimes unable to recall that traumatic event. This hotly debated issue has theoretical, clinical and forensic implications which will need to be sorted out in the future.

Finally, clinicians who work with victims of prolonged trauma such as incest and torture argue that such patients suffer from a clinical syndrome that is not adequately characterized by the PTSD construct (Herman, 1992). Although most patients in this category meet PTSD diagnostic criteria, it is argued that their primary problem is not PTSD. Instead, Herman (1992) has proposed that their major problems concern impulsivity, affect regulation, dissociative symptoms, self-destructive behaviour, abnormalities in sexual expression, and somatic symptoms, and has called this syndrome complex PTSD. Identification and treatment of these patients has been described previously (post-traumatic personality). The controversy is whether complex PTSD is distinct from PTSD and whether it should have its own diagnostic identity. After much discussion, it was decided not to include complex PTSD in the DSM-IV. The controversy has stimulated a number of research initiatives. It is expected that this issue will be revisited during development of the next revision of the DSM-IV, the DSM-V.

SUMMARY

PTSD is not difficult to detect if the clinician includes a careful trauma history as part of his or her comprehensive assessment. The major current diagnostic questions concern the possibility that there are a number of acute and chronic post-traumatic syndromes of which PTSD is the most distinct and identifiable example. Complex PTSD has been suggested as another post-traumatic syndrome which affects individuals who have protracted exposure to trauma, especially childhood sexual trauma. Another diagnostic issue concerns the relative importance of PTSD when it is associated with other co-morbid diagnoses such as depression, alcohol/substance abuse, anxiety disorders and Axis II diagnoses. A third but related diagnostic issue concerns the fact that PTSD can progress to a chronic mental illness. Such patients are so impaired that they are superficially indistinguishable from other chronic patients and can often be found on the fringes of society, in homeless shelters, and enrolled in programmes designed for patients with chronic mental illness such as schizophrenia.

The most widely used treatment for acute traumatic exposure is some CISD-type approach administered in an individual or group format. Among the treatments for chronic PTSD, group, psychodynamic, cognitive-behavioural and pharmacologic approaches are used widely, although few randomized clinical trials have been conducted on any of these treatment approaches. When PTSD is associated with Axis I disorders, both PTSD and the co-morbid problems should be treated concurrently. When PTSD is associated with a personality disorder, treatment usually needs to be long-term and complicated.

There are a number of issues that must be acknowledged and addressed by therapists who work with traumatized clientele, which stem from the powerful emotions generated in the therapists during treatment. Inappropriate coping strategies by the therapists may interfere with treatment and produce a disturbing syndrome which has been called vicarious victimization or compassion fatigue. Therapist self-care is an essential priority for these reasons.

Four controversies in the trauma field have attracted considerable attention. They are the proper balance between advocacy and therapeutic neutrality, the efficacy of EMDR as a treatment, the so-called false memory syndrome, and the possibility that complex PTSD is a unique diagnosis in its own right that is distinct from PTSD.

Box 1.1 *DSM-IV Criteria for PTSD*

> A. The person has been exposed to a traumatic event in which both of the following have been present:
>
> 1. the person has experienced, witnessed, or been confronted with an event or events that involve actual or threatened death or serious injury, or a threat to the physical integrity of self or others;
> 2. the person's response involved intense fear, helplessness, or horror. Note: in children, it may be expressed instead by disorganized or agitated behaviour.

B. The traumatic event is persistently re-experienced in one (or more) of the following ways:

1. recurrent and intrusive distressing recollections of the event, including images, thoughts or perceptions. Note: in young children, repetitive play may occur in which themes or aspects of the trauma are expressed.
2. recurrent distressing dreams of the event. Note: in children, there may be frightening dreams without recognizable content.
3. acting or feeling as if the traumatic event were recurring (includes a sense of reliving the experience, illusions, hallucinations, and dissociative flashback episodes, including those that occur upon awakening or when intoxicated). Note: in young children, trauma-specific reenactment may occur.
4. intense psychological distress at exposure to internal or external cues that symbolize or resemble an aspect of the traumatic event;
5. physiological reactivity upon exposure to internal or external cues that symbolize or resemble an aspect of the traumatic event.

C. Persistent avoidance of stimuli associated with the trauma and numbing of general responsiveness (not present before the trauma), as indicated by three (or more) of the following:

1. efforts to avoid thoughts, feelings, or conversations associated with the trauma;
2. efforts to avoid activities, places or people that arouse recollections of the trauma;
3. inability to recall an important aspect of the trauma;
4. markedly diminished interest or participation in significant activities;
5. feeling of detachment or estrangement from others;
6. restricted range of affect (e.g., unable to have loving feelings);
7. sense of a foreshortened future (e.g., does not expect to have a career, marriage, children, or a normal life span).

D. Persistent symptoms of increased arousal (not present before the trauma), as indicated by two (or more) of the following:

1. difficulty falling or staying asleep;
2. irritability or outbursts of anger;
3. difficulty concentrating;
4. hypervigilance;
5. exaggerated startle response.

E. Duration of the disturbance (symptoms in Criteria B, C and D) is more than one month.

F. The disturbance causes clinically significant distress or impairment in social, occupational, or other important areas of functioning.
Specify if:
     acute: if duration of symptoms is less than three months;
     chronic: if duration of symptoms is three months or more.
Specify if:
     with Delayed Onset: if onset of symptoms is at least six months after the stressor.

REFERENCES

Abueg, F. and Fairbank, J. (1991). Behavioral treatment of the PTSD substance abuser, in *Post-Traumatic Stress Disorder: A Behavioral Approach to Assessment and Treatment*. Edited by Saigh, P.A. New York: Pergamon Press.

American Psychiatric Committee on Nomenclature and Statistics (1980). *Diagnostic and Statistical Manual of Mental Disorders*, third edition. Washington, DC: American Psychiatric Association.

American Psychiatric Committee on Nomenclature and Statistics (1987). *Diagnostic and Statistical Manual of Mental Disorders*, third edition revised. Washington, DC: American Psychiatric Association.

American Psychiatric Committee on Nomenclature and Statistics (1994). *Diagnostic and Statistical Manual of Mental Disorders*, fourth edition. Washington, DC: American Psychiatric Association.

Archibald, H.C. and Tuddenham, R.D. (1965). Persistent stress reaction after combat: A 20 year follow-up. *Archives of General Psychiatry*, **12**, 475–81.

Armstrong, K., O'Callahan, W. and Marmar, C.R. (1991). Debriefing Red Cross disaster personnel: The multiple stressor debriefing model. *Journal of Traumatic Stress*, **4**, 481–91.

Boudewyns, P.A., Swertka, S.A., Hyer, L.A. *et al.* (1993). Eye movement desensitization for PTSD of combat: A treatment outcome pilot study. *The Behavior Therapist*, **16**, 29–33.

Breslau, N., Davis, C.G., Andreski, P. *et al.* (1991). Traumatic events and post-traumatic stress disorder in an urban population of young adults. *Archives of General Psychiatry*, **48**, 216–22.

Courtois, C.A. (1988). *Healing the Incest Wound: Adult Survivors in Therapy*. New York: W.W. Norton.

Craine, L.S., Henson, C.B., Colliver, J.A. *et al.* (1988). Prevalence of a history of sexual abuse among female psychiatric patients in a state hospital system. *Hospital and Community Psychiatry*, **39**, 300–04.

Danieli, Y. (1988). Confronting the unimaginable: Psychotherapists' reactions to victims of the Nazi Holocaust, in *Human Adaptation to Extreme Stress from the Holocaust to Vietnam*. Edited by Wilson, J.P., Harel, Z. and Kahana, B. New York: Plenum Press.

Davidson, J., Kudler, H., Smith, R. *et al.* (1990). Treatment of post-traumatic stress disorder with amitriptyline and placebo. *Archives of General Psychiatry*, **47**, 259–66.

Fesler, F.A. (1991). Valproate in combat-related post-traumatic stress disorder. *Journal of Clinical Psychiatry*, **52**, 361–4.

Figley, C.R. (1995). *Compassion Fatigue: Secondary Traumatic Stress Disorders From Treating the Traumatized*. New York: Brunner/Mazel.

Foa, E.B. and Riggs, D.S. (1993). Post-traumatic stress disorder in rape victims, in *American Psychiatric Press Review of Psychiatry*, Volume 12. Edited by Oldham, J., Riba, M.B. and Tasman, A. Washington, DC: American Psychiatric Press.

Foa, E.B., Rothbaum, B.O., Murdock, T. *et al.* (1991). The treatment of PTSD in rape victims. *Journal of Consulting and Clinical Psychology*, **59**, 715–23.

Foa, E.B., Rothbaum, B.O. and Molnar, C. (1995). Cognitive-behavioral therapy of PTSD, in *Neurobiological and Clinical Consequences of Stress: From Normal Adaptation to PTSD*. Edited by Friedman, M.J., Charney, D.S. and Deutch, A.Y. New York: Raven Press.

Friedman, M.J. (1990). Interrelationships between biological mechanisms and pharmacotherapy of posttraumatic stress disorder, in *Posttraumatic Stress Disorder: Etiology, Phenomenology, and Treatment*. Edited by Wolf, M.E. and Mosnaim, D.A. Washington, DC: American Psychiatric Press.

Friedman, M.J. (1991). Biological approaches to the diagnosis and treatment of post-traumatic stress disorder. *Journal of Traumatic Stress*, **4**, 67–91.

Friedman, M.J., Charney, D.S. and Deutch, A.Y. (1995). *Neurobiological and Clinical Consequences of Stress: From Normal Adaptation to PTSD*. New York: Raven Press.

Friedman, M.J. and Southwick, S.M. (1995). Towards pharmacotherapy for PTSD, in *Neurobiological and Clinical Consequences of Stress: From Normal Adaptation to PTSD*. Edited by Friedman, M.J., Charney, D.S. and Deutch, A.Y. New York: Raven Press.

Gusman, F.D., Abueg, F.R. and Friedman, M.J. (1991). *Operation Desert Storm Clinician Packet*. Palo Alto: National Center for PTSD.

Herman, J.L. (1992). *Trauma and Recovery*. New York: Basic Books.

Herman, J.L. and Schatzow, E. (1987). Recovery and verification of memories of childhood sexual trauma. *Psychoanalytic Psychology*, **4**, 1–14.

Horowitz, M.J. (1986). *Stress Response Syndrome*. (Second Edition). New York: Jason Aronson.

Hyer, L. (1994). *Trauma Victim: Theoretical Issues and Practical Suggestions*. Muncie, IN: Accelerated Development, Inc.

Jordan, K., Schlenger, W., Hough, R. *et al*. (1991). Lifetime and current prevalence of specific psychiatric disorders among Vietnam veterans and controls. *Archives of General Psychiatry*, **48**, 207–15.

Kofoed, L, Friedman, M.J. and Peck, R. (1993). Alcoholism and drug abuse in patients with PTSD. *Psychiatric Quarterly*, **64**, 151–71.

Koller, P., Marmar, C.R. and Kanas, N. (1992). Psychodynamic group treatment of post-traumatic stress disorder in Vietnam veterans. *International Journal of Group Psychotherapy*, **4**, 225–46.

Kulka, R.A., Schlenger, W.E., Fairbank, J.A. *et al*. (1990). *Trauma and the Vietnam War Generation*. New York: Brunner/Mazel.

Lindy, J.D. (1988). *Vietnam: A Casebook*. New York: Brunner/Mazel.

Lindy, J.D. (1993). Focal psychoanalytic psychotherapy, in *The International Handbook of Traumatic Stress Syndromes*. Edited by Wilson, J.P. and Raphael, B. New York: Plenum Press.

Loftus, E.F. (1993). The reality of repressed memories. *American Psychologist*, **48**, 518–37.

Marmar, C.R. (1991). Brief dynamic psychotherapy of post-traumatic stress disorder. *Psychiatric Annals*, **21**, 405–14.

Marmar, C.R., Foy, D., Kagan, B. *et al*. (1993). An integrated approach for treating post-traumatic stress, in *American Psychiatric Press Review of Psychiatry*, Volume 12. Edited by Oldham, J.M., Riba, M.B. and Tasman, A. Washington, DC: American Psychiatric Press.

Marmar, C.R., Weiss, D.S. and Pynoos, R.B. (1995). Dynamic psychotherapy of post-traumatic stress disorder, in *Neurobiological and Clinical Consequences of Stress: From Normal Adaptation to PTSD*. Edited by Friedman, M.J., Charney, D.S. and Deutch, A.Y. New York: Raven Press.

McCann, L. and Pearlman, A. (1990). Vicarious traumatization: A framework for understanding the psychological effects of working with victims. *Journal of Traumatic Stress*, **3**, 131–49.

Mitchell, J. (1983). When disaster strikes ... The critical incident stress debriefing process. *Journal of Emergency Medical Services*, **8**, 36–9.

Murburg, M.M. (1994). *Catecholamine Function in Post-Traumatic Stress Disorder: Emerging Concepts*. Washington, DC: American Psychiatric Press.

Pitman, R.K., Orr, S., Altman, B. *et al*. (1993, October). A controlled study of eye movement desensitization/reprocessing (EMDR) treatment for post-traumatic stress disorder. Paper presented at the Annual Meeting of the International Society For Traumatic Stress Studies, San Antonio, TX.

Raphael, B. (1986). *When Disaster Strikes*. New York: Basic Books.

Rothbaum, B.O., Fog, E.B., Riggs, D.S. *et al*. (1992). A prospective examination of post-traumatic stress disorder in rape victims. *Journal of Traumatic Stress*, **5**, 455–75.

Schnurr, P.P. (1991). PTSD and combat-related psychiatric symptoms in older veterans. *PTSD Research Quarterly*, **2**(1), 1–6.

Scurfield, R. (1993). Treatment of PTSD in Vietnam veterans, in *The International Handbook of Traumatic Stress Syndromes*. Edited by Wilson, J.P. and Raphael, B. New York: Plenum Press.

Shapiro, F. (1989). Efficacy of eye movement desensitization procedure in the treatment of traumatic memories. *Journal of Traumatic Stress*, **2**, 199–233.

Southwick, S.M., Krystal, J.H., Johnson, D.R. *et al.* (1992). Neurobiology of post-traumatic stress disorder, in *Annual Review of Psychiatry*, Volume 11. Edited by Tasman, A. Washington, DC: American Psychiatric Press.

van der Kolk, B. (1987). Reports of childhood incest and current behavior of chronically hospitalized psychotic women. *American Journal of Psychiatry*, **14**, 1474–6.

van der Kolk, B.A., Dryfus, D., Michaels, M. *et al.* (1994). Fluoxetine in post-traumatic stress disorder. *Journal of Clinical Psychiatry*, **55**, 517–22.

Williams, M.B. and Sommer, J.F. (1994). *Handbook of Post-Traumatic Therapy*. Westport, CT: Greenwood Press.

Williams, L.M. (1994). Recall of childhood trauma: A prospective study of women's memories of child sexual abuse. *Journal of Consulting and Clinical Psychology*, **62**, 1167–76.

Yassen, J. (1993). Group work with clinicians who have a history of trauma. *NCP Clinical Newsletter*, **3**, 10–11.

CHAPTER 2

Assessment and Conceptualization

Michael J. Scott

The procedural sequence for counselling survivors of trauma or indeed any clients can be summarized in the mnemonic FACT: the first letters F and A stand for 'first assess', the letter C for 'conceptualize' and the letter T for 'treat.' Assessment should always begin with an open-ended interview in which the client has the opportunity to tell his or her tale in an unfettered way with minimal interruption from the counsellor. The client's account should be set alongside the information contained in the referral letter and that available from other sources such as records and the comments of family members.

It is the counsellor's task to synthesize the information from diverse sources and to attempt to clarify any anomalies. Reliance on any one source of information can be very misleading: for example, it is common for traumatized adolescent males to minimize their symptoms. Again, a client may be referred for what appear to be severe post-traumatic stress symptoms following a very minor car accident. However, inspection of the medical records might reveal that some years previously the patient underwent a neurological examination because they were reporting some strange experiences, and the supposed PTSD symptom might be better explained as part of the early onset of schizophrenia.

The client's pre-trauma functioning is an important domain to assess. There are some traumas that will debilitate almost everyone and there are some traumas that will distress very few. It seems likely that individuals have different thresholds and an individual with a comparatively low threshold may show 'excessive' post-traumatic stress symptoms following an only moderately stressful event. It is important that the client's language is not necessarily taken at face value. For example, clients may well state that their major problem is depression, but they have not in fact been depressed and down most of the day nearly every day for the preceding month; or alternatively, they have not lost interest in most of their previous pastimes. If neither of these latter two conditions are fulfilled in terms of the DSM-IV criteria (American Psychiatric Association, 1994), they cannot meet the criteria for the condition, but that is not to say that they may not have some depressive symptoms.

There is a further difficulty in that, if the counsellor has a particular interest in

PTSD, then all clients may be looked at through this filter. But just because the client has experienced an extreme trauma, it does not follow that that trauma per se is their prime concern. For example, Martin was referred nine months after a fatal road traffic accident. He had been a front-seat passenger in a car driven by his father, who had a heart attack, so that they nearly crashed into other vehicles as well as into a lamp post. But Martin's pressing concern was that he had not done enough to revive his father who subsequently died. Although Martin continued to be fearful when driving and to be disturbed by memories of the incident, these were side issues: the focus in counselling was his trauma-related guilt.

It is not a question of clients suffering *either* PTSD *or* another disorder: clients with PTSD often suffer from other disorders such as substance abuse, and these should be carefully assessed for, and may initially be the most important therapeutic target. It is beyond the scope of this book to detail the interviews and assessments pertinent to possible co-morbid disorders such as substance abuse and panic disorder, and the interested reader is referred to Briere (1997). But substance abuse is such a common complication of PTSD that it is worth a special mention. The mnemonic CAGE can be used to help the counsellor organize an assessment of possible co-morbid substance abuse. The letter C stands for 'cut-down': the client should be asked whether they ever considered that they should cut down their consumption. The letter A stands for 'annoyed', and the client should be asked if others have ever got annoyed with him or her about their consumption of the substance. The letter G stands for 'guilt', and the client should be asked if they have ever felt guilty about their consumption of the substance. The letter E stands for 'eye-opener', and the client should be asked whether they have to consume the substance before midday. Research on alcohol abusers has shown that those who respond positively to two or more of these enquiries are likely to be substance abusers or substance-dependent. Only the person who has managed at least a month's abstinence will be able to focus sufficiently on a PTSD programme.

There should be a natural evolution from assessment to conceptualization: the former without the latter is meaningless and can result in the counsellor having an unclear focus with poor results. As a whole, the therapeutic process can be summarized using the image of an hourglass. At the top of the hourglass there is an open-ended conversation in which the clients tell the story of their trauma. As the glass narrows, a more structured interview is conducted in which questions are asked about each of the diagnostic symptoms pertinent to the disorder under consideration. This may take the form of using one of the standardized structured interviews for PTSD such as the CAPS (Blake *et al.*, 1995) or the SCID (Spitzer *et al.*, 1986). Confirmation of the result of the interview is usually established using psychometric tests, and these additionally provide a measure of the severity of the condition. At the neck of the hourglass there is a conceptualization of the client's particular difficulty. Halfway down the lower half of the hourglass, on the basis of the assessment and conceptualization, a treatment programme is implemented. Finally at the bottom of the hourglass the impact of the programme is assessed. If the programme has been unsuccessful in effect the hourglass is tipped and the process of re-assessment, re-conceptualization and reformed treatment is initiated.

WHAT COUNTS AS A GATEWAY STRESSOR TO PTSD?

In the 1987 version of the DSM (American Psychiatric Association, 1987) life events have to be classifiable as 'extreme' and 'outside the normal range of human experience' in order to qualify as an agent for PTSD. The emphasis was on the objective aspects of the trauma. With the advent of DSM-IV (American Psychiatric Association, 1994) the previous wording was abandoned in favour of a specification of the sort of life events that might lead to PTSD, and an additional requirement was inserted that the person suffered subjective distress in the aftermath of the incident. DSM-IV offers further guidance as to what may constitute a stressor that meets criterion A. On p. 424 it says:

> Traumatic events that are experienced directly include, but are not limited to, military combat, violent personal assault (sexual assault, physical attack, robbery, mugging), being kidnapped, being taken hostage, terrorist attack, torture, incarceration as a prisoner of war or in a concentration camp, natural or man-made disasters, severe automobile accidents or being diagnosed with a life-threatening illness. For children, sexually traumatic events may include developmentally inappropriate sexual experiences without threatened or actual violence or injury. Witnessed events include, but are not limited to, observing the serious injury or unnatural death of another person due to violent assault, accident, war, or disaster, or unexpectedly witnessing a dead body or body parts. Events experienced by others that are learned about include, but are not limited to, violent personal assault, serious accident, or serious injury experienced by a family member or close friend; learning about the sudden, unexpected death of a family member or close friend; or learning that one's child has a life-threatening disease.

The scope of the trauma criteria in DSM-IV is somewhat broader than in DSM-III-R. This highlights the difficulty in deciding where to draw the line between traumatic events and other undesirable events. Whilst the citation above indicates events which could prototypically lead to PTSD, there are other events which are more ambiguous, for example a mother five months pregnant who trips in a hole in the road as she gets out of a taxi and is worried about damage to her unborn child.

Norris and Riad (1997) have reviewed a number of tests and interviews for eliciting the trauma history of clients. Space precludes a detailed assessment of these measures, but it must be said that though they are useful starting points, they will not of themselves indicate whether a person meets criterion A. In addition care has to be taken that the client does not see them as overly intrusive either because the interviewer asks the question in a rapid-fire manner, or because the domain of the inquiry is not pertinent in the client's mind to the trauma for which he or she is seeking help from the counsellor. The Posttraumatic Stress Disorder Diagnostic Scale (Foa, 1995) asks clients to tick which of a set of twelve extreme events they might have experienced, with space to indicate any additional one. The client then indicates which of these traumas bothered them most. There are also questions about fear or helplessness responses. It is therefore a useful non-threatening aid in collecting information to assess the stressor criteria.

WHAT COUNTS AS A PTSD SYMPTOM?

It is important that mental-health professionals have a shared understanding of what each of the PTSD symptoms in DSM-IV (American Psychiatric Association, 1994) means. To aid this process Weiss (1997) has provided the following elaboration of the symptoms, reproduced here with the permission of Guilford Press.

Recurrent and intrusive distressing recollections of the event

In order to be coded present, the recollections must be recurrent, intrusive and distressing. These recollections are typically characterized as spontaneous and uncontrollable, and seem to have a 'life of their own'. They are unbidden, unwelcome, and unable to be easily stopped once started. Examples that meet this criterion would include a veteran driving along in a car, not focusing on any particular thoughts, who has a sudden and distressing memory of placing mutilated corpses in body bags after a rocket attack (referring to a specific wartime experience). Another example would be a victim of an earthquake who is reading a novel and suddenly has the interfering thought, 'If only I had checked the foundation of the house and had it reinforced – I could have prevented the damage and destruction', during which the memory of the house inspection is recalled.

Clinical phenomena that do not meet the criterion for intrusive recollections include the repeated ruminative thoughts of the severely depressed individual who thinks 'I am worthless' outside the context of a traumatic event, the ruminative and obsessive thoughts of the individual who feels 'I am sinful', or the intrusive thoughts of an individual with social fears who thinks 'I will make a fool of myself in front of all these people.' These are three related examples of intrusive thoughts that do not relate to traumatic life events but are specific for other disorders. Another example of a phenomenon that does not meet this criterion is the combat veteran who frequently thinks of his Vietnam experiences and may be saddened by the memories, but does so volitionally, without a sense of intrusion to the experience of the remembering.

Recurrent and distressing dreams of the event

Dreams must be recurrent and distressing. Night terrors, if present, indicate presence of this symptom, and the content of the dream should align with the traumatic exposure. The content of trauma-related nightmares may consist of relatively straightforward dreams of aspects of the event(s) (e.g., repetitive dreams of specific firefights for a veteran) or symbolic representations with some form of trauma-relevant combat theme (e.g., running in terror through a jungle with one's spouse and children while trying to escape an unseen assailant).

Clinical phenomena that do not meet the criterion include dreams or recurrent nightmares of falling off a cliff, which are of a fantasy nature and not linked to traumatic experiences. In addition, dreams of monsters or other threatening fantasy figures, or anxiety dreams related to conflicts or fears involving daily living rather than traumatic exposure, do not satisfy this criterion.

Sudden acting or feeling as if the traumatic event were recurring

This criterion taps the phenomenon of a sense of sudden reliving of the experience. Included in this are illusions, pseudohallucination, and dissociative episodes (e.g., flashbacks), even those that occur upon awakening or when intoxicated. The consequential distinction is between an intrusive memory – in which people perceive themselves to be remembering the event – and a feeling as if the event were happening again. During this experience, the individual loses the ability to distinguish the past from the present. Behaviour during reliving experiences is dissociative-like, and sometimes is unknown to the subject until described by another person who has observed the behaviour (often a spouse or close friend). Phenomena that signify the presence of this item include the case of a war veteran who hears a car backfire, hits the dirt, and sees a battle scene pass before his eyes with the dissociative quality of reliving the experience. Reliving experiences can frequently be set off by the sight of blood, or a dead, mutilated animal at the side of the road, or another stimulus reminiscent of the trauma. Another example would be someone who was subjected to severe shaking in an earthquake, who relives the earthquake experience, including the sense of distorted time and terror about safety after a heavy truck passing by shakes the building.

Intense psychological distress at exposure to cues of the event

The focus here is on psychological distress – fear, anxiety, anger, sense of impending doom – in the face of a representation that symbolizes or resembles an aspect of the traumatic event. The representation can be external, such as anniversaries, or it can be internal, such as anticipating having to approach a feared location. A classic example of this phenomenon is the assault victim who becomes fearful and anxious whenever approaching the scene of the attack. Another example is a survivor of torture with electrodes who needs to have an electrocardiogram. Being unable to face certain situations or continue with the ordinary course of daily activities because of the possibility of reminders or reexposure is the feature. The female survivor of a tornado is unable to step inside a mobile home, because it was inside such a structure that she witnessed her child being killed.

Phenomena that do not meet the criterion for distress upon reexposure are the sad feelings experienced at anniversaries of a trauma, but ones that do not impede ongoing functioning.

Physiological reactivity on exposure to cues of the event

The clinical phenomenon here includes reactivity expressed in a variety of ways: heavy or irregular breathing, lightheadedness, tingling in the extremities, tightness in the chest, knot in the stomach, damp or cold palms or feet, and other indicators of arousal. Frequently occurring in conjunction with attempts at avoidance of stimuli reminiscent of the traumatic event (e.g., a woman who was raped in an elevator breaks out in a sweat when entering an elevator), these episodes can be extremely distressing and approach a level of arousal that is exhausting.

Efforts to avoid thoughts, feelings, or conversations associated with the event

Intentional efforts to avoid thoughts or feelings, or deliberate efforts to avoid activities or situations that arouse recollections of the event must have been made, but need not have been successful. Nonetheless, in instances in which avoidance has been attempted but did not succeed, there should be indications that distress has occurred. Avoidance strategies may vary on several dimensions. They may be obvious or subtle, relatively adaptive or manifestly maladaptive. Obvious forms of avoidance include the refusal to discuss or talk about the trauma, and the use of alcohol or drugs to cloud memories. Overworking is also a strategy used to avoid thoughts and feelings about trauma. Sometimes the interviewee is self-aware of these strategies; other times, the phenomena are clinically more subtle.

Phenomena that do not meet the criterion for avoidance include the inability to remember aspects of the event, depressive social withdrawal, and overall loss of interest in things.

Efforts to avoid activities, places, or people that arouse recollections of the event

The avoidance of places, people, or things that are a reminder of the trauma, and that evoke significant distress, include certain locales that are associated with the trauma. Examples include avoiding crossing a certain bridge because it failed in an earthquake or a flood. Like avoidance of thoughts or feelings, avoidance of people, places, or activities may not be successful in reducing distress; in any case, evidence of distress is required for the avoidant activities to be meaningful expressions of the symptom.

Avoidance of social situations or people that provoke anxiety unrelated to a traumatic event (declining to give sales presentations) is an example of a phenomenon that does not meet the criteria.

Inability to recall an important aspect of the event

The clinical phenomenon here is also referred to as 'psychogenic amnesia'; this is not merely that the person could not keep track of everything that happened, but rather that the individual is aware of important details that cannot be remembered; that is, there are gaps and holes in the story as it is remembered and told. Psychogenic amnesia may be either partial or complete. High levels of distress often accompany descriptions of events in which the respondent is unable to recall important details, and this distress is usually expected to accompany this symptom.

Examples that are instances of the phenomenon include the combat veteran who cannot remember an episode in which a buddy was killed or how he survived; another is the automobile accident victim whose wife was killed, and who cannot remember being told that his spouse died. Phenomena that do not meet the criterion for psychogenic amnesia include forgetting minor details, or a victim with head injury, alcohol-induced 'blackouts', or other neurological memory failures.

Markedly diminished interest in significant activities

The essential feature here is a change in level of interest subsequent to the trauma or the onset of symptoms. Activities in which interest is lost must have been meaningful to the respondent prior to the trauma, as evidenced by continued interest or focus on the activity. Developmental changes must be ruled out in assessing this item.

Examples that fit this phenomenon include the athletically active woman who gives up all physical fitness activities after a scarring train accident; the witness to a shooting who abandons a lifelong passion for duck hunting; or the volunteer paramedic who no longer teaches CPR after having failed to revive a clearly moribund victim after a disaster. Examples that do not meet the criterion are changes in activity due to physical limitations, or the severe anhedonia of depression. Thus, if both PTSD and major depression are present, a clinical determination must be made of whether the loss of interest is clearly tied to response to the trauma.

Feelings of detachment or estrangement from others

Here, too, the essential aspect is change after the trauma. The phenomenon is common in psychological disturbance, but the key feature here is a marked increase in feelings of distance and detachment. An example is a parent, an active churchgoer, whose child is abducted: the parent continues to participate in the church, but feels alone and alienated, receives no comfort, and feels that faith has betrayed him or her. An example that is not scored as present would be the emergency/disaster worker who feels that civilians cannot appreciate what he or she has been through but does not feel socially isolated from others who have not had similar experiences.

Restricted range of affect

The restriction of affect or psychic numbing is relative to the range available to the trauma. The phenomenon is often recognized by people who are unable to have loving feelings; they are numb and do not have feelings they think they should. An example would be an earthquake survivor whose co-worker was killed, and who does not feel choked up, or moved, or sad about the lost co-worker and continues to function in a mechanical, lifeless, business-only manner.

Sense of a foreshortened future

Examples that fit this phenomenon would be a child who does not expect to have a career, marriage, children, or a long life. Other examples include the hurricane survivor who does nothing to prepare for future emergencies because he 'won't be around, anyway', and the combat veteran who drifts in and out of employment, because he does not have a sense of a job history or the implications of this for any future opportunities. This symptom is to be distinguished from a chronic lack of regard for future consequences from someone with antisocial personality disorder, for example.

Difficulty falling or staying asleep

This item is self-evident, although the patterns of sleep disturbance themselves may be of both clinical and research interest.

Irritability or outbursts of anger

This phenomenon is often observed by the interviewee with some chagrin and an apology. There is a sense of loss of control, sometimes coupled with fear of even greater expression of anger or hostility. Examples include the supervisor at work, having been robbed at gunpoint, who angrily explodes at a subordinate for having thoughtlessly told a joke about mugging. This item needs to be understood in relation to the level of pretrauma anger expressivity.

Difficulty concentrating

Trauma survivors very frequently report difficulties concentrating in both the acute and chronic phases of response. For example, a combat veteran might report that he or she found it difficult to concentrate on classroom lectures and assigned reading materials, whereas a sexual assault victim may find that he or she is no longer able to concentrate on the computational and accounting tasks of employment. The report of difficulty concentrating is to some extent a function of intrusive images and thoughts that may interfere with cognitive tasks that allow attention to wander, such as reading or mental arithmetic.

Hypervigilance

This phenomenon represents excessive attention to external stimuli beyond that required for a given realistic appraisal of the level of external threat. This symptom can often be observed during the interview, especially if the situation may have reminders of the trauma (e.g., a victim of falling books and furniture during an earthquake will not sit near the clinician's books). This item is to be differentiated from the generalized suspiciousness in a person with longstanding paranoid trends or paranoid personality disorder. Another example would be of the assault victim who continually looks over his or her shoulder when walking down streets and in stairwells.

Exaggerated startle response

This phenomenon must not predate the trauma and can sometimes be witnessed during the interview if a sudden noise or movement occurs, and the individual exhibits a startle response out of line with both the stimulus and what would typically be expected.

EXTRA CONSIDERATIONS WHEN ASSESSING FOR PTSD IN CHILDREN

The DSM-IV symptoms are more problematic when it comes to assessing children. It is difficult for children to appreciate the notion of a foreshortened future and arguably the symptom should be reframed for children, to assess whether they have greater concerns about their mortality, that is, whether they are seeking reassurances from parents about death. It is also very difficult to determine whether a child is experiencing emotional numbing. In assessing for PTSD among children the counsellor has to be aware also of developmentally appropriate manifestations of a symptom; for example intrusive recollections of a trauma might be expressed by the child playing out the incident.

Children who suffer PTSD, like adults with the condition, show impairment in family, social, occupational/school domains, but additionally they usually also manifest developmental regression. Traumatized children often regress and re-commence thumb-sucking or bed-wetting, and these can be important signs of impairment of functioning which should be noted. Following a major trauma there is often a deterioration in the child's school work and behaviour, and enquiries should be made to parents and teachers about this. Not only is the child's scholastic functioning often affected by the trauma, but their ability to relate to peers and family is impaired. Thus a comprehensive description of a traumatized child's difficulties should go beyond assessment of PTSD symptoms and include a more global assessment within the domains of school, friends and family. In a tragedy in which other people have died the child may experience trauma-related guilt and this should be assessed. It has often been noted that parents or teachers believe a child to be unaffected by the trauma, but the asking of direct questions of the child may suggest that they are more debilitated than the adults believe. In some instances the child is aware that an adult has been badly affected by a trauma and does not wish to add to their distress by openly declaring his or her own. It may be that adults unwittingly collude in the child's non-expression of distress so that they do not have to bear the anguish of knowing their plight.

STRUCTURED INTERVIEWS

A structured interview guarantees that systematic questions are asked concerning each of the DSM-IV PTSD symptoms, and these questions are posed in a neutral manner. The use of any structured interview presupposes that the counsellor has an understanding of the PTSD symptoms. This combination of standard question and an appreciation of the expression of PTSD greatly increases the likelihood that a reliable diagnosis will be made. It is beyond the scope of this book to consider the full range of structured interviews (see Briere, 1997). The focus here is on the two most commonly used in treatment studies. The Structured Clinical Interview for DSM-IV Axis 1 Disorders – Clinician Version (SCID-CV) (First et al., 1997) asks only one question for fifteen of the seventeen PTSD symptoms, e.g., 'What about having dreams about [TRAUMA]?' and for the other two symptoms there are two questions per symptom. But because of the client's response it is often necessary to ask supplementary clarifying questions to determine whether a particular symptom should be considered endorsed. The CAPS (Blake *et al.*, 1995) has useful extra questions built into it, though this probably makes for a slightly longer interview than the SCID. An additional virtue of the CAPS is that it provides a score with which to assess the severity of post-traumatic stress disorder, and it measures the frequency and intensity of each of the seventeen DSM-IV PTSD symptoms: each symptom is rated on a five-point scale and there is an explicit description of what each scale point would mean. The CAPS yields both a dichotomous measure (PTSD or not) and a continuous measure. There is a high measure of agreements between the CAPS and SCID for diagnosis of PTSD (kappa 0.77).

Newman and Ribble (1996) have produced the CAPS-C for children and it is applicable for children as young as seven. The first DSM-IV symptom, intrusive recollections, is assessed using the following questions:

Box 2.1 *Assessment of the first DSM-IV symptom according to CAPS-C*

Frequency
- Did you think about (event) even when you didn't want to? Did you see pictures in your head (mind) or hear the sounds in your head (mind) from (event)?
- What were they like? (Did you cover your eyes or ears to block out things you saw or heard in your head? What were you trying to block out?)
- How many times did this happen in the past month?
  None of the time.
  Little of the time, once or twice.
  Some of the time, once or twice a week.
  Much of the time, several times a week.
  Most of the time, daily or almost every day.

Intensity
- In the past month what have you done when these pictures, sounds or thoughts came (popped) into your mind?
- How did you feel? What did you do? (Did they bother you, scare you, or make you feel bad?)
- Did you stop what you were doing or were you able to keep doing what you were doing?
- Could you turn the pictures off or make them go away if you wanted to?
  Not a problem, none.
  A little bit of a problem, mild, minimal distress or disruption of activities, got a little upset.
  Some, moderate, distress clearly present but still manageable, some disruption of activities.
  A lot, severe, considerable distress, difficulties dismissing memories, marked disruption of activities.
  A whole lot, incapacitating distress, cannot dismiss memories, unable to continue activities.

SELF-REPORT MEASURES

As it is beyond the scope of this book to consider all the psychometric tests for PTSD, those discussed here are a cross section of measures that the first author has been involved in evaluating. For a comprehensive evaluation of the complete range of tests the interested reader might want to consult John Briere's book, *Psychological Assessments of Adult Post-traumatic States*, published by the American Psychological Association in 1997.

The purpose of self-report measures is to confirm the findings of a structured or semi-structured interview. They are also very useful for auditing changes in clients. But they can be misleading if used in lieu of a diagnostic interview. Scott, Stradling and Lee (in submission) compared the diagnostic accuracy of three self-report measures, the PENN Inventory (Hammarberg, 1992), the Impact of Event Scale (IES) (Horowitz *et al.*, 1979), and the Modified PTSD Scale (MPSS-SR) (Falsetti *et al.*, 1993). They had 207 trauma victims (123 subjects in an initial study and 84 subjects in a confirmatory second study) complete these measures, and they were assessed also by the 'gold standard' of the CAPS (Blake *et al.*, 1995) structured interview. The best performer was the PENN Inventory with correct identification of 85% of cases, using an optimal cut-off of 39 (the PENN is reproduced in Scott and Stradling, 1992), followed by the MPSS-SR with a hit-rate of 81%, using a cut-off of 59. The worst performer, yet the most commonly used measure in PTSD studies, was the IES with a hit-rate of 74%, with a cut-off of 45. The IES classified one half of those subjects who did not have PTSD as PTSD cases.

More recently Scott, Stradling and Lee (1997) have compared the PENN Inventory, Foa's Posttraumatic Stress Disorder Diagnostic Scale (PDS) (1995) and the Davidson Trauma Scale (DTS) (1997). In this study there were 82 subjects and they were each assessed using either the CAPS (Blake *et al.*, 1995) or the SCID (First *et al.*, 1997) structured interview. Preliminary analysis of this data again suggests a cut-off of 39 on the PENN Inventory with a hit-rate of 78%, closely followed by the DTS with correct identification of 76% using a cut-off of 77; then the PDS with a hit-rate of 71% using a cut-off of 32. Over one-half of subjects in these studies had PTSD; between one-half and two-thirds were victims of a motor vehicle accident and all were involved in litigation. Some care has to be taken in generalizing from these results in that the cut-offs may vary depending on the proportion of PTSD sufferers in the population studied, the types of trauma under consideration, and whether the person is pursuing litigation. But the above results are probably a useful guide for counsellors meeting trauma victims in the United Kingdom context.

It should be appreciated however that the cut-offs indicated are not sacrosanct. For example, a counsellor may well decide that in using the PENN Inventory he or she wishes to reduce the cut-off to (say) 35 to reduce further the possibility of excluding someone who may have PTSD (i.e. to reduce false negatives) from the more rigorous examination of the structured or semi-structured interview. In so doing they may possibly also 'trawl' in some cases of sub-syndromal PTSD who would doubtless also be in need of professional help. The price to be paid for this, however, will be a slight reduction in overall hit-rate, but the counsellor may well consider that clinically this is a price worth paying.

Part of the difficulty with the IES is that it was devised a year before PTSD entered the diagnostic nomenclature. The IES contains fifteen items, with seven items relating to intrusion and eight related to avoidance, but it does not include disordered arousal items, making it strictly for a measure of stress response. Despite this limitation, for the next decade it was used as a main outcome measure in treatments of PTSD and its use persists, because it is a quick and simple self-report measure for clients to complete.

In 1992 Hammarberg published the PENN Inventory. This is a 26-item measure in which the clients indicate their response to each item on a four-point scale. The PENN, though not validated against a structured standardized interview, was pitted against a structured clinical protocol. Tested on a population sample 90% of whom were combat veterans, the PENN Inventory yielded a sensitivity (the proportion of those with a disorder identified by a measure) of 90–98% and a specificity (the proportion of those without a disorder identified by a measure) of 94 to 100%, using the cut-off score of 35. (Items endorsed on the PENN can make for very fruitful discussion in the counselling session: e.g., question 12 on the PENN requires the client to indicate 'I've told a friend or family member about the important parts of my most traumatic experiences'. Or, 'I've had to be careful in choosing the part of my traumatic experiences to tell friends or family members.' Or, 'Some parts of my traumatic experience are so hard to understand that I've said almost nothing about them to anyone.' Or 'No one could possibly understand the traumatic experiences I've had to live with.')

A year later Falsetti et al. (1993) developed the Modified PTSD Symptoms Scale Self-Report (MPSS-SR). This confined itself to each of the seventeen PTSD symptoms in DSM-IIIR (American Psychiatric Association, 1987) and asked about the frequency and severity of each symptom. The MPSS-SR was validated against the SCID for DSM-IIIR (Spitzer et al., 1986). One of Falsetti et al.'s samples involved people seeking treatment from a Crime Victims Research and Treatment Centre (Resick et al., 1991) and the MPSS-SR yielded sensitivity of 93% and a specificity of 61% for a cut-off of 71.

In 1995 Foa published the PDS. The main core of this instrument asks clients to answer a question about each of the seventeen PTSD symptoms in DSM-IV and to respond to each on a four-point scale. In a study of 248 subjects it had a sensitivity of 82% and a specificity of 77%.

BEYOND PTSD?

Under the heading 'Associated Features' DSM-IV (p. 425) suggests that individuals with PTSD may describe painful guilt feelings about surviving when others did not survive or about the things that they had to do to survive, and that

> the following associated constellation of symptoms may occur and are more commonly seen in association with an interpersonal stressor (e.g., childhood sexual or physical abuse, domestic battering, being taken hostage, incarceration as a prisoner of war or in a concentration camp, torture): impaired affect modulation; self-destructive and impulsive behaviour; dissociative symptoms; somatic complaints; feelings of ineffectiveness, shame, despair, or hopelessness; feeling permanently

damaged; a loss of previously sustained beliefs; hostility; social withdrawal; feeling constantly threatened; impaired relationships with others; or a change from individual previous personality characteristics.

In the development of DSM-IV there was considerable debate about whether these symptoms constituted a disorder sufficiently separate from PTSD. However, the field studies conducted to help resolve these concerns revealed that very few subjects had these symptoms without also having PTSD, and consequently this constellation of symptoms was not given a separate diagnostic status. In effect the symptoms were relegated essentially to a footnote to the PTSD criteria. The danger of this is that they could easily be ignored. This particular combination of symptoms has been subsumed under the heading of complex PTSD and refined further by van der Kolk (1996) under the umbrella of DESNOS, Disorders of Extreme Stress Not Otherwise Specified. In part the rationale for this has been that in many cases of adult survivors of child abuse they may indeed be suffering from PTSD, but what is most debilitating to them now is not so much their memories but their inability to relate to others. DESNOS highlights this.

Briere's (1995) self-report measure, the Trauma Symptom Inventory, appears to tap much the same domains as DESNOS. There are ten clinical scales, Dissociation, Anger/Irritability, Impaired Self-Reference, Tension Reduction Behaviour, Defensive Avoidance, Intrusive Experiences, Sexual Concern, Dysfunctional Sexual Behaviour, Anxious Arousal, and Depression. He has developed norms for each of the scales based on a representative sample of the United States population, making it particularly useful in the assessment of adult survivors of child abuse. There is also a Trauma Symptom Checklist for Children (Briere, 1996).

Marmar, Weiss and Metzler (1997) have reviewed studies which show that the degree of dissociation during and a few minutes before and after a trauma is associated with the level of post traumatic stress disorder. One of the studies in their review is of particular note, in that trauma victims completed the Peritraumatic Dissociative Experiences Questionnaire (which is reproduced in Marmar, Weiss and Metzler, 1997) one week after an incident, and this predicted their PTSD symptoms five months later even after adjusting for the initial level of PTSD symptoms. The items on the PDEQ relate to

1. moments of losing track or blanking out;
2. finding the self acting on 'automatic pilot';
3. a sense of time changing during the events;
4. the event seeming unreal, as in a dream or play;
5. feeling as if floating above the scene;
6. feeling disconnected from body or body distortions;
7. confusion as to what was happening to the self – and others;
8. not being aware of things that happened during the events that normally would have been noticed;
9. not feeling pain associated with physical injury.

The DSM-IV diagnosis of the Acute Stress Disorder requires the presence of three or more dissociation symptoms as well as some intrusion, avoidance and disordered arousal features. Thus, administering the PDEQ is a way of facilitating such a diagnosis. (The diagnosis of acute stress disorder requires a minimum duration of two days and a maximum of four weeks.) Assessing for dissociation may give an early warning that a particular client may be especially difficult to counsel, particularly as, certainly within a cognitive behavioural framework, no treatment strategies for directly targeting ongoing dissociative symptoms have been elaborated or evaluated.

CONCEPTUALIZING PTSD

The counsellor's role in treating post-traumatic stress disorder or indeed any disorder can be likened to the changing of a software programme on a computer to make it more adaptive to needs. There are, for example, wide-ranging word-processing packages, some more sophisticated than others, and a computer user is likely to change from package to package as demands change. But not every software package is compatible with the computer hardware – for example, voice-recognition software needs more than a certain speed of the central processor in the hardware to function. To continue the analogy, the biological hardware of PTSD clients will impose constraints on what might be achieved psychologically. Knowledge of the hardware might also suggest new biological forms of intervention. It is therefore suggested that an adequate conceptualization of post-traumatic stress disorder is only possible by an exposition of the biological (neuroanatomy and neurochemistry) and a consistent psychological description. What follows is a synthesis of the psychological and biological perspectives.

From a psychological point of view PTSD appears to involve classical conditioning in that anything associated with the original trauma subsequently evokes distress: e.g., a Hillsborough victim becomes disturbed to find himself in a crowd of football supporters watching a match on TV when he enters a pub. According to Mowrer's (1960) two-factor theory, classical conditioning and operant conditioning are combined to produce a fear response. In the case of the Hillsborough victim with PTSD he might leave the pub to reduce his anxiety but this reinforces his avoidance behaviour – operant conditioning. Had he stayed in the pub and similar situations, gradually his fear response would have diminished, i.e., he would have become habituated to his fear. More recently Foa et al. (1992) have proposed an emotional processing model in which PTSD symptoms arise from a fear structure stored in long-term memory. The structure consists of a network of information about stimuli, their meanings, and responses to those stimuli (i.e., avoidance, escape). The fear structure is activated by retrieval cues producing arousal and intrusive recollections of the trauma. Avoidance and numbing symptoms are thought to arise from mechanisms for deactivating the structure.

Clients with PTSD and those with a phobia are similar in that they exhibit a fear response. Just as it has proven possible to help clients with phobias by gradually exposing them to their fears, so helping PTSD victims encounter situations reminiscent of their trauma can also facilitate their recovery. But the nature of the unconditional stimulus in PTSD is more extreme than in a phobia, e.g. rape versus a spider. This means that the initial impact on the brain's emotional computer, the amygdala, is likely to be greater, and the amygdala is also the brain's alarm system.

The amygdala is closely connected to the hypothalamus, which controls the body's fight-or-flight response. If a memory is burned into the amygdala with enough force, it may be almost uncontainable and trigger such dramatic bodily reactions that a person may re-experience the precipitating trauma, complete with the full sensory replay that characterizes PTSD. LeDoux (1998) has suggested that the amygdala-based system can produce a sort of physical reminiscence, reconstituting the body state, palpitations, sweating etc. that arose with the original trauma. Further, the amygdala can store non-conscious memories in that the person has no explanation for the sensations. Most recent conscious memories are stored in the hippocampus, from where those of them that are destined to become permanent brain furniture are dispatched to long-term memory.

It is known that the greater the magnitude of the stressor, the greater the amount of cortisol secreted from the adrenal glands, and that depressed patients consequently have significantly higher levels, compared with non-psychiatric control subjects. Yet, strangely, patient groups with PTSD appear to have lower cortisol levels (Yehuda, 1998), and there are also other ways in which this patient group is 'abnormal': they have increased glucocorticoid receptor sensitivity; stronger negative feedback inhibition; and the hypothalamic-pituitary axis (HPA) system becomes progressively more sensitized, i.e., their neurochemistry is different from that of depressed or stressed patients. This may suggest that above a certain threshold of severity of the unconditional stimuli (which may vary from individual to individual because of their biology or trauma history), the amygdala appears to enter a different mode or node. It is as if it resonates, and the sensory aspects of the trauma appear frozen together, so that subsequently, if one part of the memory is retrieved, the whole experience is re-ignited. It is possible that dissociation may serve as a marker that the person's threshold has been reached. Dissociation involves the victim (consciously or non-consciously) distancing themselves from the trauma so that it might appear as if it was happening in slow motion; it is a coping response geared to gradual assimilation of the event.

LeDoux (1998) has suggested that if the sights, sounds and smells associated with the trauma occur subsequently, that is, if there are further conditional stimuli, there is a profound fear response via reactivation of the powerfully potentiated amygdala circuits. The sensory aspects are so highly bonded that when one aspect is triggered all parts ignite. Conditional stimuli activate the amygdala unconsciously, but at the same time reach the temporal lobe memory system and can lead to the recall of the initial trauma. These conscious memories, together with the awareness of now being in this state of strong emotional arousal, then gives rise to conscious anxiety and worry. These cognitions about emotional arousal in turn flow from the neocortex and hippocampus to further arouse the amygdala. (The function of the amygdala is to integrate information from the sub-cortical pathways and from the cortex, in particular from the hippocampus, which is concerned with long-term explicit memory.) The bodily expression of the amygdala's response keeps the cortex aware that emotional arousal is ongoing, and further facilitates the anxious thoughts and memories. The brain enters into a vicious cycle of the emotional and cognitive excitement and like a runaway train just keeps picking up speed. LeDoux (1998) suggests that there are sub-cortical pathways to the amygdala and these are quick and dirty transmission routes, making for fast responses but failing to distinguish between stimuli such as shots, lightning and slamming doors. These sub-cortical pathways to the amygdala may dominate over those from the cortex to the amygdala in PTSD. There are many more pathways from the amygdala to the hippocampus than from the latter to the former, making overriding of the amygdala always potentially problematic – it is as if there is a motorway up to the hippocampus and a back road downwards. The hippocampus is part of the cortex of the brain and is responsible for locating events in time and space. Patients who suffer PTSD following a trauma show reduced hippocampal volume and its functioning is impaired, though this is not thought to be permanent. Not only is the neurochemistry of PTSD clients different to that found in depressed or stressed clients, but so also is their neuroanatomy, with the latter groups not showing a reduction of hippocampal volume. The therapeutic tasks are to try to gain conscious wilful control of the sub-cortical pathways to the amygdala to whatever extent is possible, and to try to 'soothe' the amygdala with corrective information from the cortex. It may also be the case (LeDoux, 1998) that non-conscious control of the sub-cortical pathways to the amygdala takes place, that is, there is implicit learning if the person is repeatedly exposed to their trauma in a safe context, and this could be why exposure therapy for PTSD appears to work.

Approaching PTSD from a psychological perspective, Brewin, Dalgleish and Joseph (1996) postulated two levels of representation of trauma-related information: situationally accessible memories (SAMS) and verbally accessible memories (VAMS). The SAMS appear to be an analogue for an amygdala-based system and the VAMS an analogue for the hippocampus/cortical long-term store. The SAMS may be triggered non-consciously by exposure to cues associated with the trauma. The VAMS represent the individual's conscious experience of the traumatic event. They have suggested that the SAMS are not available for editing in the same way as VAMS information. Brewin, Dalgleish and Joseph argue that their Dual Representation Theory (DRT) has the power to account for the range of PTSD symptoms. For example, dissociative memories or 'flashbacks' would be considered to be the result of the activation of SAM representations, whereas the person's ability to recount the trauma, for example in counselling, would be a function of the accessibility of VAM representations. Brewin, Dalgleish and Joseph suggest that individuals need consciously to integrate the verbally accessible information in VAM with the pre-existing beliefs and models. In addition information in SAM has to be activated by exposure to cues concerning the events, and new non-threatening information incorporated into it. The distillation of corrective information in VAM is an obvious therapeutic goal; trauma victims might discover this information via the social support of friends or family or through counselling. But as Power and Dalgleish (1997) point out, the DRT model does not explain how the trauma information is integrated with previous views of self and world. However, from a biological perspective, the hippocampus/cortical long-term store interface is clearly involved in such a synthesis.

Both biological and psychological accounts described highlight the interplay of two levels, primarily perceptual (SAMS/amygdala-based) and a conceptual level (VAMS/hippocampus and cortical long-term store). The counselling approach described by Scott in the next chapters therefore has as its starting point the teaching of clients to accept their sensory experience related to the trauma, then to locate this within a coherent view of the trauma, and then to integrate the trauma itself within the overall context of life. Intrusive imagery, it is suggested, is maintained by an inability to contextualize the trauma. Avoidance behaviour can be seen as an attempt to ensure that memories of the incidents are not cued in the first place. Disordered arousal arises when the output from the amygdala continues to indicate danger, resulting in the accompanying physiological tension. Attentional resources are allocated almost entirely to being on guard (hypervigilance) leaving little energy over for routine activities, i.e., the person experiences impaired concentration and can become distant and cut off from others. As a consequence of this deployment of attentional resources ambiguous information is interpreted in a threatening manner, serving to maintain the state of vigilance.

The memory of the trauma is not simply a visual representation of the incident – it is an emotional memory (van Oyen, 1997) so that a client with (say) a sub-syndromal level of Post Traumatic Stress Disorder may experience a worsening of their intrusive imagery (and therefore a worsening of their PTSD) as a result of increased arousal e.g. because of the subsequent development of panic attacks. Similarly a client who had recovered from PTSD may again be debilitated by the trauma if they experience a subsequent more minor incident that nevertheless intensifies emotional arousal. Conceptualizing the memory as an emotional memory better explains the variability in intrusive imagery and why it is sometimes that PTSD clients seem more disturbed by images of what could have happened than what did happen, and why it is that many of the nightmares of trauma victims are not an exact re-enactment of the incident though clearly related to it. This also means that it is not necessary to postulate, as Foa (1992) and Brewin, Dalgleish and Joseph (1996) have done, that PTSD always involves a trauma that violates the person's previously held beliefs. It then becomes understandable that a person already exposed to years of warfare can still suffer PTSD following a particular event.

REFERENCES

American Psychiatric Association (1987) *Diagnostic and Statistical Manual of Mental Disorders*, third edition revised. Washington, DC: American Psychiatric Association.

Blake, D.D., Weathers, F.W., Nagy, L.M., Kaloupek, D.G., Gusman, F.D., Charney, D.S. and Keane, T.M. (1995) The development of a clinician administered PTSD scale. *Journal of Traumatic Stress*, 8, 79–90.

Brewin, C.R., Dalgleish, T. and Joseph, S.A. (1996) A Dual Representation Theory of Posttraumatic Stress Disorder. *Psychological Review*, 103, 670–86.

Briere, J. (1995) *Trauma Symptom Inventory Professional Manual*. Odessa, FL: Psychological Assessment Resources.

Briere, J. (1996) *Trauma Symptom Checklist for Children (TSCC)*. Odessa, FL: Psychological Assessment Resources.

Briere, J. (1997) *Psychological Assessment of Adult Post-traumatic States*. American Psychological Association.

Davidson, J.R. T., Book, S.W., Colket, J.T., Tupler, L.A., Roth, S., David, D., Hertzberg, M., Mellman, T., Beckham, J.C., Smith, R., Davison, R.M., Katz, R. and Felldma, M. (in press) Assessment of a new self-rating scale for post-traumatic stress disorder. *Psychological Medicine*.

Falsetti, S.A., Resnick, H.S., Resick, P.A. and Kilpatrick, D.G. (1993) The Modified PTSD Symptom

Scale: A brief self-report measure of post traumatic stress disorder. *Behaviour Therapist*, **17**, 66–7.

First, M.B., Spitzer, R.L., Gibbon, M. and Williams, J.B. W. (1997) *Structured Clinical Interview for DSM IV Axis 1 Disorders – Clinician Version (SCID-CV)*. Washington, DC: American Psychiatric Press.

Foa, E.B., Zinberg, R. and Rothbaum, B.O. (1992) Uncontrollability and the unpredictability in PTSD: an animal model. *Psychological Bulletin*, **112**, 218–38.

Foa, E.B. (1995) *Posttraumatic Stress Disorder Diagnostic Scale (PDS) Manual*. Minneapolis MN: National Computer Systems.

Hammarberg, M. (1992) PENN Inventory for post-traumatic stress disorder: psychometric properties. *Psychological Assessment*, **4**, 67–76.

Horowitz, M.J., Wilner, N. and Alvarez, W. (1979) Impact of The Scale: a measure of subjective distress. *Psychometric Medicine*, **41**, 209–18.

LeDoux, J. (1998) *The Emotional Brain*. London: Weidenfeld and Nicolson.

Marmar, C.R., Weiss, D.S. and Metzler, T.J. (1997) 'The Peritraumatic Dissociative Experiences Questionnaire' in *Assessing Psychological Trauma and PTSD*, ed. J.P. Wilson and T.M. Keane. New York: Guilford Press.

Mowrer, O.H. (1960) *Learning Theory and Behaviour*. New York: Wiley.

Newman, E. and Ribble, D. (1996) 'Psychometric review of the Clinician Administered PTSD Scale for Children' in *Measurement of Stress, Trauma, and Adaptation*, ed. B.H. Stamm. Lutherville, MD: Sidran Press.

Norris, F.H. and Riad, J.K. (1997) 'Standardised Self-report Measures of a Civilian Trauma and Post-traumatic Stress Disorder' in *Assessing Psychological Trauma and PTSD*, ed. J.P. Wilson and T.M. Keane. New York: Guilford Press.

Power, M. and Dalgleish, T. (1997) *Cognition and Emotion*. Psychology Press.

Resick, P.A., Falsetti, S.A., Resnick, H.S. and Kilpatrick, D.G. (1991) *The Modified PTSD Symptom Scale Self-report*. St Louis, MO: University of Missouri and Charleston, SC: Crime Victims Treatment and Research Centre, Medical University of South Carolina.

Scott, M.J. and Stradling, S.G. (1992) *Counselling for Post-traumatic Stress Disorder*. London: Sage Publications.

Scott, M.J., Stradling, S.G. and Lee, S. (1997) The utility and accuracy of three self-report measures of post-traumatic stress disorder. Presented to Annual Meeting of ISTSS November 1997.

Spitzer, R.L. and Williams, J.B.W. (1986) *Structured Clinical Interview for DSM-IIIR Nonpatient version*. New York: Biometrics Research Department, New York State Psychiatric Institute.

van der Kolk, B.A. (1996) 'The black hole of trauma' in B.A. van der Kolk, A.C. McFarlane and L. Weisaeth (eds), *Traumatic stress: The effects of overwhelming experience on mind, body and society* (pp. 5–23). New York: Guilford Press.

van Oyen, C. (1997) Traumatic intrusive imagery as an emotional memory phenomenon: a review of research and explanatory information processing theories. *Clinical Psychology Review*, **5**, 509–36.

Weiss, D.S. (1997) 'Structured Clinical Interviews in Assessing Psychological Trauma and PTSD' in *Assessing Psychological Trauma and PTSD*, ed. J.P. Wilson and T.M. Keane. New York: Guilford Press.

Yehuda, R. (1998) 'Neuroendocrinology of Trauma and PTSD' in *Psychological Trauma*, ed. R. Yehuda. American Psychiatric Press.

CHAPTER 3

Guidelines for Crisis Counselling

Michael J. Scott

Crisis counselling is somewhat different to the systematic cognitive-behavioural counselling for PTSD which is the major concern of this book. A crisis counsellor often only has one session with a client and is typically functioning in an emergency capacity. The role is more one of orientating than of treating, mapping out for the client the sort of difficulties that might be encountered and the directions from which means to resolve the problems might be found. The goal of crisis counselling is to help the client to get their bearings. To orientate the client it is necessary that the counsellor rapidly establishes rapport. This may involve listening repeatedly to the same tale without expressing criticism of the client. The crisis counsellor will often have to help the client answer a number of pressing questions:

'What is or has been happening to me?'
'What is going to become of me?'
'What if I don't get better?'
'Am I safe?'

In addition the counsellor has to provide guidance as to how the client might help themselves and how this might be facilitated by significant others, for example friends or solicitors. The crisis counselling should be low key as the client has had enough drama to cope with. An information leaflet can be constructed which answers these four questions and gives the necessary advice. This is a useful way of implicitly reminding the client that they are not alone with their difficulties and that there is life after trauma. Having said that, it would be difficult to write a separate leaflet for each conceivable natural disaster or type of trauma and an 'all-purpose' leaflet will inevitably be couched in generalities. The crisis counsellor's task is to try to tailor the sort of information in the leaflet to the needs of the particular client. The adaptation to individual needs is described using the four questions as a framework.

'WHAT IS OR HAS BEEN HAPPENING TO ME?'

The crisis counsellor should not assume that the client labels the trauma in the way one might anticipate from the 'facts' of the matter. Thus for example the client who has been raped might choose to label her experience as being 'sexually assaulted' or 'molested'. Use of the milder term by the client may serve as temporary protection from the enormity of what has been experienced, allowing for a gradual assimilation. From a crisis counselling point of view there is no merit in insisting that the correct label is used from the outset. However, other professionals such as the police and solicitors, of necessity, need factual details and have to apply the realistic label. In such circumstances the crisis counsellor can help as a useful intermediary or buffer between the client and the legal system.

Any PTSD symptoms the client reports can be described initially by the crisis counsellor as 'a normal response to an abnormal situation'. In some cases however the client's distress will be enhanced because the trauma has reawakened memories of earlier trauma. These clients are especially at risk, and steps should be taken if possible to monitor their progress more carefully and ensure that therapeutic counselling is available if symptoms persist.

'WHAT IS GOING TO BECOME OF ME?'

It is reasonable and probably helpful for the crisis counsellor to be realistically hopeful about the outcome for clients presenting in crisis in the immediate aftermath of a trauma. The majority of those experiencing the trauma will have recovered within three months. However, the counsellor has to be careful not to overstate the case, as a significant minority, as much as 40% cent, do not. Which group the client will fall into will depend on pre-trauma history, support network and coping style. Again, in instances where these are negative, some provision for ongoing monitoring and possible treatment should be made.

'WHAT IF I DON'T GET BETTER?'

The crisis counsellor can make two responses to this question. The first is that it is early days and the client is crossing bridges before arriving at them. Second, if they do not recover in the next two to three months there is specialist help available. Where and how the specialist help is available should be specified.

'AM I SAFE?'

This is a particularly important question for clients whose experiences may repeat themselves; for example, a battered wife might need a great deal of reassurance that she is secure in her hostel accommodation and that her husband would be unlikely to have knowledge of or access to the hostel.

The crisis counsellor should give general advice to the client about engaging in normal activities, albeit in small doses for the time being; then pacing their return to normality, which needs approaching like a marathon rather than a sprint. It is useful in this connection to make the point that initially they may feel distant from important others in their lives, perhaps because the others 'haven't been through the trauma', but if they keep in contact, even at reduced levels, some of the joys of the previous relationship will return.

In the immediate aftermath of a major trauma a client may believe themselves to be functioning perfectly well. Nevertheless, the counsellor should make the client aware of the sorts of problems that can occur later so that they have a potential framework for understanding their experiences. If possible the crisis counsellor should go beyond the client's self-report and elicit the views of those close to him or her as to changes in irritability, startle responses and hypervigilance. This information may contradict the client and the client can be asked what they make of the contradiction.

In crisis the client is too overwhelmed by events to begin systematic counselling and needs space to try out their own coping responses. But the orientating framework can serve to enhance those coping responses and provide an emergency procedure should the natural coping mechanisms fail (and simply knowing that a facility is available is often perceived as a source of support even if the client makes no call on the facility). It should be remembered that most PTSD clients actually present for systematic help many months after the 'crisis'. PTSD clients rarely begin systematic work at the time of crisis.

CHAPTER 4

Post-traumatic Stress Disorder: A Cognitive-contextual Approach

Michael J. Scott

Most people are psychologically affected by an extreme trauma and for a significant minority the debility is long-term, often expressed as Post-traumatic Stress Disorder (PTSD). A cognitive-contextual approach is described in which the prime focus is upon teaching the client how to interact adaptively with the memory of the trauma by: a) facilitating a switch from a primarily perceptual to a more conceptual level of processing the trauma itself; and b) placing the trauma in the context of past life experiences and determining its relevance for the future. The approach is illustrated by the treatment of a PTSD-diagnosed motor-vehicle accident victim.

Extreme traumas have long been thought of as precipitants for a distinct pattern of symptom responses. In Homer's *Odyssey*, warriors' diaries revealed gruelling accounts of intense panic and disturbance both during and following battlefield encounters (Trimble, 1985). The two world wars introduced a variety of synonyms for traumatic stress such as shell shock, war neurosis, combat exhaustion and fight fatigue. However, it was not until 1980 (APA, 1980) that these terms were subsumed under the heading of Post-traumatic Stress Disorder (PTSD) and diagnostic criteria elaborated. Studies on non-combat populations, such as survivors of fire, explosion, flood and concentration camps, showed them also to be experiencing PTSD symptoms (Scott and Stradling, 1992). Probably most of the PTSD clients that counsellors encounter are victims of all too commonplace assaults or motor-vehicle accidents rather than of a newsworthy trauma. Recent data from the US national co-morbidity study (Kessler *et al.*, 1996) indicates PTSD prevalence rates are 5% and 10% among American men and women respectively.

DEFINING PTSD AND ACUTE STRESS DISORDER

The most recent revision of PTSD criteria is contained in the *Diagnostic and Statistical Manual of Mental Disorders*, fourth edition (APA, 1994), which has the following stressor criterion, criterion A, for PTSD:

> A *The person has been exposed to a traumatic event in which both of the following were present.*
> (1) The person experienced, witnessed, or was confronted with an event or events that involved actual or threatened death or serious injury, or the threat to the physical integrity of self or others.
> (2) The person's response involved intense fear, helplessness, or horror.

Criterion A acts as the gateway to PTSD, in that even if a person has all the symptoms of PTSD, they cannot be diagnosed as suffering from the condition unless they meet the stressor criterion. The first part of criterion A acknowledges that the stressor must be objectively extreme whilst the second part signifies that it must also be subjectively experienced as extreme.

DSM-IV (APA, 1994) groups the symptoms of PTSD under three headings: B *intrusion* – the traumatic event is persistently re-experienced in one (or more) of five possible ways; C *avoidance* – persistent avoidance of stimuli associated with the trauma and numbing of general responsiveness, as indicated by three (or more) of seven possible ways; D *disordered arousal* – persistent symptoms of increased arousal as indicated by two (or more) of five possible ways. Criterion E requires that criteria B, C and D have to have lasted more than 1 month. (If criteria A-D have been fulfilled but symptoms have lasted less than a month then the term Acute Stress Disorder (ASD) is used instead.) Criterion F requires that the disturbance causes clinically significant distress or impairment in social, occupational or other important areas of functioning.

The distinction between PTSD and ASD is made because there is a great deal of naturally occurring improvement in trauma victims' symptoms in the weeks and months immediately following the trauma. For example, Rothbaum, Foa, Riggs, Murdock and Walsh (1992) found that 94% of women entering a longitudinal study following rape met criteria for PTSD at approximately two weeks post-rape, and about 50% at twelve weeks. Similarly, Blanchard *et al.* (1995) found that one-half of patients suffering from PTSD after a motor-vehicle accident recovered within six months.

There is a great deal of natural adaptation to extreme trauma: while 75% of the population experiences a criterion A stressor sometime in their life, the lifetime prevalence of PTSD is only 7.5% (Kessler *et al.*, 1996).

DEVELOPMENT OF A COGNITIVE-CONTEXTUAL MODEL OF PTSD

The general finding is that in the immediate aftermath of an extreme trauma the majority of people are destabilized, but within a few months at least half of those affected have regained their balance. If the mechanism by which such adjustments are made can be understood, then this may have important implications for those suffering long-term debility, chronic PTSD. What is it then that successful adaptors are able to do that others are not?

It is suggested that the primary mechanisms involved in fostering adaptive inter-action with a trauma memory are twofold: first, a shift from a primarily perceptual or primitive level of thinking to a more conceptual level; and second, the location of the trauma experience in an overall benign life experience. The adaptive interaction takes place at two levels: (a) the trauma itself – in which the victim shifts from a primarily perceptual processing, e.g. 'his eyes were just bulging out of his head, as he hung there, staring right through me', to a primarily conceptual level, e.g. 'at least I did all I could to help him', and (b) the prototypicality of the trauma – in which the trauma is seen as an exception to previous life experiences and of little or no relevance to the future.

Initial difficulties in contextualizing the trauma itself may arise because in the aftermath the visual-spatial and verbal stores in working memory dictate actions, reversing the normal hierarchy between the stores and the central executive. The restoration of the central executive requires a switch to a more conceptual level of processing. It is well established that those with a previous history of emotional disorder are more likely to suffer PTSD in the wake of an extreme trauma. This finding is consistent with the above model in that those with a psychiatric history are more likely to see their trauma as 'typical' of life and a further justification for vigilance.

INTERACTION OF PTSD SYMPTOMS

Perhaps the key difference between PTSD-diagnosed survivors of trauma and non-PTSD-diagnosed survivors of trauma is that the former are hypervigilant. (The hypervigilance is associated with an exaggerated startle response, and together these represent hallmarks of PTSD.) It is the vigilance–hypervigilance dimension that is likely to be most salient from an evolutionary perspective. The maintenance of a hypervigilant state requires justification, and this is furnished by the graphic intrusive imagery of the trauma. These 'images' are 'toxic' and consequently there is a tendency to avoid them, but this avoidance means that they are not contextualized at any level. Hypervigilance means preoccupation, preventing the performance of previously valued roles and the pursuit of what have hitherto been life goals. This leads to irritability and usually a deterioration of relationships.

CASE STUDY

PTSD is often discussed in the context of major disasters, but a counsellor is much more likely to encounter the disorder in the context of a motor-vehicle accident or an assault victim. The case study chosen is therefore of a client involved in a road-traffic accident. It is in fact an amalgam of such cases so as to illustrate the approach.

Paula was referred by her general practitioner, seven months after a road-traffic accident, because he was concerned at her persisting PTSD symptoms.

Session one

This session was devoted primarily to an assessment of Paula. Assessments of possible PTSD clients are a delicate matter in that part of the condition is cognitive avoidance, i.e. they typically make strenuous efforts to avoid thinking about or having conversations about the incident. This means that it is unlikely that the counsellor will obtain a comprehensive picture of the trauma at first interview in routine practice. Indeed, if the counsellor presses too hard for detail the client may become too distressed and may default from counselling.

It emerged that Paula had been driving her car, with her friend Marian as a front-seat passenger, and without warning they were hit on the driver's side by another vehicle. Their car spun down the road and she remembers thinking, 'This is it.' Their car came to a halt just short of another vehicle. From her initial description of the trauma it was clear that both the objective and subjective requirements of the gateway stressor criterion (criterion A) in DSM-IV were met. The symptoms she reported in the DSM-IV symptom clusters were: (1) *intrusion* – several times a week she experienced uncued recollections of the incident which disrupted whatever activity she was engaged in at the time. Flashbacks to the incident became particularly intense when travelling as a passenger in a car. She had dreams about the incident once or twice a week which caused her to wake up and it took her about an hour to return to sleep. (2) *Avoidance* – she always tried to avoid thinking about the incident, distracting herself by making a drink or performing a household task. Paula would abruptly change the conversation if others mentioned anything connected with the incident. She had not driven since the accident. Paula had also lost interest in, and felt detached from, both friends and family. (3) *Disordered arousal* – she was hypervigilant and particularly so as a pedestrian crossing roads and as a passenger in a car. When startled by an unexpected noise it now took her from five to ten minutes to calm down. She had become uncharacteristically irritable and her concentration was impaired, e.g. she was only able to read newspaper headlines. Paula had sufficient symptoms in the three clusters to meet the symptom requirements for a clinical 'case' of PTSD in DSM-IV.

To gauge the severity of her condition the counsellor administered the PENN Inventory (Hammarberg, 1992). This covers the whole range of PTSD symptoms. By contrast, the more commonly used Impact of Events Scale (Horowitz *et al.*, 1979) embraces only intrusion and avoidance symptoms. On the PENN Inventory she scored 48 which is well above the cut-off of 34 which is usually used to indicate clinical 'caseness' of PTSD with about 90% accuracy. The PENN score was used as the measure of progress. In addition, Paula completed the Hospital Anxiety and Depression Scale (Snaith and Zigmond, 1983) which indicated that there was a severe depression associated with the PTSD. This level of depression is a likely concomitant of severe post-traumatic stress disorder. Paula was aged 49, happily married, with three adult children living at home, and had no previous emotional difficulties.

Towards the end of the first session the counsellor introduced the 'Managing Post-traumatic Stress Disorder' handout, which is reproduced on pages 46–47. It was agreed that for homework Paula would tackle items (1) writing about the trauma for up to ten minutes a day at a fixed time, and (5) using a 'set of traffic lights' at the first signs of irritability. The rationales for these procedures were explained to Paula and are summarized in the handout.

Session two

Paula arrived for the second session in a very tearful state. She had been unable to write about the trauma and had 'gone through the lights on red' with the routine for tackling irritability. She was particularly distraught that she was being 'unfair' to her family. The prospect of writing about the accident had clearly produced excessive arousal and this is incompatible with the formation of a new view of the incident. Strian and Klicpera (1978) have shown that excessive arousal interferes with the acquisition of new information and thus impedes habituation. This is a major theoretical problem for those who would advocate flooding techniques for PTSD clients. Unfortunately it is difficult to know in advance what degree of inter-action with the memory of the trauma will be overwhelming. (In one case the author recently successfully treated a World War II veteran who could only manage to write a sentence a day about his trauma!)

In Paula's case the counsellor said that he would like to get as full a picture as possible of the incident on tape, and asked her to dictate in the first person, as if it was happening now, the details of the incident. This met with no resistance on Paula's part; it seemed that the presence of the counsellor made the issue 'safe', thus avoiding excessive arousal and providing an appropriate context for a possible reconceptualization. As Paula dictated her experience the counsellor watched closely for signs of increased arousal. At one point she paused and became tearful as she recalled seeing her friend Marian covered in blood. After seven minutes she felt that she had fully related her experience. In the first session there had been no mention of her upset at seeing Marian and it seemed likely that this aspect was at the core of her trauma. Consequently, the counsellor asked her:

Counsellor	What was it about seeing Marian that got to you?
Paula	I am responsible for that! (Followed by tears)
Counsellor	How do you mean responsible?
Paula	If I had not been driving, it would not have happened.

This exchange indicates considerable trauma-related guilt and makes it less surpris-ing that she is so depressed. Cognitive restructuring was then used first of all to contextualize the incident itself.

Counsellor	Did you ever have the experience when the children were small they fell over and cut themselves, blood everywhere, but after you cleaned them up, found it was only a small scratch?
Paula	Yes.
Counsellor	What would you have done if one of them kept on fussing about all the blood?
Paula	I would have told him it was only a scratch.
Counsellor	So what you have done there is to switch your son from the details of what happened, to what it means, which in his case was not a lot.
Paula	I can see what you are getting at, but I still feel responsible.

In this extract the counsellor has avoided excessive arousal, by moving away to a non-threatening but analogous situation from which Paula can begin to reappraise the situation and locate it within her own autobiographical narrative. The counsellor then went on to tackle the issue of responsibility:

Counsellor When the children were small did you ever, say, promise to take them to the park, you got them ready, you just set foot over the door and it starts to rain? Would you have felt guilty in that situation?
Paula Yes, I suppose I would.
Counsellor So, if things turn out badly, e.g. the children were disappointed, you would automatically blame yourself?
Paula Hmm, I think I do.
Counsellor If you saw your daughter get in a state with your grandchild in just such an incident what would you say to her?
Paula I would probably tell her not to be stupid. She is not in charge of the weather.
Counsellor So your daughter, a mere mortal, is not responsible for everything bad that happens but you are?
Paula Oh, I can see what you mean, it's daft. (Laughing)
Counsellor In the same way, I cannot work out how you can have been responsible for the consequences of Marian being in your car. You went driving as innocently as if you were taking children to the park.
Paula But I still feel responsible.
Counsellor It is perfectly possible to feel guilty and not to be guilty. If you have only the time and strength to rescue one of two people from a river you may well feel guilty, but that does not mean you are guilty.

In such cases it is a question of helping people regard the guilt feelings as a 'mental cold', an irritant not to be taken too seriously, and they carry on life much as they usually do, if a little below par, with the reassurance that eventually the cold/guilt feelings fade.

Paula But the feelings are so strong. I think people are lying when everybody, including Marian, tells me I have nothing to blame myself for.
Counsellor If you were truly guilty how come there is no hint of your prosecution?
Paula I guess you're right, but I think the letter is delayed. I know I am being silly.

Paula has used emotional reasoning to conclude that she is guilty. This is just one of ten thought processes that can lead to emotional distress (they are summarized with examples in Scott and Stradling (1992), p. 43). Once the counsellor has identified that a particular maladaptive thought process is leading to significant impairment it can then become a prime target for intervention.

For homework the client was asked to listen to the trauma tape daily and play it over again at the same sitting until she became bored with it. In addition she was asked to complete item (2) on the handout, i.e. to 'Yes . . . But' the memory each time it intruded outside of playing the tape. It was agreed that she would tell herself, 'Yes, it was horrible to see Marian covered in blood and to feel as if I was going to die, BUT her injuries were very minor, I am still here to tell the tale.'

Session three

In the previous session the counsellor's focus had been mainly on shifting Paula from a primarily perceptual processing of the trauma itself to a more conceptual level. The focus in the third session was on putting the incident in the wider context of her life, i.e. to attending to the prototypicality of the trauma. The session began as always with a review of the previous session's homework. Unfortunately Paula reported that since playing the tape she felt no better. On closer enquiry, however, she had not played the tape in the manner prescribed. She had, in fact, played it as background whilst she did other tasks, and pretended that it was someone else who was talking, i.e. she had engaged in considerable cognitive avoidance. To put it another way, she had avoided saying 'YES' to the trauma. This is a doomed enterprise because the primarily perceptual processing will continue anyway. A trauma has to be fully acknowledged before it can be contextualized. This is, however, not the same as 'reliving' the trauma which is likely to produce excessive arousal. Most sufferers from PTSD find the idea of reliving the trauma abhorrent, and to the extent that exposure treatments approximate in the client's mind to 'reliving' they are likely to default from a homework or counselling as a whole. Listening to the tape for Paula was intended as an active process involving 'Yes . . . Buts', not a passive process. (It is suggested that habituation, a decrement in responsivity, is a spin-off of reconstruction and not something that simply occurs after prolonged imaginal exposure.) The counsellor suggested that for homework she listened to the tape in the prescribed manner, but could avoid excessive arousal by having her husband present, and Paula agreed to this.

Paula's pressing concern at this session was her disturbed sleep, and this was tackled next. Several times a week she dreamt of the accident, but in the dream she actually crashed into the car that she missed and she woke in a sweat 'on impact'. This had led to a fearfulness about going to sleep. It is sometimes possible to change the context of a bad dream by changing the perspective from which it is viewed when awake. In Paula's case the counsellor suggested that because crashing into the other car was a fantasy it was reasonable to replace it with another less fearful fantasy. It was agreed that at about 9 p.m. she would begin to imagine her car going towards the other car but, as it gets nearer, it changes into 'Mr Blobby' who is bemused by the impact, opens the door of the car to Paula, takes her hand and walks her down the road. The counsellor decided to postpone work on the prototypicality of the trauma to the next session.

Session four

The earlier sessions had focused primarily on Paula's re-experiencing PTSD symptoms and her trauma-related guilt. In the fourth session it was intended to tackle the postponed work on the prototypicality of the trauma and then turn to the avoidance and disordered arousal PTSD symptoms. As usual, however, the session began with a review of the previous session's homework. It had been two weeks since the previous session and Paula had found in the first week of listening to the trauma on the tape her score was at her worst point (high is worst) when she had finished. It was explained that her score at the end had to be less than at the worst point. To achieve this she might have to rewind the tape and begin playing it again so as to end at a less distressing point. In the days preceding this fourth session her typical scores were six (at the beginning), nine (at the worst) and seven (when she exited). The aspect of the tape that makes the client feel worst can vary from day to day, indicating that in listening to it they are involved in a reconstruction process. In addition her bad dreams had reduced to one a week.

The counsellor began work on the prototypicality of the trauma by asking her how she had looked at life the day before the accident. PTSD clients' memories of life before the trauma are usually positive but over-general. In Paula's case she could only reply that she had been 'happy'. The counselling task was to have her access positive memories in graphic detail so as to provide a benign context for the trauma. Paula described the joyful chaos of meeting her husband on a blind date and then the birth of their first child. It is necessary when clients recall these positive events that they are encouraged to elaborate. The counsellor then suggested that these incidents are all part of the picture of her life, but there is also the accident which is a part of the picture, and that it was important to keep all parts of the picture in the 'frame' at the same time. He added that the temptation was to use a mental filter and 'home in' on just the negative part of the picture. To do this, it was explained, would be rather like watching recorded highlights of a football game in which they showed only the fouls and she would think it was a 'dirty game', whereas if she had been at the game she would have said, 'YES . . . this foul and that foul did happen, BUT it was yet another brilliant display by my team.'

The vividness of an experience gives a mistaken impression about its likelihood. It was explained to Paula that if she had a neighbour who died of some rare, but horrible, disease then she might well find herself initially checking herself for symptoms, but eventually the fact of reminding herself that, say, only ten people a year die of the disease in the UK would 'percolate' trickling to a 'gut' level and then it would cease. There does appear to be a time gap for this more abstract conceptual thinking to dominate the primitive more perceptual thinking. The counselling task is to help the client think in terms of statistical probability rather than of the vividness of the experience. In this connection the counsellor suggested that if she were to attempt to drive around her block with her husband would she bet him £50 that she would have an accident? Her answer was that she would not, and the counsellor replied that she could not therefore believe it, but she did feel it. It was pointed out to Paula that ordinarily she acted on what she would 'put money on', for example she would bet the counsellor £50 that the ceiling under which they were sitting would not fall in, and so she continued to sit in the room. Further, that life becomes impossible if one does not act on that which is statistically most probable. The next task was to assess the probability of another such accident. Paula had driven for twenty years, and she concluded that the chances of another such accident were probably less than one in a thousand. She agreed that if a horse were in a race at these odds she would not bet on it. For homework it was agreed that Paula would 'YES . . . BUT' the trauma memory, item (2) on the Managing PTSD handout.

The 'YES . . . BUT' procedure is an important prelude to tackling avoidance behaviour. There are a number of grounds for tackling avoidance behaviour that have little to do with reliving the trauma. The first is that avoidance behaviour stops engagement in activities that produced a sense of achievement or pleasure, thus producing *both irritability and depression*. The second is that avoidance behaviour serves to maintain a belief that it is relevant to life to disengage from certain everyday activities. The trauma memory, like all memories, is stored in the brain in a use-dependent fashion. If, therefore, behaviours are engaged which suggest that the existing trauma memory is 'useless', i.e. it has no action implications, then it is likely to be less easily activated.

A driving hierarchy was constructed with Paula in the form of a ladder: the bottom rung of the ladder was driving a friend home five minutes away, and the top rung driving twenty miles to a seaside resort. It was agreed that for homework she would begin by tackling the first rung of the ladder and hopefully after each session she would tackle a further rung.

Sessions five to eight

PTSD is a condition with high levels of co-morbidity in some instances, e.g., in clients with substance-abuse problems, the co-morbid disorder will need tackling first because of its effects on cognitive processing, but in most instances a simultaneous focus is recommended. (Strategies for tackling the co-morbid disorders of substance-abuse, panic attacks and obsessive compulsive disorder are described in Scott, Stradling and Dryden (1995).) The counsellor's intent in these sessions was to intro-duce general mood management strategies that were particularly relevant to Paula's depression. The session began with a review of the previous session's homework. On the positive side she was less troubled by intrusions of the memory of the accident by using the 'YES . . . BUT' strategy but her driving was more problematic. She had made the agreed five-minute drive each day to her friend's but she arrived in such an agitated state that it was taking her thirty minutes to unwind. This task was simply sensitizing her to the experience rather than producing an habituation response. In an attempt to avoid excessive arousal the counsellor had made the first step in overcoming the avoidance behaviour as small as possible, but unfortunately the prescribed task was not allowing her the opportunity to collect sufficient data that there was no real threat.

Accordingly the first rung on the ladder was revised to a twenty-minute drive to a shopping centre. By the next session she had successfully completed this task without undue distress and by the eighth session she was able to drive the twenty miles to the seaside resort. Paula's irritability had substantially reduced by the eighth session and she was able to utilize the 'traffic light' routine, item (5) on the Managing PTSD handout. In this session the counsellor sought to normalize Paula's life by asking her to timetable, into her week, activities that she had previously found uplifting. These included going to keep-fit, and socializing with friends. One of Paula's depressive symptoms was a motivational deficit, hence the need to 'timetable' in activities. It was explained that initially she should praise herself for attempting activities and that any enjoyment was a bonus, but if she continued to be active she would catch the taste of life again. Because motivation is a problem in depression it is important that tasks are made of manageable proportions so that the client will likely have a success experience. In Paula's case she initially decided to have a chat on the telephone with a friend rather than spend an evening with them.

The second mood management strategy taught to Paula was a 'Thought Record'.

This consists of (a) the identification of the situation that has led to a downturn in mood, (b) the determination of the 'automatic thoughts', i.e. what it sounded 'as if' she had said to herself to feel the way she did (the automatic thoughts may be at the forefront of her mind or may be at the edge of awareness, the latter requiring more effort to identify), (c) a standback assessment of the automatic thoughts, assessing the degree of truth in them, and elaborating more reasonable ways of thinking and behaving in response to the situation. It was explained to Paula that completing the Thought Record as soon as possible after an upset helped resolve everyday hassles and stop their accumulation. (The cumulative effect of hassles is one of the pathways to depression, often leading to depression about depression because the person realizes that no one hassle by itself is sufficient to 'justify' the depression.)

At each of these sessions the counsellor reviewed Paula's activity scheduling and use of the Thought Record in the standard cognitive therapy fashion (see Scott, 1989).

Sessions nine and ten

These sessions were devoted respectively to relapse prevention and follow up, the latter planned to take place six weeks after the former. By the ninth session Paula had significantly improved. She was no longer troubled by intrusive imagery of the accident, she was driving up to twenty miles by herself, but she was still, in her view, 'overcautious' and a little concerned that she might cause an accident by driving too slowly. Paula was much less irritable than she had been since the accident but not as placid as previously. These improvements were reflected in her PENN score of 22 which was below the cut-off usually used to indicate a clinical case of PTSD. It was explained to Paula that she should not, however, regard herself as 'cured', but as 'scarred' by the experience with a 'fault line' – while she could function well enough probably most of the time, certain events could happen, like seeing a road traffic accident, causing her to crack temporarily along the fault line and she would only regain her balance if she used the tools she had been taught to do a 'repair job'. This 'job' could take days and it was crucially important for her to be gentle with herself while she carried it out. In this way the counsellor sought to inoculate her against subsequent 'failure' experiences. The ninth session ended with the counsellor giving Paula a follow-up appointment together with a telephone number to contact him in an emergency if she really could not manage to apply the tools taught. This provided her with the reassurance that she did have a 'safety net'. In the event Paula rang to cancel the follow-up appointment because she was feeling very well indeed and it was agreed to leave it open for her to contact the counsellor 'if she really needed it'. Had the follow-up session taken place the counsellor would have focused on any periods of destabilization and highlighted the relevance of particular tools already taught in more speedily regaining her equilibrium.

It may be that in the successful treatment of PTSD the counsellor does not so much change the trauma memory, as suggested by Foa and Kozak (1986), as develop a compensatory schema consisting of (a) any elements of the trauma that carry action implications in the real world (e.g., if a client had been somewhat over the speed limit at the time of the accident there might be an action disposition to drive more slowly, signposted by a non–debilitating image of the accident), and (b) their own benign life experiences. When relapse occurs it is the trauma memory that is activated, and the client experiences this as being controlled by the memory. The therapeutic task is to ensure that the compensatory schema assumes the ascendancy, and the client experiences this as themselves controlling the memory. Indeed the whole counselling enterprise can be explained to the client as being about them controlling the memory rather than the memory controlling them or, in the language of cognitive psychology, restoring the central executive to its rightful place.

THE CONTEXT FOR A CONTEXTUAL APPROACH

Paula was treated entirely on an individual basis, but a group module for PTSD clients can lessen the sense of isolation of trauma victims and make for a more efficient use of professional resources (see Scott and Stradling, 1997).

If before the trauma a client already has adaptive ways of thinking about suffering and death, then there may be a foundation for the construction of the compensatory schema. Religious beliefs may constitute an organized schema that can be readily pressed, albeit with some elaboration, into service as a compensatory schema. An eighteen-month longitudinal study of adaptation to the death of an infant (McIntosh, 1993) found that strong religious beliefs prospectively predicted greater cognitive processing activity and enhanced well-being.

One of the difficulties with much PTSD research is that it is based in the Western industrialized nations with researchers and, often, clients of a particular world-view, disguising the possibility that ethnicity and culture may well affect both the development and treatment of the condition.

APPENDIX A

Managing Post-traumatic Stress Disorder

(1) MANAGING THE MEMORY

If you try to block out the memory of the incident you will find that it does not really work, it keeps coming back. To help you control the memory rather than the memory control you, each time the memory comes to mind say to yourself 'now is not the time and place, I will sort that out properly with pen and paper at, say, 11 a.m., I will write down whatever I can about what happened and how I felt.' Spending a couple of minutes at a fixed time writing about it (or talking about it to someone) tells your mind that you are in charge of the memory and it acts as a safety valve for the memory. Otherwise it is all 'bottled up' inside you and you feel ready to explode. The first days of writing about it can be very upsetting so you might just do a minute or two to begin with. As the days go on it gets easier and after two or three weeks you will find the memory does not get to you in the way it used to.

(2) 'YES . . . BUT' THE MEMORY

With Post-traumatic Stress Disorder people get sucked into the details of the incident like a 'black hole' that can swallow you up and stop ordinary living. When a detail of the incident comes to mind, calmly acknowledge the horror of the details, e.g. 'yes it was horrible that . . .' but then put the horror into context, e.g. 'but the incident was a one off, nothing like it had ever happened to me before, I have many more good experiences in life that tell me life can be good.'

(3) UNLOCK POSITIVE MEMORIES

With Post-traumatic Stress Disorder positive memories are locked away in your mind – you know they are there but they are vague. To make the positives come alive spend a couple of minutes each day going into great detail about two particular events, e.g. a holiday or the birth of your first child. Either write them down or talk about them.

(4) TIMETABLE UPLIFTS

Timetable into your week things that could be potentially uplifting. Have a go at them even if you don't feel like it. If you keep active eventually the taste of life comes back. To begin with you might have to do things in small doses, e.g. visit a friend for twenty minutes for a coffee rather than stay all evening.

The timetable is a way of reminding yourself that despite the disruption caused by the incident it is possible to get a sense of achievement and pleasure out of life, though what you do may be different to before.

(5) MANAGING IRRITABILITY

When you notice the first signs of anger, imagine a set of traffic lights on red and shout 'STOP!' As the lights go to amber ask yourself, 'Am I absolutely sure he/she did that deliberately to wind me up? Is it really the end of the world that X has just happened?' When the lights go to green go into another room to calm down. Perhaps make a drink.

REFERENCES

American Psychiatric Association (APA) (1980). *Diagnostic and Statistical Manual of Mental Disorders*, III edition. Washington, DC: APA.

American Psychiatric Association (1994). *Diagnostic and Statistical Manual of Mental Disorders*, IV edition. Washington, DC: APA.

Blanchard, E.B., Hickling, E.J., Vollmer, A.J., Loos, W.R., Buckley, T.C. and Jaccard, J. (1995). Short-term follow-up of post-traumatic stress symptoms in motor vehicle accident victims. *Behaviour Research and Therapy*, **33**, 369–78.

Foa, E.B. and Kozak, M.J. (1986). Emotional processing of fear: Exposure to corrective information. *Psychological Bulletin*, **99**, 20–35.

Foa, E.B., Rothbaum, B.O., Riggs, D.S. and Murdock, T.B. (1991). Treatment of post-traumatic stress disorder in rape victims: a comparison between cognitive-behavioural procedures and counselling. *Journal of Consulting and Clinical Psychology*, **59**, 715–23.

Hammarberg, M. (1992). PENN inventory for post-traumatic stress disorder: psychometric properties. *Journal of Consulting and Clinical Psychology, Psychological Assessment*, **4**, 67–76.

Horowitz, M.J., Wilner, N. and Alvarez, W. (1979). Impact of event scale: a measure of subjective distress. *Psychomatic Medicine*, **41**, 209–18.

Kessler, R.C., Sonnega, A., Bromet, E., Hughes, M. and Nelson, C.B. (1996). Post-traumatic stress disorder in the National Comorbidity Study. *Archives of General Psychiatry*, **52**, 1048–60.

McIntosh, D.N. (1993). Religion as schema, with implications for the relation between religion and coping. *The International Journal for the Psychology of Religion*, **5**, 1–16.

Rothbaum, B.O., Foa, E.B., Riggs, D.S., Murdock, T. and Walsh, W. (1992). A prospective examination of post-traumatic stress disorder in rape victims. *Journal of Traumatic Stress*, **5**, 455–75.

Scott, M.J. (1989). *A Cognitive-Behavioural Approach to Client's Problems*. London: Tavistock/Routledge.

Scott, M.J. and Stradling, S.G. (1992). *Counselling for Post-Traumatic Stress Disorder*. London: Sage Publications.

Scott, M.J., Stradling, S.G. and Dryden, W. (1995). *Developing Cognitive-Behavioural Counselling*, London: Sage Publications.

Scott, M.J. and Stradling, S.G. (1997). *Brief Group Counselling: Integrating Individual and Group Cognitive-Behavioural Approaches*. London: John Wiley & Sons.

Snaith, R.P. and Zigmond, A.S. (1983). The hospital anxiety and depression scale. *Acta Psychiatrica Scandinavia*, **67**, 361–70.

Strian, F. and Klicpera, C. (1978). Die Bedeutung psychoautonomischer Reaktionen im Entstehung und Persistenz von Angstzustanden. *Nervenartz*, **49**, 576–83.

Trimble, M. (1985). Post-traumatic stress disorder: history of a concept. In: C. Figley (ed.), *Trauma and its Wake*. New York: Brunner/Mazel.

CHAPTER 5

Cognitive-behavioural Treatment of Post-traumatic Stress Disorder from a Narrative Constructivist Perspective
A Conversation with Donald Meichenbaum

Michael F. Hoyt

One of the founders of the 'cognitive revolution' in psychotherapy and a major proponent of the constructivist perspective, Donald Meichenbaum is Professor of Psychology at the University of Waterloo in Ontario, Canada. A prolific writer, researcher and international lecturer, he is the author of the classic *Cognitive-Behavior Modification: An Integrative Approach* (1977). His other books include *Stress Reduction and Prevention* (Meichenbaum and Jaremko, 1983), *Pain and Behavioral Medicine: A Cognitive-Behavioral Perspective* (Turk, Meichenbaum and Genest, 1983), *The Unconscious Reconsidered* (Bowers and Meichenbaum, 1984), *Stress Inoculation Training: A Clinical Guidebook* (Meichenbaum, 1985), and *Facilitating Treatment Adherence: A Practitioner's Guidebook* (Meichenbaum and Turk, 1987).

The following conversation took place in San Francisco on 4 May 1994, where Meichenbaum was to present a two-day workshop on 'Treating Patients with Post-traumatic Stress Disorder' for the Institute for Behavioral Healthcare. We had just been looking at the typescript of his forthcoming magnum opus, *A Clinical Handbook/Practical Therapist Manual for Treating PTSD* (1994),[1] an extraordinary compendium of information for clinicians and researchers working with persons suffering the effects of traumatic stress.

Hoyt   The first question I want to ask you, Don, is how did you come to think of treating PTSD [Post-traumatic Stress Disorder] as a narrative constructive endeavour?

Meichenbaum   For a number of years, I have been involved in treating adults, adolescents and children with behavioural and affective disorders who were depressed, anxious, angry and impulsive. Based on my research and clinical experience with these populations, I was invited to present a number of training workshops. Then a very interesting set of invitations came my way when I was given the opportunity to consult and conduct research on a variety of different distressed populations. I was asked to consult on a treatment programme within the US military on spouse abuse. I also consulted with mental-health workers who conducted debriefing of natural disasters, occupational accidents and combat. I also consulted at residential treatment programmes for children and adolescents, some 40% of whom met the DSM criteria for PTSD. In addition, I was supervising various mental-health workers (psychiatrists, psychologists, social workers, family physicians) who were treating clients who had a history of victimization experiences – child sexual abuse, rape, domestic violence. As I became more and more involved with these populations and spent many hours listening to the therapy tapes, looking at the debriefing experiences, I became quite fascinated with the nature of the 'stories' that people offered to describe their traumatizing experiences and how they coped – that is, the narratives and the accounts that they constructed.

Hoyt   What about the stories?

Meichenbaum   I became fascinated with how people describe their experience and how their accounts changed over time. While victimization experiences can affect individuals at various levels (e.g. physiologically, behaviourally, socially), given my cognitive-behavioural background and my interest in cognition and emotion, I became particularly interested in the nature of the 'stories' that people tell themselves and others, and the manner in which they offer accounts of their experience. When something bad happens to you, when some natural or man-made disaster occurs, when some form of victimization experience occurs to you or to your family, ordinary language and everyday vocabulary seem inadequate to describe your experience and reactions. In their own ways, these 'victimized' individuals became 'poets' of sorts, using metaphors to describe their experiences. They conveyed their experiences by using phrases such as 'This is like . . .', 'I feel like a . . .', and so forth. The victimized individual may describe herself as a 'prisoner of the past', as a 'doormat', a 'whore', as a 'time bomb ready to explode', and the like. Just imagine the impact on yourself and on others if you go about describing your experiences in such metaphoric terms.

As a result of these initial clinical impressions, I undertook the task of analysing the nature of the metaphors and the narrative accounts that clients offered over the course of their therapeutic sessions. I also analysed the literature on PTSD in order to discern what were the narrative features of individuals who did *not* suffer PTSD following exposure to traumatic events (Meichenbaum, 1994; Meichenbaum and Fitzpatrick, 1993). Based upon both the clinical analysis and the literature review, I came to appreciate the heuristic value of a constructive narrative perspective, not only for PTSD, but for other clinical disorders as well. Obviously, I am not the first to propose such a constructive narrative perspective. Let me note that there are people like Harvey (Harvey, Weber, and Orbuch, 1990), Gergen (1991; McNamee and Gergen, 1992), Schafer (1992), White and Epston (1990), and O'Hanlon (O'Hanlon and Weiner-Davis, 1989) who have also advocated for a constructive narrative perspective.

Hoyt   Let me read you a quotation from an article you wrote with Geoffrey Fong (Meichenbaum and Fong, 1993, p. 489). You said, 'The constructivist perspective is founded on the idea that humans actively construct their personal realities and create their own representational models of the world. There is a long tradition of philosophical and psychological authors who have argued that the paradigms, assumptive worlds, and schemas that individuals actively create, determine, and in some instances constrain how they perceive reality.'[2] When someone becomes a victim, has a horrible trauma, how does that affect them? What changes, especially in terms of their world view?

Meichenbaum The answer to what changes after you've been victimized depends on which piece of the puzzle you look at – sort of like the old metaphor of the elephant, whether you examine the tusk, the tail, or whatever. Clearly, there is increasing evidence that something changes physiologically (see van der Kolk, 1994). This is especially true of chronic, prolonged exposure, or what are called *Type II stressors* (e.g., abuse, domestic violence, Holocaust victim). Such exposure leads to what are called 'disorders of extreme stress' that affect one's sense of trust in family and beliefs about self and the world. To use Janoff-Bulman's (1985, 1990) model, traumatic events can 'shatter' your basic assumptions about the world; traumatic events can violate and invalidate your core beliefs. Another thing that trauma does is overly sensitize you to trauma-related cues, and this hypervigilance feeds into, and is in turn affected by, the ruminations, flashbacks, and avoidance behaviours that characterize PTSD. Trauma biases the ways in which you selectively attend to events. There is a great deal of data that I review in the PTSD clinical handbook (Meichenbaum, 1994) that examines the impact of trauma from an information-processing and a constructive narrative perspective.

Hoyt   Is this primarily a protective mechanism: 'I need to be on alert so it won't happen again'?

Meichenbaum I think there are functional and adaptive values in such behaviour. To become vigilant and to over-respond after exposure to a trauma can be adaptive initially. But what happens to the people who have difficulty recovering, who evidence maladjustment, is that they continue to behave in ways that may be no longer necessary. From my point of view, a central feature of individuals with PTSD can be characterized as a 'stuckness' problem. That is, people get 'stuck' using techniques such as dissociation that were at one time effective in order to deal with trauma such as incest, or dealing with the aftermath of rape, or dealing with combat. What happens is that some individuals continue to respond in the same fashion even when it is no longer needed. It is my task as a therapist to help clients understand and appreciate the adaptive value of how they responded. But

I also help them appreciate what is the *impact*, what is the *toll*, what is the *price* to them and others of continuing to respond in this fashion when it is no longer needed. This approach helps clients reframe their reactions (their 'symptoms') as adaptive strengths, rather than as signs of mental illness. In a collaborative fashion, this approach 'inoculates' them, in some sense, to the impact of future stressors. We work together to help them not only change their behaviour, but also to tell their 'stories' differently.

Hoyt   In your writing about stress inoculation training (SIT), you describe three phases: namely, education, skills acquisition and consolidation, and application training. The first phase, of education, sounds like you are having clients work to better understand the impact of their . . .[3]

Meichenbaum   I even go beyond understanding, to nurturing the client's discovery process by using Socratic questioning. In the PTSD handbook (Meichenbaum, 1994), I have included the best Socratic questions you can ask in therapy. Moreover, I believe that I am at my 'therapeutic best' when the client I am seeing is one step ahead of me, offering the advice that I would otherwise offer. I try to train clinicians how to emulate that fine inquirer of sorts – namely, Peter Falk playing the popular TV detective character, Columbo. I want clinicians, at times, to play 'dumb'. For some clinicians this is not a difficult nor challenging role. (*Laughter*) I encourage clinicians to use strategically their bemusement, their befuddlement; I want them to be collaborators. The goal is to help the client in the initial phase of stress inoculation to understand better what they have been through; how are things now; how would they like them to be; and what can *we* do, working together, to help them achieve their goals? The educational phase of SIT lays the groundwork whereby the client can come to say, 'You know, I'm stuck.' A related objective of this initial phase is to help clients move from global metaphorical accounts of their experience and reactions to behaviourally prescriptive descriptions that lead to change, and to nurture a sense of hope to undertake this change.

Hoyt   In essence, I think you're saying that as clinicians we're trying to help clients re-author their narratives, rather than us undertaking the role of correcting their accounts (see Simon, 1993, p. 72). We're there as sort of an amanuensis, as an assistant to take it down, rather than simply to correct their narratives or to tell them they're looking at it wrong.[4]

Meichenbaum   Correct. The metaphors that describe my therapeutic approach include 'rescripting', 're-authoring', 'helping clients generate a new narrative', and 'being a coach'. I don't just record the clients' accounts; rather, I help them alter their personal stories. Such change occurs as a result of my helping clients attend to and appreciate the strengths they possess, or what they have done to survive. A second way is to help them engage in 'personal experiments' in the present that provide them with 'data' that they can take as evidence to 'unfreeze' the beliefs they hold about themselves and the world. The results of such ongoing experiments that occur both within and outside of the therapeutic setting provide the basis for the client to develop a new narrative. This co-constructive process is one that emerges out of experientially meaningful efforts by the client. In terms of strengths and coping efforts, I help people who have PTSD to appreciate that their intrusive thoughts, hypervigilance, denial, dissociation, dichotomous thinking and moments of rage each represent coping efforts, and metaphorically reflect the 'body's wisdom'. For example, intrusive thoughts may reflect ways of making sense of what happened, as attempts to 'finish the story', to answer 'why' questions. Denial may be an attempt to 'dose oneself', dealing with limited amounts of stress at a given time – a way to take a 'time out'. Hypervigilance may be seen as being on continual 'sentry duty' when it is no longer needed.

In other words, it is not that people get anxious, angry or depressed per se; those are natural human emotions. Rather, it is what people say to themselves about those conditions that is critical. The collaborative process of therapy is designed to help the client 'say' different things to herself, as well as to others. A key element of cognitive-behavioural interventions is that an effective way of having people talk to themselves differently is to have them *behave* differently. Thus, a critical feature of cognitive-behavioural interventions such as stress inoculation training is to encourage and even challenge clients to perform personal experiments *in vivo*, so, as I mentioned, they can collect data that will 'unfreeze' their beliefs about themselves and about the world. Cognitive-behavioural therapy is *not* just a 'talking cure'. It is a proactive, enabling form of intervention that fits an 'evidential' theory of behaviour change (see Meichenbaum, 1977, 1994).

But such change is *not* enough. It is critical for clients to take credit for the changes that they have brought about. There is a need for the therapist to ensure that the clients take data resulting from personal experiments as evidence, and thus assume a greater sense of responsibility for the changes that they have brought about. This process of 'ownership' is evident in the new narratives that clients relate. I listen carefully to the clients' stories. I listen for their spontaneous use of metacognitive self-regulatory verbs as part of their new accounts. Improvement is evident when clients use such verbs as 'I noticed . . . caught myself . . . interrupted . . . used my plan . . . felt I had options . . . patted myself on the back . . . became my own coach . . . anticipated high-risk situations . . . tried my other options'. When clients incorporate these expressions into their narratives, then they have become their own therapists, and truly have taken (appropriated) the clinician's 'voice' with them.

Hoyt This is the power of new *experience* – not just explanation of what's wrong, but disconfirming the expectations with a new experience.[5]

Meichenbaum But for meaningful change to occur, it has to be 'affectively charged'. I am referring to the time-honoured concept of 'corrective emotional experience' (Alexander and French, 1946). People can readily dismiss, discount, dissuade themselves of the 'data'. They don't really accept data as 'evidence', and it is critical therapeutically to work with clients in order to ensure that they take the data they have collected as evidence to unfreeze their beliefs – to get into the nature of the clients' belief system and to nurture an internal dialogue that they would find most adaptive, as compared to being 'stuck' in maladaptive patterns of thinking and behaving.[6]

Hoyt Watching you work, I'm always impressed by how much caring and effort goes into developing a therapeutic alliance and a collaborative relationship with the client. It appears to be the vehicle that carries the rest of your work.

Meichenbaum I agree. I think the therapeutic relationship is the glue that makes the various therapeutic procedures work. Some of the things that I try to highlight for a clinical audience watching my videotapes is how often I 'pluck' and reflect the client's key words, use Socratic questioning, and often over the course of the session, I let the client finish my sentences. The most valuable tool that a clinician has is the art of questioning. As Tomm (1987a, 1987b, 1988) has highlighted, the questions we ask clients have presuppositions, and as a result the clinician can use questions effectively and strategically to move clients towards self-generated solutions.

Let me also highlight, however, that in this movement toward solutions, a major clinical concern which is critical is that of timing. If the clinician only focuses on the positive, if you have clients move toward solutions too quickly, then the clients may *not* feel you have heard their emotional pain, nor appreciated the seriousness of their situations. You need to encourage clients to tell their stories, at their own pace, and to be in charge. But out of the telling of their stories, out of the narrative sharing – and there's a lot of therapeutic value in sharing one's story – new stories emerge that also reveal strengths and resources. As the radio commentator Paul Harvey highlights, there is a need to hear 'the rest of the story'. Clients come in and tell us their stories. Their stories are often filled with expressions of hopelessness and helplessness. They often convey a tale of having been victimized by individuals, by events, by their feelings and thoughts. It is my job, as the therapist, not only to hear their stories and empathize with them, but also to help them appreciate what they have done to survive and to cope with their feelings – namely, help them attend to 'the rest of the story'. For 'the rest of the story' is often the tale of remarkable strengths.

Keep in mind that the story of how people cope with stressful events such as incest, rape, the Holocaust, war experiences, urban and domestic violence, and man-made and natural disasters is inherently the story of resilience and courage of human beings. That is, if you look at the impact of disasters, most people are going to 'make it' and *not* evidence long-term debilitating effects. So even in the worst scenarios, people evidence remarkable strengths. As a therapist, I need clients to attend to that part of their stories. There are a number of clinical techniques designed to accomplish this goal and to incorporate these features into their personal narratives. Thus, the 'bad things' that happened to people are only one chapter in their life stories. And, as Judith Herman (1992) indicates, it is *not* the most interesting chapter of their autobiographies.

Hoyt Oftentimes brief therapists (and others) rush past the painful material, trying to reframe or restructure so quickly that the person doesn't feel heard or validated. Do you think there's also – maybe following from Aristotle – a need for catharsis and abreaction? Is that part of the cure, or is it . . .

Meichenbaum That is a challenging question. I can offer my clinical impressions, given the limited database that exists (see Meichenbaum, 1994). The question about differential forms of treatment is complex. How one should proceed therapeutically is dependent upon which target group you are looking at. If you are treating people who have experienced traumas that are brief, sudden, yet life-threatening, such as automobile accidents, robberies, rape, and sudden disasters, or what have been characterized as 'Type I stressors' (Terr, 1994) . . .

Hoyt   You mean relatively discrete, sudden-onset stressors.

Meichenbaum   Yes. The data suggest that having clients go through re-experiencing pro-cedures as a means of 'coming to terms' with what happened is therapeutic and beneficial. Indeed, there are a variety of very creative clinical tech-niques, including direct therapy exposure, guided imagery procedures, graded *in vivo* procedures, and the like, that are helpful. They fit your Aristotelian catharsis model and provide a means of 'working through' that can prove valuable.

Hoyt   What about people with more prolonged trauma?

Meichenbaum   When, however, you are treating a different traumatized clinical group, where the PTSD is chronic and the traumatic events occurred many years ago, the treatment decision to undertake 'memory work' of having clients 'go back' may *not* be the most effective treatment strategy. Having clients recount and re-experience traumatic events, even in the area of incest, may not be the most therapeutic approach. Because in the attempt to conduct so-called 'memory work', there is the danger that the therapist can inadver-tently, unwittingly, and perhaps even unknowingly, help clients co-create memories. With such prolonged traumas that have a number of secondary sequelae, it is important to address the secondary consequences such as depression, interpersonal distrust, sexual difficulties, addictive behaviours, and the like that may accompany PTSD. The full cognitive-behavioural therapeutic armamentarium needs to be employed to address these signs of co-morbidity. A 'here-and-now' therapeutic focus, as compared to a 'there-and-then' approach, may prove most helpful. Research is needed to determine how to blend the need for 'memory work' with a coping skills model. But keep in mind that from a constructive narrative perspective, even when clients are doing so-called 'memory work', they are not relating nor 'uncovering' history, but rather they are co-constructing history in a mood-congruent fashion. As Donald Spence (1982) observes, it is the 'narrative truthfulness', not the 'historical truthfulness', of clients' accounts that needs to be the focus of therapeutic interventions.[7]

Hoyt   You have worked clinically with many diverse groups, and you have taught and given workshops internationally. How do these guidelines vary across these diverse settings?

Meichenbaum   That question raises the important issue of how important it is to be culturally sensitive in formulating a treatment plan. Let me give you an example. As I review in the clinical handbook on PTSD (Meichenbaum, 1994), there are 'testimony' procedures that are sometimes used in treating people who have been victims of torture. These procedures have individuals 'go public' with what traumas they have experienced and what retribution should occur. For instance, one group of torture victims for whom this testimony procedure has been used came from Argentina, Chile, and other South American countries. Agger and Jensen (1990) have described how having these survivors write out testimonies, bear witness, go back and relive what happened, was highly therapeutic. On the other hand, there is another group of victims of torture who come from South-East Asia – Cambodia and other countries – who have also received treatment. Therapists such as Mollica (1988) and Kinzie (1994) have indicated that a somewhat different therapeutic approach – one that is designed to deal with their 'here-and-now' problems, their practical employment and living situations, rather than do 'memory work' – is more effective. The torture victims' cultural orientation suggested that treatment should *not* encourage clients to go back and relive their victimization experiences per se.

Thus, being sensitive to cultural differences should influence the nature and form of the intervention. When I am in doubt, I spell out the treatment options and collaborate with the client in formulating, implementing, and evaluating the therapeutic options. This is especially important when the database for alternative treatments is so limited. For instance, Solomon and her colleagues (1992) reviewed some 255 studies on the treatment of PTSD. Out of those 255 studies, there were only eleven clinical trials that employed randomized control groups. Eleven! Five of these were in the area of psychopharmacology with PTSD clients. These five double-blind studies employed a total of 134 subjects, mostly combat veterans. There were only six well-controlled psychotherapy outcome studies. As you can see, we are at such a preliminary stage in the area of PTSD treatment that anyone who gets on a soapbox and says that 'Memory work interventions are essential', or who claims that 'This is the way to conduct intervention', should be received with a great deal of scepticism and caution, no matter what the therapeutic approach they advocate. It is critical for clinicians to appreciate the scope of our limited knowledge. I also think, however, that straight-forward empiricism is *not* going to advance the field. We need a theoretical framework to explain therapeutic approaches. One such theoretical framework is that of a constructive narrative perspective.

Hoyt　　　How would you distinguish the constructive narrative perspective from the other wing of cognitive therapy that sometimes is called 'rationalist'?

Meichenbaum　I really take issue with the so-called 'rationalist' perspective. It is *not* that people distort reality, nor make cognitive errors, that contributes to their difficulties. Instead of one reality that is distorted, as some 'rationalists' would advocate, I believe that there are multiple potential 'realities'. Instead, the focus of therapy is to help the client appreciate how he or she has constructed his or her realities, and what is the impact, the toll, the price, of such constructions. Most importantly, what are the alternative (more adaptive) constructions? I am not alone in highlighting the distinction between the 'rationalist' and 'constructive' perspectives. For instance, see the ongoing debate between Michael Mahoney and Albert Ellis, and others.[8]

Hoyt　　　How does this apply in the case of individuals who have been traumatized or victimized?

Meichenbaum   For instance, consider the client who has been victimized sexually. Envision the clinical impact of this individual characterizing herself as being 'damaged goods' or as 'soiled property'. Such labels, such metaphors, may be culturally reinforced. Whatever the origins and influences of such labels, the consequences of such narrative constructions are likely to lead to dysphoric feelings and distressing behaviour. In therapy, I would help the client share her story either in individual or group therapy; validate her feelings; but at the same time help the client appreciate the toll, impact and price she pays if she goes around telling herself that she is 'soiled goods', that she is 'damaged property', that she is 'useless'. In this way, she can come to also appreciate that she speaks to herself in the same manner that the perpetrator spoke to her. She may inadvertently reproduce the 'voice' of the perpetrator, as in the case of the victims of domestic violence. She needs to develop her own voice. One goal of treatment is to no longer let the perpetrator continue to victimize her when he is no longer present. Instead, what is the best revenge?

Hoyt   Living well.

Meichenbaum   To live life well. In therapy, we need to explore with clients operationally what it means to live life well. Moreover, given the cognitive-behavioural approach, therapists also consider with clients what are the barriers, the obstacles, the potential reasons why clients may *not* do anything that they said they are going to do.[9] Thus, when clients say, 'I need to live well', there is a need to help clients translate such general admonitions into behaviourally prescriptive statements such as 'Between now and next time, how will that show up? What will you do differently?' There is also a need to build relapse prevention procedures into the treatment regimen – anticipating high-risk situations, as well as ways of handling possible setbacks, so lapses don't escalate into full-blown relapses.

Hoyt   Some clients will get stuck in what I call a 'persistent negative narrative', and oftentimes I think that a horrible stress event confirms for them some underlying schema, some assumptive thoughts they have. To use the example you were just giving, she says, 'I *am* soiled property, useless; I *am* a piece of dirt; and this just proves it'. How do we then get the person to move out of that belief about herself? Do we go back through the earlier assumptions?

Meichenbaum   I don't know the answer to your question, and I don't think the field knows either, but let me offer a clinical strategy that I would be prone to use in such a situation. When the client responds with 'I'm soiled property', or 'I'm useless', or words to that effect, it's usually said with a great deal of emotion. What I would be prone to do as a therapist is to not only attend to the client's words, but to the affect in which it is said. So I would say, 'Soiled property? Tell me about that.' I would pluck the key words and put them back in the client's lap, and encourage her to elaborate. I would also attend to the feelings with which this was said. The feelings might convey a sense of being overwhelmed, or feelings of being depressed, and the like. I want to learn about the circumstances that led to such self-perceptions and accompanying feelings.

Next, as part of my clinical approach, I 'commend' the client for being depressed. After empathetically listening to their distress, I might say something like: 'Given what you've been through (citing specific examples), if you were not depressed at times, if you did not feel at times like you were "soiled property", or at times as if you were "useless", then I think I would be really concerned and conclude that something was seriously wrong.' In this fashion, I attempt to validate the client's experience. I am going to go beyond that and even compliment the client for the symptoms of being depressed. For instance, I might say to the client, 'What does your being depressed say about what's going on? . . . Perhaps it conveys that you are in touch with your feelings, that you are reading your situation, that you're responsive to what you have experienced.'

Hoyt The first step is to join with, to validate, to recognize . . .

Meichenbaum And also to commend the client because her depression and the resultant withdrawal, the labelling of being 'soiled property', at one time may have been adaptive. I need to help the client see that when she calls herself 'soiled property', that maybe that self-attribution was an impression management stance and her way of trying to control the situation. So even if she says, 'You know, I was a zombie with no emotions', I try to have her appreciate that the dissociative responses that she used were adaptive. The critical step in helping her to alter her view of herself is whether I can help her appreciate that what she is continuing to do now, even in 'safe' relationships, is no longer her only option. The problem is that she is stuck. It is not that she is 'deficient' nor 'sick'. I am helping her move away from a so-called 'deficit model' where she continually questions her self-worth and even her sanity – 'Am I losing my mind?' Instead, I want her to appreciate, I want to help her cognitively reframe her experiences as a form of 'survival skills'. The problem is that she is continuing to do what 'worked' in the past, but it may no longer be necessary.

In order to facilitate this transition, I encourage the client to consider the question: What is the impact, toll, price she is paying for being stuck? The answer to this question is *not* discussed in the abstract, but rather the client is encouraged to feel experientially, in the session, the costs of being stuck. Moreover, if the client is stuck, I then ask, in my best Columbo-like style: 'What, if anything, can you do to change your situation?' *If* I have laid the groundwork well – by means of

1. plucking key metaphorical terms;
2. validating the client's experience and the accompanying feelings;
3. commending the client for her presenting symptoms;
4. helping her cognitively reframe these symptoms as a form of coping and as a set of survival skills;
5. examining collaboratively how such survival skills worked in the past, but how she continues to do so now, even in situations in which the client is no longer in danger; and
6. considering the devastating impact, the emotional toll, and the interpersonal price of her being stuck –

it is *then* not a big step for the client to offer suggestions about possible ways that she can get unstuck. Remember, my therapeutic goal is to have the client come up with solutions about how to change. If she can come up with possible solutions that could be tried, then she will feel enabled and empowered, and moreover, since she came up with the ideas, there is a greater likelihood that she will follow through. Can I give you another example?

Hoyt   Please.

Meichenbaum   In fact, I have two cases that come to mind. First, I wish to describe a challenging case of a woman who has experienced a disastrous accident. She was with her fiancé – the only man she had fallen in love with after several previous broken relationships. They were returning from a party and decided to take a short cut and cross some train tracks. They were running along the train track to get to the other side where this woman lived, and a horrendous thing happened. As the train approached, she yelled out to her fiancé, 'Let's beat it,' and she darted in front of the oncoming train safely. Her fiancé tripped and did not make it. He was hit by the train and instantly killed. His body was severed.

Hoyt   Oh, my gosh.

Meichenbaum   It was horrendous. In a dissociative state, she picked up his body parts. It was one of the most horrific stories that I have ever heard. She is suffering from PTSD, depression, and suicidal ideation, as she feels responsible and guilty about his death. Her intrusive thoughts are overwhelming.

I have another case of a mother who had a 10-year-old daughter. They were at home alone. In the middle of the night, she woke up thinking that someone had broken into her home. Since she had experienced such a robbery in the past year, she became fearful. In a state of panic, she reached into her night table to grab hold of a recently obtained pistol that her husband had given her. With gun in hand, she was running into her daughter's room when her bedroom door slammed open and hit her hand, and the gun discharged.

Hoyt   Don't tell me.

Meichenbaum   Yes. It was her daughter. The mother shot her daughter and blew her daughter's brain away.

Hoyt   That is terrible!

Meichenbaum   Michael, what are you going to say or do in therapy with these clients? In each instance, I listened sympathetically to the tale of the horrendous events. And eventually asked the mother, 'What did you see in your daughter that made your relationship with her so special? Please share with me the nature of the loss.' In fact, I asked the bereaved mother to bring to therapy a picture album of her daughter and to review with me the special qualities of her daughter. The picture album permitted the client to tell the story of her relationship with her daughter in some developmental (time-line) context, and thus not delimit her memories to only the time of the shooting – which she played over and over again, with the accompanying narrative of 'If only . . .', 'Why didn't I tell my husband I didn't want to own a gun?',

'Why my daughter?', 'Tell me it is only a dream', 'How could I have?' and so forth. Moreover, the review of the picture album provided the opportunity to query further what she saw in her daughter, and, in turn, what did her daughter see in her. Following this exchange, I asked the client, 'If your daughter, whom you described as being "wise beyond her years", were here now, what advice, if any, might she have to help you get through this difficult period?' Fortunately, with some guidance I was able to help the client generate some suggestions that her daughter might have offered.[10] I then noted, 'I can now understand why you described your daughter as being "wise beyond her years". She does sound special.'

Moreover, if the client followed through on her notion to commit suicide in order to stop the emotional pain, what would happen to the memory of her daughter? Did she feel that she owed her daughter more? Like many victims of traumatic events, this client found a mission in order to cope with her distress. She undertook the task of educating parents about the dangers of keeping guns in their homes.[11] She became an expert on the incidence of accidental homicides, and developed a foundation named after her daughter designed to decrease the likelihood that this could happen to other children. She felt that if she could save one other child, then her daughter would not have died in vain. Through her actions, she was writing a new script, fashioning a new more adaptive narrative. In therapy, we also addressed her feelings of guilt. I will have to refer you to my clinical manual on treating PTSD (Meichenbaum, 1994) to see the discussion of how such guilt reactions can be addressed therapeutically.

Hoyt	I can see what you mean by arranging the conditions whereby clients come up with suggestions themselves, although you could have offered all of the advice that the daughter might have offered.
Meichenbaum	You're right, but there is a greater likelihood that clients will follow through if they come up with the ideas than if you, the therapist, give them the ideas. I use a phrase to caution therapists not to act as 'surrogate frontal lobes' for their clients.
Hoyt	(*Laughter*) I like that – 'surrogate frontal lobes'. It's better to support the client's own construction. What did you do with the client whose fiancé died in the train accident?
Meichenbaum	I used a similar therapeutic strategy, but I had to alter it somewhat. As in the case of the grieving mother, I asked the client who lost her fiancé to help me appreciate what happened exactly, and more importantly – 'To help me understand what you saw in your fiancé, Jimmy. What was life like with him? What did you see in him that attracted you to him? . . . What do you think he saw that attracted him to you? . . . If Jimmy were here now, what advice, if any, would he have for you in this difficult time? . . . What do you think would be the best legacy, the best way to remember Jimmy – not only for yourself, but for others who knew him?'

Whereas this strategy worked with the bereaved mother, it did *not* work with this client. When I asked her to come up with advice that Jimmy might offer, she drew a blank. The image of Jimmy's grotesque death was so vivid and current (even some six months after the accident) that she could not assume any distance psychologically, to consider ways to handle her distress. So, instead, I pursued a somewhat different line of questioning. Since the image of Jimmy, her fiancé, was too emotionally laden to elicit suggestions about potential coping procedures, I asked her when else she might have experienced a personal loss. She described the loss of her grandmother, whom she loved a great deal. I then asked her what did she see in her grandmother that made the relationship so special. 'What do you think your grandmother saw in you? . . . If your wise grandmother were here now, what words of support, what advice, if any, do you think your grandmother might have for you?' (Interestingly, this grandmother sounded like a good cognitive-behavioural therapist!) I then conveyed that 'Now I understand why your grandmother was so special.'

From my perspective, the 'name of the game' is to use the art of questioning to enable and empower clients to come up with possible coping strategies.

Hoyt	Thibaut and Kelley (1986), the social psychologists, wrote about *'bubbe psychology'*, the native good sense of a wise grandmother.
Meichenbaum	But note that in this instance I could have told this client every single thing that the grandmother would have offered, but it would not have been as helpful. It is not just a case of giving information. There is data we review in the Meichenbaum and Turk (1987) book on facilitating treatment adherence that if people come up with ideas themselves and the accompanying reasons for behaving in this fashion, then, as the therapist, you have a greater likelihood of clients' following through than if you, the therapist, offer such advice. Whatever merit there is to our discussion, the readers should take away the notion that they should not be a 'surrogate frontal lobe' for their clients. They should *not* do the thinking for them, nor put the words in their mouths; they should be respectful, collaborative, and remember that most people evidence the potential for a great deal of resilience and courage.
Hoyt	What about the client who did not have the positive experience that they can draw from with the lost object? The person who says, 'I've always had low self-esteem. I'm no good. I deserve what I got.' It stimulates earlier relationships that were very negative; the family abused them. What would you have done if she had said, 'My father told me I'd never be happy'?
Meichenbaum	In fact, that is what happened. Did you see the videotape of this case that I show in my workshop?
Hoyt	No, I haven't.
Meichenbaum	Because you are right on target. One of the things she says is that her father called her up and conveyed that she is a 'total screw-up' because she went down to the tracks. Not only that, but this guy, Jimmy, wasn't that good anyway, so the accident is a 'blessing in disguise'. Not very sympathetic, to say the least. In fact, she goes on to report a whole series of troubled parental interactions. During the course of therapy, the client came to realize that part of the reason she is so depressed is that she is talking to herself, reproducing the same narrative that her father said. Part of the reason that she is suicidal and depressed is not only due to this

horrendous event, but she is playing the same 'CD' she heard during her entire childhood. For the client who lacks positive developmental experiences, the therapist can help the client appreciate that she is reproducing someone else's script, that she is playing their narrative. The challenge or question is whether she can develop a voice of her own to write her own narrative.[12] Does she have the courage to do that? But a cognitive-behavioural approach goes further by ensuring that the client has the intra- and interpersonal skills to implement such a new script or construct a more adaptive narrative. Moreover, built into the treatment regimen are such therapeutic procedures as problem-solving training, cognitive restructuring techniques, 'homework' assignments, relapse prevention, 'personal experiments' and self-attributional procedures. It is *not* enough to have clients produce a new narrative, but this new narrative must be tied into behavioural acts that lead to 'data' that is taken as 'evidence' to alter the client's view of oneself and the world. While I advocate a constructive narrative perspective, it is important to appreciate that I also employ the full clinical array of cognitive-behavioural procedures that have been found to be so efficacious in treating clients with a number of psychiatric disorders.

Hoyt   In psychodynamic terms, they might say that you try to help her 'extroject the pathologic introject' in order to get the 'voice' of her father out of her head (Hoyt, 1994).

Meichenbaum   As you know, mental health workers have their own metaphors to describe therapeutic interventions. There are innumerable potential metaphors. The bottom line is that people come into therapy with a 'story', and you, the therapist, try to help them change their 'stories'. Now, clinical theorists can impose their metaphors to describe this process – for example, 'extroject the introject'. Other theorists use metaphors derived from learning theory, such as 'deconditioning' and 'habituation', or from information-processing theory in terms of 'assimilating/accommodating', 'schemas', etc. As I note in the PTSD handbook (Meichenbaum, 1994), there are many alternatives. My own approach is to remain much more phenomenologically oriented, using the client's metaphors. From my perspective, it is better to 'unpack' the client's metaphor rather than to impose the therapist's metaphors. By 'unpack', I mean help the client to appreciate the adaptive features of how he or she has constructed reality in the past, but to also consider anew what is the impact, toll and price of continuing to view the world in such a fashion – moreover, to consider in some detail what exactly can be done to change his or her 'construction', as well as the ways he or she behaves. From this perspective, the client's altered narrative becomes the 'final common pathway' to behavioural change. (It seems that we can't get away from using metaphors when describing our own, as well as others', behaviour.)

Hoyt   Are you saying that it is better to find *their* central metaphor rather than having to first educate them to believing our system?[13]

Meichenbaum   Yes. You want to help 'unpack' their metaphor, to have them appreciate the impact, the toll, the price of the stories they tell. Note that this joint exploration is *not* just something intellectual.[14] You need to have the client *feel* in therapy the impact, the toll, the price. And out of such discussions, you can then play your Columbo role. I'll give you an example. A client comes in and says that she 'stuffs her feelings'. I say, 'Stuff feelings? Tell me about that.' And we behaviourally and operationally define what 'stuffed feelings' means. It's important to listen for such verbs as 'stuffed'.

Hoyt   That is where the action's at, literally and figuratively.

Meichenbaum   Right. I usually listen very attentively to how clients tell their stories. I especially listen for how clients use transitive verbs. When I hear such verbs being used such as 'stuffed', or 'noticed', 'caught', 'put myself down', etc., I pluck these from their narrative and reflect it back to them in an inquiring fashion: 'Stuffed feelings?' I explore what she does. And then we consider what is the impact of such behaviour. Once we do that, I say, 'What could you do about it?' You don't have to be a rocket scientist for the client to then say, 'Well, maybe I should not stuff the feelings.' Then I say, 'Not stuff the feelings. That's interesting. What did you have in mind?' Once again, I am laying the groundwork where the client is going to codefine the problem and collaboratively generate possible solutions. We are now collaborating in this constructive narrative process. Another example is when clients spontaneously offer an example of some strength, some successful coping effort, and I then use this 'nugget' (as I perceive it) to ask: 'Are you saying that *in spite of* all that you experienced (give specific examples), you were able to do (to try, to achieve – give specific examples)? How did you come to the decision that X? How did you manage to do X? Where did this courage come from?'

The strategy I employ to help clients 'restory' their lives is (1) to solicit from the clients an example of their strengths; (2) ask an 'in spite of' question, and (3) ask a 'how' question. In turn, we can explore how clients can employ these coping skills and take credit for the change they bring about.

This is *not* just a 'repair' process, as Schafer (1992) describes. The metaphor of 'repair' implies that an individual's narrative is broken, like a tyre, and one has to fix it. It conveys that the narrative one is using was 'wrong'; it was 'broken' and needs to be 'fixed'. Thus, I try to stay away from the term 'narrative repair', but rather, talk about the 'constructive narrative process' that clients are now engaged in. The client's narrative may have been adaptive at one time. It wasn't broken; it doesn't need fixing. I don't have to 'fix the client's head'. Instead, I help clients to become better observers and become their own therapist. As Tomm (1989) suggests, I ask the client, 'Do you ever find yourself, out there, asking yourself the kind of questions that we ask each other right here in therapy?' I convey to clients that the treatment goal is to become your own therapist, your own coach. In this way, the clients can learn to take the therapist's voice with them[15] and appropriate, own and internalize the suggested changes. They can now write their own stories. That is what the therapeutic process is all about.

Our research task now is to demonstrate that doing all this makes a difference. The PTSD manual that I have spent the last two years writing

(Meichenbaum, 1994) is designed to operationalize these procedures, so that investigators will be able to validate empirically what I have been describing. I thank you for the opportunity to share these ideas.

NOTES

1 This 600-page manual is now available directly from Donald Meichenbaum (University of Waterloo, Department of Psychology, Waterloo, Ontario N2L 3G1, Canada).

2 Meichenbaum and Fong (1993, p. 489) go on: 'Common to each of these proponents is the tenet that the human mind is a product of constructive symbolic activities and that reality is a product of the personal meanings that individuals create. Individuals do not merely respond to events in and of themselves, but they respond to their interpretation of events and to their perceived implications of these events ... Constructivists assume that all mental images are creations of people, and thus, speak of "invented reality". How individuals construct such meanings and realities, how they create their world view is the subject of narrative psychology.'

3 Meichenbaum (1993, 1994; Meichenbaum and Fitzpatrick, 1993; Meichenbaum and Fong, 1993) describes key features of SIT as including the following:

a. Establishment of a nurturant, compassionate, non-judgemental set of conditions in which distressed clients can tell their stories at their own pace.

b. Normalization of distressed individuals' reactions.

c. Reconceptualization of the distress process.

d. Breaking down or disaggregating global descriptions of clients' stress into specific, concrete, behaviourally prescriptive stressful situations.

e. Performance of personal experiments that produce experientially meaningful occurrences, in a gradual manner. These experiments should test the limits on how clients will respond to re-entering the stressful situation, via imagery, via behavioural rehearsal, and eventually in real situations.

f. Encouragement of taking credit for positive outcomes of coping efforts.

g. Relapse prevention, including teaching ways to anticipate, accept, and cope with lapses so that they don't escalate into full-blown relapses.

4 What's 'right' is what works for the client. Again, to quote Meichenbaum and Fitzpatrick (1993, p. 698): 'There are two important features to recognize about this reconceptualization or new narrative reconstruction process. First, the scientific validity of the specific healing theory that is developed is less important than is its plausibility or credibility to the client. Second, this entire 'narrative repair' effort is conducted in a collaborative inductive fashion and not imposed upon, nor didactically taught, to distressed individuals. The distressed client must come to develop and accept a reconceptualization of the distress that he or she has helped cocreate.'

5 As discussed in *The First Session in Brief Therapy* (Budman, Hoyt, and Friedman, 1992), the introduction of *novelty* is a key element across different therapeutic approaches. As the adage has it, 'If we don't change directions, we'll wind up where we are heading!' (Hoyt, 1990, p. 128).

6 Some of the ways people who have experienced traumas get 'stuck' are catalogued by Meichenbaum and Fitzpatrick (1993, p. 697). These include the following:

a. making unfavourable comparisons between life as it is and as it might have been had the distressing event not occurred;

b. engaging in comparisons between aspects of life after the stressful event versus how it was before, and also continually pining for what was lost;

c. seeing themselves as 'victims' with little expectation or hope that things will change or improve;

d. engaging in 'undoing' counterfactual thinking of 'only if'; 'If I only had'; 'I should have'; and continually trying to answer 'Why' questions for which there are no satisfactory answers;

e. failing to find any meaning or significance in the stressful event;

f. dwelling on the negative implications of the stressful event;

g. seeing themselves as continually at risk or vulnerable to future stressful events;

h. feeling unable to control the symptoms of distress (i.e., viewing intrusive images, nightmares, ruminations, psychic numbing, avoidant behaviours, hyperarousal, and exaggerated startle reactions as being uncontrollable and unpredictable);

i. remaining vigilant to threats and obstacles.

7 For some additional discussions of the role of memory in therapeutic reconstruction, see Bonnano (1990), Bowers and Meichenbaum (1984), Rennie (1994), Russell and van den Broek (1992), Sarbin (1986), J.L. Singer (1990), and J.A. Singer and Salovey (1993).

8 Summaries can be found in Guidano and Liotti (1985), Lyddon (1990), Mahoney (1991), Mahoney and Lyddon (1988), and Meichenbaum (1992a). Controversies abound, and readers interested in watching some of the recent jousting may want, in addition to these references, to look at Ellis (1990, 1992a, 1992b, 1993a, 1993b), Lyddon (1992), Meichenbaum (1992b), and Wessler (1992, 1993).

9 See Meichenbaum and Turk (1987) for a discussion of various clinical procedures designed to facilitate treatment adherence, reduce noncompliance, and enhance client motivation.

10 Note that this line of 'internalized other' questioning (White, 1988, 1989; Tomm, 1989; Nylund and Corsiglia, 1993) evokes the daughter as an ally rather than as a source of remorse (Hoyt, 1980, 1983).

11 Each year there are approximately 1,400 such deaths in North America (Meichenbaum, 1994).

12 See Gilligan (1982; Gilligan, Roger and Tolman, 1991) for a discussion of the idea of claiming one's 'voice', especially in the lives of women. The work of White and Epston (1990) is pertinent; for further application of the narrative therapeutic use of 'voice' in the treatment of eating disorders, see Epston (1989) and Zimmerman and Dickerson (1994). Goulding (1985; Goulding and Goulding, 1979) also asks, 'Who's been living in your head?', and describes many ways to take charge of those 'voices'. Related ideas of 'voice' as internalized others include Firestone's (1988) 'voice therapy' and Minuchin's (1987) discussion of his family therapy teachers and mentors as 'the voices in my head'.

13 Since 'the map is not the territory' (Korzybski, 1933), we can understand virtually all communication to be metaphor. Using clients' metaphors is a way of joining. Moreover, it appreciates their experience and allows it to unfold as they know it. Recognizing the validity of their reality avoids 'resistance'. They don't have to fight or defend against the therapist's incursion. It moves forward. Aristotle said, 'The greatest thing by far is to have command of metaphor.' (See Barker, 1985; Combs and Freedman, 1990; Kopp, 1995.)

14 This same point – the power of experience in relearning – was emphasized by Freud (1914/1958) in his essay 'Remembering, Repeating and Working-Through', and, as discussed above, is also central in the concept of the 'corrective emotional experience' (Alexander and French, 1946). Cutting across different theoretical approaches, the induction of novelty requires a shift in narrative and thus generates change (Budman, Friedman and Hoyt, 1992).

15 'My voice will go with you' was an expression Milton Erickson would use to encourage continued benefit (Rosen, 1982).

REFERENCES

Agger, I., and Jensen, S.B. (1990). Testimony as ritual and evidence in psychotherapy for political refugees. *Journal of Traumatic Stress*, **3**, 115–30.

Alexander, F. and French, T.M. (1946). *Psychoanalytic Therapy: Principles and Application*. New York: Ronald Press.

Barker, P. (1985). *Using Metaphors in Psychotherapy*. New York: Brunner/Mazel.

Bonnano, G. (1990). Remembering and psychotherapy. *Psychotherapy*, **27**, 175–86.

Bowers, K. and Meichenbaum, D. (eds) (1984). *The Unconscious Reconsidered*. New York: Wiley.

Budman, S.H., Friedman, S. and Hoyt, M.F. (1992). Last words on first sessions. In S.H. Budman, M.F. Hoyt and S. Friedman (eds), *The First Session in Brief Therapy* (pp. 345–8). New York: Guilford Press.

Budman, S.H., Hoyt, M.F. and Friedman, S. (eds) (1992). *The First Session in Brief Therapy*. New York: Guilford Press.

Combs, G. and Freedman, J. (1990). *Symbol, Story and Ceremony: Using Metaphor in Individual and Family Therapy*. New York: Norton.

Ellis, A. (1990). Is rational-emotive therapy (RET) 'rationalist' or 'constructivist'? In A. Ellis and W. Dryden (eds), *The Essential Albert Ellis*. New York: Springer.

Ellis, A. (1992a). Discussion. In J.K. Zeig (ed.), *The Evolution of Psychotherapy: The Second Conference* (pp. 122–7). New York: Brunner/Mazel.

Ellis, A. (1992b). First-order and second-order change in rational-emotive therapy: A reply to Lyddon. *Journal of Counseling and Development*, **70**, 449–51.

Ellis, A. (1993a). Constructivism and rational-emotive therapy: A critique of Richard Wessler's critique. *Psychotherapy*, **30**, 531–2.

Ellis, A. (1993b). Another reply to Wessler's critique of rational-emotive therapy. *Psychotherapy*, **30**, 535.

Epston, D. (1989). *Collected Papers*. Adelaide: Dulwich Centre Publications.

Firestone, R.W. (1988). *Voice Therapy: A Psychotherapeutic Approach to Self-Destructive Behavior*. New York: Human Sciences Press.

Freud, S. (1958). Remembering, repeating and working-through. In J. Strachey (ed. and trans.), *The Standard Edition of the Complete Psychological Works of Sigmund Freud* (Vol. 12, pp. 145–56). London: Hogarth Press. (Original work published 1914.)

Gergen, K.J. (1991). *The Saturated Self*. New York: Basic Books.

Gilligan, C. (1982). *In a Different Voice*. Cambridge, MA: Harvard University Press.

Gilligan, C., Roger, A., and Tolman, D. (1991). *Women, Girls, and Psychotherapy*. Cambridge, MA: Harvard University Press.

Goulding, M.M. (1985). *Who's Been Living in Your Head?* (rev. edn). Watsonville, CA: Western Institute for Group and Family Therapy Press.

Goulding, M.M. and Goulding, R.L. (1979). *Changing Lives through Redecision Therapy*. New York: Brunner/Mazel.

Guidano, V.F. and Liotti, G.A. (1985). A constructivist foundation for cognitive therapy. In M.J. Mahoney and A. Freeman (eds), *Cognition and Psychotherapy* (pp. 101–42). New York: Plenum Press.

Harvey, J.H., Weber, A.L. and Orbuch, T.L. (1990). *Interpersonal Accounts: A Social Psychological Perspective*. Oxford: Blackwell.

Herman, J. (1992). *Trauma and Recovery*. New York: Basic Books.

Hoyt, M.F. (1980). Clinical notes regarding the experience of 'presences' during mourning. *Omega: Journal of Death and Dying*, **11**, 105–11.

Hoyt, M.F. (1983). Concerning remorse: With special attention to its defensive function. *Journal of the American Academy of Psychoanalysis*, 11, 435–44.

Hoyt, M.F. (1990). On time in brief therapy. In R.A. Wells and V.J. Giannetti (eds), *Handbook of the Brief Psychotherapies* (pp. 115–43). New York: Plenum Press. (Reprinted in M.F. Hoyt, *Brief Therapy and Managed Care: Readings for Contemporary Practice* [pp. 69–104]. San Francisco: Jossey-Bass, 1995.)

Hoyt, M.F. (1994). Single-session solutions. In M.F. Hoyt (ed.), *Constructive Therapies* (pp. 140–59). New York: Guilford Press. (Reprinted in M.F. Hoyt, *Brief Therapy and Managed Care: Readings for Contemporary Practice* [pp. 141–62]. San Francisco: Jossey-Bass, 1995.)

Janoff-Bulman, R. (1985). The aftermath of victimization: Rebuilding shattered assumptions. In C.R. Figley (ed.), *Trauma and Its Wake*. New York: Brunner/Mazel.

Janoff-Bulman, R. (1990). Understanding people in terms of their assumptive worlds. In D.J. Ozer, J.M. Healy and A.J. Stewart (eds), *Perspectives in Personality: Self and Emotion*. Greenwich, CT: JAI Press.

Kinzie, J.D. (1994). Countertransference in the treatment of Southeast Asian refugees. In J.P. Wilson and J.D. Lindy (eds), *Countertransference in the Treatment of PTSD*. New York: Guilford Press.

Kopp, R.R. (1995). *Metaphor Therapy: Using Client-Generated Metaphors in Pyschotherapy*. New York: Brunner/Mazel.

Korzybski, A. (1933). *Science and Sanity* (4th edn). Lakeville, CT: International Non-Aristotelian Library.

Lyddon, W.J. (1990). First- and second-order change: Implications for rationalist and constructivist cognitive therapies. *Journal of Counseling and Development*, 69, 122–27.

Lyddon, W.J. (1992). A rejoinder to Ellis: What is and is not RET? *Journal of Counseling and Development*, 70, 452–4.

Mahoney, M.J. (1991). *Human Change Processes*. New York: Basic Books.

Mahoney, M.J. and Lyddon, W.F. (1988). Recent developments in cognitive approaches to counseling and psychotherapy. *The Counseling Psychologist*, 16, 190–234.

McNamee, S. and Gergen, K.J. (eds) (1992). *Therapy as Social Construction*. Newbury Park, CA: Sage.

Meichenbaum, D. (1977). *Cognitive-Behavior Modification: An Integrative Approach*. New York: Plenum Press.

Meichenbaum, D. (1985). *Stress Inoculation Training: A Clinical Guidebook*. Elmsford, NY: Pergamon Press.

Meichenbaum, D. (1992a). Evolution of cognitive behavior therapy: Origins, tenets and clinical examples. In J.K. Zeig (ed.), *The Evolution of Psychotherapy: The Second Conference* (pp. 114–22). New York: Brunner/Mazel.

Meichenbaum, D. (1992b). Response: Dr Meichenbaum. In J.K. Zeig (ed.), *The Evolution of Psychotherapy: The Second Conference* (pp. 127–8). New York: Brunner/Mazel.

Meichenbaum, D. (1993). Stress inoculation training: A twenty-year update. In R.L. Woolfolk and P.M. Lehrer (eds), *Principles and Practice of Stress Management* (2nd edn, pp. 373–406). New York: Guilford Press.

Meichenbaum, D. (1994). *A Clinical Handbook/Practical Therapist Manual for Treating PTSD*. Waterloo, Ontario, Canada: Institute Press, University of Waterloo.

Meichenbaum, D. and Fitzpatrick, D. (1993). A constructive narrative perspective on stress and coping: Stress inoculation applications. In L. Goldberger and S. Breznitz (eds), *Handbook of Stress* (pp. 695–710). New York: Free Press.

Meichenbaum, D. and Fong. D.T. (1993). How individuals control their own minds: A constructive narrative perspective. In D.M. Wegner and J.W. Pennebaker (eds), *Handbook of Mental Control* (pp. 473–90). New York: Prentice Hall.

Meichenbaum, D. and Jaremko, M.E. (eds) (1983). *Stress Reduction and Prevention*. New York: Plenum Press.

Meichenbaum, D. and Turk, D. (1987). *Facilitating Treatment Adherence: A Practitioner's Guidebook*. New York: Plenum Press.

Minuchin, S. (1987). My many voices. In J.K. Zeig (ed.), *The Evolution of Psychotherapy* (pp. 5–14). New York: Brunner/Mazel.

Mollica, R.F. (1988). The trauma story: The psychiatric case of refugee survivors of violence and torture. In R. Ochberg (ed.), *Post-Traumatic Therapy and Victims of Violence*. New York: Brunner/Mazel.

Nylund, D. and Corsiglia, V. (1993). Internalized other questioning with men who are violent. *Dulwich Centre Newsletter*, No. 2, 30–5.

O'Hanlon, W.H. and Weiner-Davis, M. (1989). *In Search of Solutions: A New Direction in Psychotherapy*. New York: Norton.

Rennie, D.L. (1994). Storytelling in psychotherapy: The client's subjective experience. *Psychotherapy*, **31**, 234–43.

Rosen, S. (1982). *My Voice Will Go with You: The Teaching Tales of Milton H. Erickson*. New York: Norton.

Russell, R.L. and van den Broek, P. (1992). Changing narrative schemas in psychotherapy. *Psychotherapy*, **29**, 344–54.

Sarbin, T. (ed.) (1986). *Narrative Psychology: The Storied Nature of Human Conduct*. New York: Praeger.

Schafer, R. (1992). *Retelling a Life*. New York: Basic Books.

Simon, R. (1988). Like a friendly editor: An interview with Lynn Hoffman. *Family Therapy Networker*, September/October. (Reprinted in L. Hoffman, *Exchanging Voices: A Collaborative Approach to Family Therapy* [pp. 69–79]. London: Karnac Books, 1993.)

Singer, J.A. and Salovey, P. (1993). *The Remembered Self: Emotion and Memory in Personality*. New York: Free Press/Macmillan.

Singer, J.L. (ed.) (1990). *Repression and Dissociation*. Chicago: University of Chicago Press.

Solomon, S.D., Garrety, E.T. and Muff, A.M. (1992). Efficacy of treatments for posttraumatic stress disorder: An empirical review. *Journal of the American Medical Association*, **268**, 633–8.

Spence, D. (1982). *Narrative Truth and Historical Truth: Meaning and Interpretation in Psychoanalysis*. New York: Norton.

Terr, L.C. (1994). *Unchained Memories: True Stories of Traumatic Memories, Lost and Found*. New York: Basic Books.

Thibaut, J.W. and Kelley, H.H. (1986). *The Social Psychology of Groups* (rev. edn). New Brunswick, NJ: Transaction.

Tomm, K. (1987a). Interventive interviewing: Part I. Strategizing as a fourth guideline for the therapist. *Family Process*, **26**, 3–13.

Tomm, K. (1987b). Interventive interviewing: Part II. Reflexive questioning as a means to enable self-healing. *Family Process*, **26**, 167–83.

Tomm, K. (1988). Interventive interviewing: Part III. Intending to ask lineal, circular, strategic and reflexive questions. *Family Process*, **27**, 1–16.

Tomm, K. (1989). Externalizing the problems and internalizing personal agency. *Journal of Strategic and Systemic Therapies*, **8**, 54–9.

Turk, D., Meichenbaum, D. and Genest, M. (1983). *Pain and Behavioral Medicine: A Cognitive-Behavioral Perspective*. New York: Guilford Press.

van der Kolk, B.A. (1994). The body keeps the score: Memory and the evolving psychology of post-traumatic stress. *Harvard Review of Psychiatry*, 1, 253–65.

Wessler, R.L. (1992). Constructivism and rational-emotive therapy: A critique. *Psychotherapy*, **29**, 620–5.

Wessler, R.L. (1993). A reply to Ellis's critique of Wessler's critique of rational-emotive therapy. *Psychotherapy*, **30**, 533–4.

White, M. (1988). Saying hello again: The incorporation of the lost relationship in the resolution of grief. *Dulwich Centre Newsletter*, No. 1. (Reprinted in M. White, *Selected Papers* [pp. 29–36]. Adelaide: Dulwich Centre Publications, 1989.)

White, M. (1989). *Selected Papers*. Adelaide: Dulwich Centre Publications.

White, M. and Epston, D. (1990). *Narrative Means to Therapeutic Ends*. New York: Norton.

Zimmerman, J.L. and Dickerson, V.C. (1994). Tales of the body thief: Externalizing and deconstructing eating problems. In M.F. Hoyt (ed.), *Constructive Therapies* (pp. 295–318). New York: Guilford Press.

CHAPTER 6

Brief Group Counselling and Post-traumatic Stress Disorder

Michael J. Scott and Stephen G. Stradling

The most common model of stress is a transactional one (see Meichenbaum, 1985), in which stress is regarded neither as a property of the individual nor of the environment but of the interaction between them. Accordingly, whether a particular person has a PTSD response to a trauma will depend not only on the extremity of the trauma (e.g. did they lose a close relative? were they seriously physically injured with likely long-term debility?) but also on various aspects of the individual (e.g. have they had previous extreme trauma? were there previous emotional problems?). Thus an individual may respond unfavourably to a less extreme trauma if they have a number of personal vulnerability factors. By contrast, some events, e.g. rape, are so extremely intrusive that they would evoke an initial traumatic response in almost anybody. Here, however, the individual factors may exert an important influence on recovery.

In traditional cognitive-behavioural approaches to the treatment of PTSD the individual has been regarded as in need of exposure to the full memory of the trauma for as long as it takes to produce a habituation response. Therapeutic efforts have been devoted almost entirely to ensuring adequate exposure with little regard for the uniqueness of the individual and their history. Theoretical formulations such as those of Foa and Kozak (1986) acknowledge that the end result of interventions has to be that the individual comes to ascribe a more adaptive meaning to the trauma and their response to it, but have been unclear as to why prolonged exposure was the *sine qua non* for providing the necessary corrective information.

From a biological perspective it appears that in extreme trauma there is damage to the hippocampus. One of the functions of the hippocampus appears to be to co-ordinate the various sensory aspects of an experience, the smells, sights, etc., locate the experience in space and time, and provide an overall meaning. PTSD clients appear to have a smaller hippocampal volume than non-PTSD survivors of trauma (van der Kolk, 1996). Thus PTSD clients are likely to have a more fragmented memory of the trauma. The amygdala registers affect-laden memories, and these are usually kept in check by the hippocampus, but damage to the hippocampus from cortisol release would prevent this. Cortisol damage to the hippocampus is thought to be reversible.

INITIAL ASSESSMENT

For patients recently traumatized – within the previous few weeks – a group debriefing is probably the appropriate response whether they meet the actual criteria for acute stress disorder or not. The rationale for a debriefing is that early intervention may prevent the development of more serious problems later, particularly PTSD. But there is little evidence of its effectiveness overall (Kenardy *et al.*, 1996) and whether it exerts a preventive function may depend on the type of debriefing. Guidelines for conducting a debriefing are given in Scott and Stradling (1992) and are based on the premise that no pressure should be exerted on anyone to disclose their thoughts or feelings. After the debriefing people are given a contact number should their symptoms not resolve. Though there is a strong humanitarian case for making professional services available to victims in the wake of a trauma, the goal should be to enhance individuals' natural coping mechanisms.

Given the improvements in PTSD symptoms that often occur in the first six months post trauma, it is probably a better use of resources to restrict a group programme to those who were traumatized at least six months earlier, though exceptionally one might admit clients traumatized as recently as three months ago.

The assessment interview should be structured around the DSM-IV criteria for PTSD (see Box 1.1, pp. 10–11) with appropriate questions asked under each heading. There are well-validated structured interviews for PTSD such as the Clinician Administered PTSD Scale (CAPS: Blake *et al.*, 1990) but they are time-consuming, the CAPS typically taking an hour for clients who prove to have PTSD and 30–40 minutes for those who do not. It is useful to have a category of sub-syndromal PTSD. The commonest presentation of sub-syndromal PTSD is of insufficient avoidance symptoms for a diagnosis of PTSD but sufficient of the other two symptom clusters – intrusion and disordered arousal. Sub-syndromal clients can benefit from a couple of individual counselling sessions focusing on their prominent symptom clusters but a group programme is usually too extensive an intervention for them. Material can be extracted from the group programme given below that addresses the particular concerns of the individual sub-syndromal client. It is important that these clients are not dismissed simply because they do not meet full PTSD criteria and that their needs are addressed in a systematic way, because even sub-syndromal PTSD can greatly restrict an individual's activities and relationships.

Post-traumatic Stress Disorder is a disorder with considerable co-morbidity, the (US) National Comorbidity Survey (Kessler *et al.*, 1996) suggesting a lifetime prevalence of major depression of 48%, alcohol or drug abuse 65%, generalized anxiety disorder 16% and panic disorder 11%. Screening for other disorders is therefore important. If there is an addiction, treatment of this is necessary before addressing the PTSD. Often the client is using the alcohol or drugs to block out the memories and ensure sleep, so that though they may be willing to attend a PTSD group they may be unwilling to abstain first. It is recommended that in such cases the client's needs are addressed in individual counselling.

Groups can be homogeneous with regard to the original trauma, e.g. consisting entirely of rape victims. In routine practice most counsellors will have a mixed PTSD caseload of motor-vehicle accident victims, those who have been variously assaulted, and survivors of disasters. The programme described here is for such a mixed group, but that is not to say it is not perfectly valid to run a group exclusively for, say, incest survivors or combat veterans. A group mixed by trauma and sex is problematic for clients who have been the victim of a sexual assault and in the authors' view should be avoided.

AUDITING THE PTSD GROUP PROGRAMME

The PENN Inventory (PENN: Hammarberg, 1992) covers all the PTSD symptoms and is a useful measure of change. The most commonly used PTSD outcome measure is the Impact of Event Scale (IES: Horowitz et al., 1979). However, it does not assess disordered arousal symptoms and should be more properly viewed as a stress response measure. Both instruments are reproduced in the appendices to Scott and Stradling (1992). The Modified PTSD Scale (Falsetti et al., 1993) is a PTSD self-report measure which asks questions about the frequency and severity of each of the seventeen DSM PTSD symptoms. We have examined the diagnostic accuracy of these three measures (Scott et al., 1997) in a study in which 150 clients completed the instruments and were also assessed using the CAPS interview in conjunction with the DSM-IV criteria. The PENN Inventory was the most accurate. Using a cut-off of 37, it gave false positives of 15% and false negatives of 20%. The Impact of Event Scale was the least reliable.

Because of the high incidence of moderate to severe depression amongst PTSD clients it is useful to also measure progress with a depression self-report measure such as the Beck Depression Inventory (Beck et al., 1961). Clients scoring highly on the BDI (26+) may have considerable trauma-related guilt and/or difficulty adjusting to the loss of some previously valued role in the wake of the trauma. The high levels of co-morbidity mean that the counsellor will often have to incorporate, within the PTSD group programme, strategies for other disorders.

CONVEYING THE METAPHOR

Clients suffering from Post-traumatic Stress Disorder often report that they are 'not the same person' as they were before, and in contrast to most other emotional disorders they suffer an abrupt discontinuity of identity. Close relatives and friends become acutely aware of this change. The autobiography of the PTSD client is typically in two halves. The first half relates to how they viewed themselves and their personal world up to the time of the trauma and the second half presents a very different, post-trauma, view of themselves and their world. Prior to the trauma clients usually assumed most situations were safe until proven otherwise. In the aftermath of trauma clients routinely assume danger and therefore engage in hyper-vigilance and avoidance behaviour. The treatment of PTSD involves assisting the client in rewriting their autobiography so that there is a consistent view of themselves and their personal world. This must come from contextualizing the trauma in their pre-trauma experiences.

Historically in the treatment of PTSD the tendency has been for counsellors to try and normalize a client's feelings by telling them that they are a normal emotional response to an abnormal situation, but this is only a partial and potentially misleading truth. Whilst virtually all persons exposed to an extreme trauma show PTSD reactions in the week or so afterwards, over half are no longer suffering PTSD three to six months later. This means that the 'normal' response is not to be in a state which merits consideration for admission to a PTSD counselling programme. The major goal of the programme is then to help them do what the other, 'recovered', victims of the trauma have done. In essence the client is told that they are engaged in a battle: either they learn to control (contextualize) the memory of the trauma or the memory will control them. The warring factions are their present self looking at life through the glasses of the experience of the trauma, and their pre-trauma, 'no glasses', self. The question is who will win, or at least what peace agreement may be brokered.

Because the PTSD client is viewed by themselves and by significant others as 'not the same person', they usually feel very isolated and communication is fraught. They are, however, often more at ease with other similarly traumatized victims and can identify with them, often saying of others' experiences 'I have been there'. For this reason a PTSD group programme can seem an attractive option to a client and can act as a stepping stone for reconnecting them to the world around them. Meeting other PTSD clients helps many to be able to put into words for the first time their emotional experience of PTSD.

Reconnecting the client with the world is a major goal of the programme and an important first step towards this is involving a partner, close friend or relative of the client in the initial interview. This significant other has to be warned not to take the changes in the client's behaviour – e.g. increased irritability – personally, how to act as a 'coach' using the handout material given to the client, and what the likely prognosis is. Armed with this information they can then mediate between the client and the client's personal world. Significant others may play an important role in helping those with PTSD reactions contextualize their trauma and this may be the most salient aspect of support post-trauma.

Engagement of the client and the significant other in the therapeutic process is facilitated by the counsellor providing a readily understandable post-trauma metaphor.

Leader When you experience an extreme trauma it is as if the alarm in your nervous system is knocked. It is now in this position (use a pencil to illustrate, at 60° clockwise from the vertical) when it should be in that position (rotate the pencil to 60° anticlockwise from the vertical) and your alarm begins to go off for the slightest reason. With the alarm in this new position you are likely to get angry over the smallest thing, e.g. your partner not handing you a cup of coffee but placing it down on the table. One of the things we will teach you is how to begin to ignore the false alarms, so that you get on better with the people around you. But we cannot reset the alarm in one sweep (illustrate by a movement of pencil from +60° to ×60°) it is always two steps forward and one back (again illustrate by movement of the pen through 20° and back 10°). It is rather like driving lessons: some weeks you think you are doing fine and are going to pass your test and then other weeks you think that you are not going to make it, but gradually you do make it.

PARTICULAR PROBLEMS IN ENGAGING THE PTSD CLIENT

One of the difficulties with engaging PTSD clients in counselling is that sometimes they know of other trauma victims who have recovered without recourse to professional help and believe that they also ought to be able to do so by themselves. This can be tackled by explaining that some people are more vulnerable than others to the effects of trauma. The chief vulnerability factors for PTSD are listed in Box 6.1.

Box 6.1   *PTSD Vulnerability Factors*

PTSD VULNERABILITY FACTORS

1. Genetic
2. Early deprivation
3. Prior psychiatric illness
4. Prior stress
5. Personality factors

   Thus two individuals exposed to the same trauma but differing on any one or more of the above factors will likely have a different outcome. Some individuals may have so little vulnerability that it would take a very extreme trauma – say the loss of a close relative – to usher in PTSD, whilst a highly vulnerable individual experiencing, say, a minor car crash may suffer PTSD because of the way in which it reignites some past life-threatening trauma (prior stress) from which they thought they had recovered. Listing the vulnerability factors shows the client that their response to trauma cannot be divorced from their history.

   Given that one of the symptom clusters in PTSD is disordered arousal, it may be that one of the salient personality factors that makes for vulnerability is a predisposition to emotional arousability. Coren's (1988) Arousability Predisposition Scale has twelve items which include 'Sudden changes of any kind produce an immediate emotional effect on me', 'I find that my heart keeps beating fast for a while after I have been stirred up', 'I startle easily', and 'I am easily frustrated'. Emotional arousability may also be an important determinant not only of onset of PTSD but also of recovery.

   Some clients' excessive self-blame can militate against engagement and they frequently say 'It is not as if I had any physical injury'. This point can be dealt with by telling clients that it seems that PTSD victims have a slightly reduced (4–12%) hippocampal volume compared to non-PTSD survivors of trauma and this probably relates to their difficulty in handling the memory. But the damage caused to the hippocampus in extreme trauma is not necessarily irreversible. So they are not responsible for the problem of suffering their condition any more than someone who develops diabetes, they are only responsible for sorting out what, for them, is the best way of handling it.

   Cognitive avoidance is an intrinsic part of PTSD and because of this the client is likely to be highly anxious about disclosing the trauma to the counsellor and even more so to other group members. It is therefore important to stress that the prime focus of the group is teaching members how to handle the memories that intrude anyway and that any disclosure is entirely in the hands of the client. A related issue is that of secondary traumatization, a fear that hearing of others' traumas will retraumatize them. This can be addressed by telling them that victims of trauma like themselves do not like talking about their trauma and that therefore they would only hear of others' traumas in such measured doses that it would not overwhelm them.

A further problem in engaging some PTSD clients is the issue of safety. In some instances their assailant is perhaps out on bail or intimidating the client, perhaps through a third party. In other instances the assailant has served a prison sentence because of the attack and is back in the client's locality. The issue of client safety is paramount and in a few instances it is not possible to proceed with a programme until the threat recedes.

It can also be more difficult to engage a PTSD client in a programme when it is five years or more since the trauma. At this stage it is often the depression symptoms and relationship difficulties that are uppermost in their mind, since they have reached a new equilibrium with the trauma. But it is likely to be an unhealthy equilibrium, fuelling their inter- and intrapersonal problems. Their PTSD can be likened to someone with a back injury initially unable to walk who then, with the help of a walking stick, manages to get about a bit. The question is whether they want a back operation and the attendant initial discomfort (the treatment programme) to enable them to function much as before their trauma, or whether they are going to be content to continue to hobble about with a stick.

Some chronic PTSD clients are best advised not to make a decision about a programme immediately but to go away and think it over and get back to the counsellor if they wish to avail themselves of it. It should be stressed however that the evidence to date (Kessler *et al.*, 1996) on the natural history of PTSD suggests that it is very unlikely that at this stage there would be any naturally occurring improvement in their condition. However, giving these clients time to make a decision results in a more stable decision and may help prevent premature disengagement from the group, which is disquieting not only for the individual but for other group members.

TARGETS

The goals of the group are:

1. to help clients interact adaptively with their memory of the trauma;
2. to test out their beliefs on the dangerousness of ordinary situations;
3. to restore connections with those in their personal world;
4. to adapt or reinstate pre-trauma goals.

FORMAT OF TEN-SESSION GROUP AND INDIVIDUAL PROGRAMME FOR PTSD

Session one. Introductions and handling the trauma memory

The programme begins, as do all the group programmes, by stressing the need for confidentiality. Some members of a group PTSD programme may require simultaneous individual sessions if there is substantial trauma-related guilt that they are unable to address in the group, for example if they were the perpetrator of a crime or if the trauma has reawakened feelings associated with childhood physical or sexual abuse.

The availability of such sessions should be made known at the outset. In any one group probably only one or two members will avail themselves of this. The refreshment break at the end of each session provides a setting for determining the appropriateness of such an arrangement. In addition an individual session is required between the first and second group session to troubleshoot any problems with the group format and ensure engagement with the memory of the trauma.

Clients with PTSD have lost a sense of who they are, and the development of a coherent and historically consistent sense of self is an important therapeutic goal. A first step in the reconstruction process is to ask each member of the group to get to know the person next to them for ten minutes. Each member then has the task of introducing their partner to the group. The instructions to participants for this exercise are deliberately vague, with no indication given of whether they mention their trauma or not, but the implication is that they are not just defined by their trauma experience.

The feedback to the group at large may however indicate the degree of cognitive avoidance of the trauma by particular clients and this should be noted by the group leaders. This exercise can build group cohesion if leaders can underline some similarities of, say, interests, work experience or family arrangements. Spending some time on these non-trauma-related issues makes the group members feel safe and makes manifest defining characteristics of their current identity other than as trauma victims. When several clients have declared information about their trauma the leaders should again point to similarities in either the objective nature of the trauma, e.g. two members have experienced motor-vehicle accidents, or the subjective similarities, e.g. some thought that they were going to die, all showed feelings of helplessness. Those who have disclosed aspects of the trauma to the group act as important models for those yet to disclose.

In instances where clients are only disclosing the trauma the leaders should seek elaboration of the non-trauma-related self, again by implication saying that they are more than their trauma. This can be encapsulated by the leaders saying that the client is not just a victim or, better, a survivor, but a whole person with a history.

The format of the introductions section of this first session provides a backcloth to the main theoretical rationale for the programme, which is that individuals are able to cope with an extreme trauma to the extent that they are able to take account of the trauma whilst simultaneously elaborating on their pre-trauma experiences of their personal world and to produce a benign, integrated story of their life.

The second major topic covered in this session is handling the memory of the trauma. Before describing to group members new ways of handling the trauma memory it is necessary that they come to an understanding of the futility of their current coping strategy. To do this the leaders should go round the group and elicit each individual's coping strategies and list them on a board. The coping strategies almost always involve cognitive and/or emotional avoidance. Some commonly elicited strategies are given in Box 6.2.

Box 6.2 *Typical Strategies for Coping with Intrusive Memories in PTSD*

TYPICAL COPING STRATEGIES

Go and make a drink
Go for a walk
Get into a conversation with someone about something else
Do something in the garden
Avoid the spot where the incident occurred
Drink to forget

The next step is to enquire whether the strategies work and, if so, for how long. Most clients readily agree that the avoidance only works briefly and the trauma memory soon returns. The group leaders can amplify this as follows.

Leader   Trauma memories are, as it were, on an elastic band – the more you push them away the harder they spring back and you get more injured in the end. Ultimately the band snaps and you snap at yourself and others. At this point you get lost in the details of the trauma, e.g. the smell of the dead body, eyes like a cod. It is then like disappearing down a 'black hole', the memory is controlling you rather than you controlling the memory. Your waking and sleeping hours are controlled by the memory. You pay a very heavy price for trying to block the memory. On the other hand you understandably do not want it to dominate your life. There is however a better way of handling the trauma memory.

Co-leader The key is to regard the trauma memory a bit like a local thug, perhaps a bully you can remember from your schooldays. It is not very bright to totally ignore or become aggressive with the thug. You may have developed the skill of exchanging pleasantries with him but you take care not to get involved with him. You perhaps learnt to develop a matter-of-fact style in the face of this potential adversary so that life could go on. In a similar way when people have experienced extreme trauma they have to cultivate such a style, but it takes practice and, initially at least, you will still feel uncomfortable. To begin with it will be a question of coping with the memory rather than mastering the memory.

Group members are then introduced to the specifics of interacting adaptively with the memory of the trauma by reading through and discussing Items (1) and (2) on the Managing PTSD handout of Box 6.3.

Box 6.3 *Managing PTSD Handout*

MANAGING POST-TRAUMATIC STRESS DISORDER

1. *Managing the memory* If you try to block out the memory of the incident you will find that it does not really work, it keeps coming back. To help you control the memory rather than have the memory control you, each time the memory comes to mind say to yourself 'Now is not the time and place. I will sort that out properly with pen and paper at [say] 11 a.m. when I will write down whatever I can manage about what happened and how I felt.' Spending a couple of minutes at a fixed time writing about it (or talking about it to someone) tells your mind that you are in charge of the memory and it acts as a safety valve for the memory otherwise it is all bottled up inside you and you feel ready to explode. The first days of writing about it can be very upsetting so you might just do a minute or two to begin with. As the days go on it gets easier and after two or three weeks you will find the memory does not get to you in the way it used to.

2. *'Yes . . . But' the memory* With post-traumatic stress disorder people get sucked into the details of the incident like a 'black hole' that can swallow you up and stop ordinary living. When a detail of the incident comes to mind, calmly acknowledge the horror of the details '**Yes** it was horrible that . . .' and then put the horror into context '**but** the incident was a one-off, nothing like it had ever happened to me before, I have had many more positive experiences in life that tell me life can be good'.

3. *Unlock positive memories* With post-traumatic stress disorder positive memories are locked away in your mind, you know they are there but they are vague. To make the positives come alive spend a couple of minutes each day going into great detail about two particular events, e.g. a holiday or the birth of a child. Either write or talk about them.

4. *Timetable uplifts* Timetable into your week things that could be potentially uplifting. Have a go at them even if you don't feel like it. If you keep active eventually the taste for life comes back. To begin with you might have to do things in small doses, e.g. visit a friend for twenty minutes for a coffee rather than stay all evening. The timetable is a way of reminding yourself that despite the disruption caused by the incident it is possible to get a sense of achievement and pleasure out of life, though what you now do might be different to before.

5. *Managing irritability* When you notice the first signs of anger imagine a set of traffic lights on red and shout 'STOP!' to yourself. As the lights go to amber ask yourself 'Am I absolutely sure they did that to deliberately wind me up? Is it really the end of the world that [X] has just happened?' When the lights go to green go into another room to calm down, or perhaps make a hot drink.

The first item on the handout can be introduced by continuing the school bully analogy.

Leader It is as if you have reached the limits of your tolerance with the school bully and you have agreed to see him at a certain time and place. Avoiding him has meant that your life had become very restricted. You have considerable misgivings, however, about the wisdom of such a meeting even though you know it is the only way you can move forward. But in writing about your trauma you are now taking control – you choose the time and duration. It does not matter if you begin with just a sentence a day.

Though Item (1) on the handout seems straightforward, cognitive avoidance can occur in a number of guises. The trauma may be reported rather like a police report with little of the idiosyncratic thought processes or the emotions specified. To counter this, clients are asked to write their account in the first person, 'I am lying on the motorway . . .' Sometimes the avoidance takes the form of writing a diary of how the incident has affected them. The leaders should anticipate these forms of avoidance by ruling them out in advance of setting Item (1) as a homework exercise. The incident has first to be acknowledged in order to be subsequently contextualized. Clients' engagement with the trauma memory is such a crucial and painful issue that an individual session should be arranged between the first and second group sessions in order to review this interaction.

Item (2) on the handout, the 'Yes . . . But' strategy, can be introduced along the following lines.

Leader PTSD symptoms are often experienced like a wave of terror coming over you. To begin with you will not be able to stop the waves coming, if you try to you will just get more frustrated. Do not try to pretend that the terror has not come, do not get cross with yourself for its arrival, you are not responsible for its visit, but you have to say 'Yes' to the visitor, acknowledge it as calmly as possible, accept the physical sensations, the images, whilst acknowledging their full horror. You must properly say 'Yes' before 'Butting' the memory and putting the visitor in its place. There are usually two aspects to a 'Yes . . . But'. The first is another angle on the incident itself. For instance you might move from saying 'I was driving. There was blood on my friend after we were hit. I hurt her' to 'Yes my friend was hurt. But I did not assault her.' The second 'Yes . . . But' puts the incident into the context of your life and locates it to a specific time and place and makes the point that it only has relevance in that unique situation, i.e. it is not typical of life. Say 'Yes, that was an awful experience. I would not wish it on my worst enemy. But it was on March 10th 1996 at 9.50 p.m. It belongs then. It was totally different to anything before and is almost certainly a once in a lifetime experience. I will see it as having visited Hell, but the good news is I have returned'. It is very important not to expect too much of the 'Yes . . . Buts', certainly initially. At most they will to begin with take the edge off the sensations you experience. With practice and probably some gradual alteration of your particular 'Yes . . . But' they percolate down in the words of the TV advert 'to the parts that other strategies cannot reach' and you begin to feel real change. But it is a percolation process you cannot hurry.

This should be followed by asking the group whether they already use any 'Yes . . . Buts'.

Ian	Yes, I try and tell myself 'Yes but my accident could have been much worse, the road is usually much busier, with schoolchildren crossing' but that just gets me really wound up when I think of the possible carnage.
Leader	The right 'Yes ... But' is one that leaves you less distressed. Yours, Ian, is making it worse. Your mind is going dancing and playing a catastrophic video and it is no wonder you feel distressed. What we have got to get you to do is to play a reality video.
Ian	What, you mean like concentrating on the fact that I survived?
Leader	Yes, perhaps your 'Yes ... But' should be in two parts. First 'Yes, the incident was awful. But I have survived' and then 'Yes, I can still remember the feelings of helplessness as the cab went towards the house. But nothing else like it has happened in twenty years driving. It was a one off.'
Ian	It makes me sweat when I think of the helplessness.
Co-leader	We can't wipe away those initial physiological reactions but what we can do is to help you put them in their place.
John	But Ian's right isn't he? Someone could have died. You can't just forget that. As you know that child did die when I was driving the Heavy Goods Vehicle.
Leader	You have a point, John. We can't dismiss the possibility of an extreme outcome, but extreme outcomes are extremely unlikely. You can only live in the present by playing a reality video of the most likely sequence of events, i.e. the sequence of events that you would put money on happening. If you play catastrophic videos we would not continue to sit under this ceiling because it is possible that it might fall in.
Co-leader	Horrible traumas can give you a mistaken impression of how likely an incident is. If you have someone living next door who you see die of some horrible rare disease you might start to inspect yourself for signs afterwards. It is understandable, but finally you have to stop the checking and calmly remind yourself of how rare it is and that there is no reason to believe that you should be singled out as especially vulnerable any more than the rest of the human race.

Individual session (core). Locking on to the trauma memory

Up to the point of entering the programme, clients' interactions with the memory of their traumas will have been automatic, a fight or flight response. The suggestion that they stay with the memory long enough to contextualize it is likely to evoke fears that they will be overwhelmed. Consequently their feelings of being unsafe are likely to have been heightened at the start of the programme. It is therefore recommended that an individual session is scheduled after the first group session.

In this session the counsellor should be aware of the contrast between what the client has written about the trauma and their verbal description of the trauma elicited at the first assessment session. It is important that the counsellor has to hand an almost verbatim copy of what the client said at the assessment, together with the counsellor's notes of any particularly strong emotions evoked at any point in the proceedings or any physiological reaction such as sweating. The client's initial description of both the objective and subjective aspects of their trauma will typically have taken at least fifteen minutes to elaborate.

The client should first of all be congratulated on anything that they have written and praised for attempting to engage with the material. What the client has written should be read back by the counsellor who should pause at any point where the client gets markedly distressed.

At such points of intensification of emotion the counsellor asks 'What was going through your mind there that caused you to get upset?' In this way the counsellor is able to identify the core of the client's distress. Clients have usually left something out of their written account and in some instances may not have written anything. The client is then asked why they left out various aspects that were obviously 'hot' for them at the initial assessment. In this way the client is engaged in elaborating in turn on various aspects of the trauma, e.g. 'You were saying at the initial interview that sometimes as you are going to sleep you get a picture of yourself lying face down on the motorway, and you have to open your eyes because you can not bear what you see. What do you see, the car coming over your leg?'

In the second half of the interview the client is encouraged to add to what they have written. Where a client has been unable to write anything, the counsellor has to take over the job of authorship. The writing has to be done as if the client were giving the account of the trauma, seeking the client's approval for every sentence – 'Have I got that right? Have I missed the point? Is there something that I have missed out?' The aim is to have, by the end of the session, an account of the trauma of about 150 words in the client's terminology which is reasonably comprehensive – the client's story of the event. Such an account should take no more than about 90 seconds to read through. The client is then set for homework the task of modifying or changing what is written to produce another 90-second version that they would be prepared to read out at the next group session to 'put other group members in the picture', emphasizing that they are in control of what, if anything, they will read out. They are free to present an expurgated or unexpurgated version of their trauma at the next session. Fears of doing this can be assuaged by noting that 'Everybody will be in the same boat.'

An alternative strategy to use when the client has been unable to write anything is a technique described by Ochberg (1996) (see chapter 11). The client is asked to gaze at some fixed point in the room and then to remember the various aspects of the trauma – without verbalizing them – as the counsellor counts from 1 to 100. They are advised to focus on less distressing aspects of the trauma when the count is around 20–30, reaching the worst parts with the count around 50, then back to less distressing parts of the memory as the end of the count approaches. At around 90 the counsellor says 'Back here' to help bring the client back to the present. Afterwards the client is asked what went through their mind, and usually gives a comprehensive account of the trauma. The counsellor can then write down this account, checking the details with the client, and this becomes the client's story.

However, some clients' cognitive avoidance is so great that they cannot even verbalize their trauma. Using the Ochberg technique it is possible to overcome this by asking, for example, 'What was going through your mind at 20–30?' or at even earlier points in the count, thereby gaining entry to the client's trauma.

When clients are insistent that they could not tell the group about the trauma the counsellor should then endeavour to make an audiotape of their trauma from the account given, lasting perhaps two to three minutes. They are then asked for home-work to 'bore' themselves with (i.e. desensitize themselves to) the memory, using the Trauma Tape form (Box 6.4), stressing that they should eschew rumination and postpone consideration of the trauma to the daily time for listening to the tape.

What the Ochberg technique and the counsellor-recorded trauma tape have in common is that they render it safer for the client to address the memory of the trauma by linking the therapist's voice to the account of the trauma. The fundamental message to be conveyed by this session is that the counsellor can provide the client with sufficient safety within which to address the trauma.

At this individual session it is also important to elicit feedback on their initial experience of the group and to troubleshoot any difficulties. Similarities between the client and other group members in terms of the objective trauma, their subjective response to the trauma or difficulties in reconnecting with people and engaging with life should be emphasized in the interests of developing group cohesion. This cohesion is especially important with chronic PTSD clients who have often been unable properly to communicate their experience to anyone and whose often antisocial behaviour has led to a very solitary existence. Their membership of the group testifies that they still 'belong' in a way that purely individual counselling for the condition cannot.

Session two (core). Review of revisiting the trauma and review of 'Yes . . . Buts'

This session begins with the leader inviting members to tell their trauma story from what they have written 'for just a minute or so', inviting first of all someone who seemed least disturbed at the individual session in the construction of their narrative. In this way a process of telling their trauma rather than reliving the experience is modelled for other, perhaps more distressed, group members. After each narrative is read out (those who do not feel comfortable enough even after gentle encouragement to read their transcript are allowed not to do so) the story is discussed in the group for about ten minutes. The leaders begin the discussion by thanking the person for sharing it, using some metaphor that highlights the importance of trying to verbalize the experience.

> *Co-leader* Thanks for that Ian, it is often difficult to begin to put into words the horror, but if you can name the enemy – the memory, the feelings – you can begin to deal with it. It's been stuck in your throat for years stopping you swallowing life and you're beginning to get it up. Unless you have a safety valve for the release of the memory it all builds up inside and you feel that you are going to explode. This is why probably most of the group are having 'explosions' with friends and family, there is a need for a safety valve.

This thanking should take place through any sobs of distress of the client, legitimat-ing that distress but at the same time underlining the fact that they have taken an all-important first step along the road to recovery.

The discussion of the narrative is begun gently by the leaders locating the incident

Box 6.4 *Trauma Tape*

TRAUMA TAPE

Play the trauma tape each day. It is easier to get around to listening to it if you decide in advance on a particular time, say 11.00 a.m. (do not play it anywhere near bedtime). At the end of each playthrough, before you rewind it, write down a number 0 to 10 in the table below that describes how you are feeling: 0 is feeling very low, 3 would be pretty low, 5 is so-so, 7 pretty good, and a 10 would be feeling superb.

Play the tape over and over for about 15 minutes. Only finish with it when you are not feeling too low.

Week 1	Mon	Tue	Wed	Thur	Fri	Sat	Sun
1							
2							
3							
4							
5							
6							
7							
8							
9							
10							

Week 2	Mon	Tue	Wed	Thur	Fri	Sat	Sun
1							
2							
3							
4							
5							
6							
7							
8							
9							
10							

Week 3	Mon	Tue	Wed	Thur	Fri	Sat	Sun
1							
2							
3							
4							
5							
6							
7							
8							
9							
10							

in time and place then leaving space for other group members to comment. Their initial comments usually reflect an identification with the narrator's subjective response to the incident, validating their own experience. This is often followed by a challenge to the client's interpretation of the trauma.

> Ian   What do you mean, John, you should have been going slower? You were only going 30–40 m.p.h.
>
> John   But if I had maybe the driver of the other vehicle would not have been killed.
>
> Ian   If you had driven any slower at rush hour you would have caused another accident before it. I know I get frustrated with slow drivers.

In the above extract Ian attempted to switch John from a primarily perceptual processing of the trauma, namely that the driver of an oncoming car that was over-taking another vehicle was killed, to a more abstract conceptual level. The co-leader was able to build on this.

> Co-leader   That sounds like a 'Yes . . . But'; 'Yes it was tragic that the other driver died, my guts wrench when I think about it. But if I had been driving any slower I may have caused an accident earlier.' Would you be able to try out that 'Yes . . . But' when these waves of feelings hit you, John?
>
> John   I will give anything a try.

The second part of this session is a review of the practice of 'Yes . . . Buts'.

> Ian   Sometimes the 'Yes . . . But' seemed to work but sometimes the situation took over. My worst one was somebody stopping sharply at a junction. I became so angry that I had to stop the car and get myself together. Then I felt stupid because there was no real danger. So I am only making absolutely essential journeys.
>
> Leader   To begin with it can be a fair bit after the event that you come up with a 'Yes . . . But'. At the start you have to really consciously spell out the 'Yes . . . Buts'. Then with practice they become almost automatic and nip your distress in the bud. So congratulate yourself, Ian, for coming up with your 'Yes . . . But'; 'Yes it is frightening when cars are approaching from a side road. But I do know that I am safe.' It is rather like learning to drive a car – first of all you have to really spell out what you have to do. Then after a time you can do it without thinking.

This exchange highlights the intended switch from deliberate, effortful processing, operating at a declarative level with the 'Yes . . . Buts', to an increasingly automated procedural processing at a pre-conscious level. It is this latter which will more likely influence the initial physiological response to an alarming situation.

Sessions three and four: Review of earlier sessions and contrasting the trauma with previous life experiences by contextualizing rules for living then and now

These sessions begin with a review of the rewritten stories, then the focus moves to an account of a typical week before the trauma, presented as a 'getting to know each other more fully' exercise. The idea of the latter is to build a bridge over the trauma, access the former self and its *modus operandi*. Then, in the interactions with other group members, to provide a corrective emotional experience which 'draws across the bridge' former ways of operating and rules for living that enhance the quality of life. In these sessions the dual focus on the trauma and pre-trauma experiences mirrors the necessary contextualizing of the trauma.

In their rewritten scenarios clients often introduce material that has not been presented before and this should be focused on by one of the group leaders.

Co-leader   That's new Ian, I didn't know that someone had been standing in the pub doorway as you went towards it.

Ian   Yes, I can still see the look of horror on his face as he saw me approaching as if it was yesterday.

Co-leader   Was he injured?

Ian   No, he got inside pretty damn quick, but when I think of what could have happened to him I go sick.

Here again the client's account of the trauma is staying at a perceptual level, 'the sight', the somatic response 'sick'. The therapeutic goal is to transform it to a conceptual level.

Leader   If the man in the doorway was present here now what do you think he would be saying of the experience?

Ian   Scary!

Leader   Do you think he would be worrying about the incident?

Ian   No, he was OK.

Leader   He might be saying, 'Yes, it was scary for a moment. But there was no real danger to me.'

Ian   I could borrow his 'Yes . . . But'.

Leader   If you like. Try it on for size, see if it fits.

Group members are asked to rewrite their trauma scripts again for presentation at the next session.

The leaders next need to ask group members in turn to describe a typical week before the trauma. It is important to get group members to be as specific as possible about their pre-trauma experiences, hence the focus on a typical week. Most clients with PTSD, left to their own devices, speak of their pre-trauma days in generalities, e.g. 'I was happy then' or alternatively 'Life has always been a pain' and compare it with their current difficulties in relating to others and the world, expressed in more specific terms, e.g., 'We drove to Wales last week-end heading for the Falls. I got a bit lost, threw a tantrum, gave up and came home. What a waste. It was not fair on my wife.' The task of the leaders is to help group members stay sufficiently in the pre-trauma experiences to elaborate on the taken-for-granted assumptions that underpinned that behaviour and to distil what pre-trauma coping strategies might be salvaged. The following extract demonstrates the approach.

Leader	What was a typical week for you, Sarah, before you were attacked in the Off Licence?
Sarah	I used to go to a pub or the Taxi Club a couple of times a week. But I have not bothered to renew my membership of the Club, I haven't the time for people now.
Leader	So you used to enjoy being with people?
Sarah	Oh yes, my husband used to complain that he could not take me anywhere without my knowing someone. I used to love nothing better than a good chat.
Leader	Do you think that the people you used to chat to have changed?
Sarah	No, it's me.
Co-leader	What is it about you that's changed?
Sarah	Everything. I am not the same person.
Co-leader	Is that really true? You have still got red hair. Maybe the only real difference is that you are afraid?
Sarah	You are right. I will not go out by myself because I think my assailant will harm me.
Co-leader	But he wore a mask, didn't he?
Sarah	I just see those eyes peering out. It makes me shudder.
Co-leader	But why should he seek you out and want to harm you?
Sarah	The police said from the route he took and other robberies in the area he probably lives locally.
John	But why should he have a go at you, Sarah? I would have thought he would want to stay well out of your way.
Sarah	I just feel vulnerable.
Leader	You had worked as manageress of the Off Licence for ten years before, hadn't you, Sarah? Did you go to work expecting to be safe?
Sarah	Oh yes, I had some good times.
Leader	So your belief that you were safe worked, it paid off?
Sarah	Maybe I was just lucky.
Leader	What, lucky on something like 3,000 days?
Sarah	I see what you mean.
Leader	If you were able to tell yourself what you took for granted before the incident, that you could expect to be safe going out that day, maybe you could begin to enjoy people's company again.
Sarah	Maybe, but then there are these panic attacks every time I try and go out by myself.
Leader	Can we discuss your handling of them over coffee at the end and we might also need to build in an individual session or two to address them?
Sarah	That is fine.

At the end of the above exchange the client mentions a common co-morbid problem – panic disorder. If more than one member of the group has such a disorder then the group leaders can more easily legitimate some time in the session devoted to the issue. However if, as is often the case, only one person is affected it is better dealt with using the above strategy of scheduling in an additional individual session.

Sometimes clients have done something during the traumatic event that made the outcome less awful than it might otherwise have been. The client's attention should be drawn to this to assist in reducing the sense of helplessness evoked by the trauma memory.

Leader	Sarah, you mentioned that you struggled not to be pushed back into the shop by your assailant. Your fear was that once inside the shop he would try and open the safe, would not believe you when you told him it was on a timelock, and in his frustration would have killed you with his knife. In the event you stopped him from pushing you back through the door. You did well there. Even in that extreme situation you were able to make a difference. Has anyone else managed to influence things in that sort of way?
Mary	Yes, I did wake up my sister and the other hotel residents when the fire broke out. I thought that we weren't going to get out but we did.
Co-leader	The fire occurred at about 1.00 a.m. when most of the residents were asleep, is that right?
Mary	Yes.
Sarah	God, if you had not done that they would have died.
Mary	I only did what I had to.
Leader	Yes, but you made a difference to the traumatic event, you did influence things. In some situations like those of Ian and John it was impossible to influence the event, but in yours, Mary and Sarah, you did.
Mary	I guess so.

Sometimes, however, it is an exaggerated sense of control that is at the heart of a client's trauma-related guilt. For example, a rape victim might blame herself for walking down an isolated lane and this guilt needs to be addressed. One approach to this is to enquire whether it was reasonably foreseeable in this case, whether a significant proportion of women would have walked down that lane at the time. The strategy is then to suggest that it was not unreasonable at the time. This focus on the constraints and circumstances existing at the time of the trauma is crucial to the client assuaging themselves of trauma-related guilt. Confronted with a trauma many clients freeze or rush to perform an action that in retrospect was not the best option. In the case of frenzied activity oxygen has to be pumped to the large muscles in order to take action, depriving oneself of the composure needed for a carefully thought-out response.

Mary	I tried desperately to revive the old lady who had fallen asleep in the lounge, but I think I just should have pulled her out instead.
Co-leader	But how do you know that if you had pulled her out and then tried to revive her she wouldn't have died anyway?
Mary	I don't, but I just feel so guilty.
Ian	I don't think the lady would be blaming you.
Mary	I know, but that's not the point.

Co-leader	What is the point?
Mary	I feel incredibly guilty.
Leader	Maybe all we can do is alter your reaction to those guilt feelings rather than try and take them away. Treat them as a mental cold, uncomfortable, but not to be taken too seriously. A 'Yes . . . I do feel extremely uncomfortable with these guilt feelings. But I do not have to buy into them, I can carry them, acknowledge them.'
Mary	I wish I could, but next weekend is the second anniversary.
Leader	But you can 'Yes . . . But' that day. 'Yes, March 26th can be a horrendous day if I remember the fire. But it could also be a really good day to remember if, say, I took a weekend flight to Monte Carlo!' You can re-write history.
Mary	Monte Carlo!! Will you pay? Coming with me, Sarah?
Co-leader	It's just making sure the trauma memory doesn't have the last word.

These sessions finish by asking clients not only to re-write the script of their trauma, but also, and separately, to spend ten to fifteen minutes each day writing about positive experiences from their pre-trauma life.

Sessions five and six: Reconnecting with others and establishing goals

The close relationships of PTSD clients are inevitably strained and they are often goalless. These sessions get under way, as always, with a review of the homework assignments.

Co-leader	Can anyone tell us about some positive incident from before the trauma?
John	Yes, I wrote about the Liverpool v Newcastle game, it was an absolute classic. Liverpool won 4–3 in the end. When I was writing about it I felt more my old self than for ages.
Co-leader	But that's not your old self John, that is you. The you who is sensible enough to be a Liverpool supporter rather than an Everton supporter!
Ian	Steady on!
John	Been a Liverpool supporter since I went to the match with my Dad as a child.
Co-leader	Ah! A Liverpool supporter through and through. But that says as much about you and your life as ever the trauma does.
John	I know, I just feel sick still when the incident comes to mind.
Sarah	But there's more to you than that accident, John. I reckon you're a big softy.
John	What?
Mary	That's a compliment.
Leader	Think about it, John.

Relating and juxtaposing trauma and pre-trauma experiences both for homework and in the session provides the means for contextualizing the trauma.

Close relationships are strained by the development of uncharacteristic irritability, emotional numbness and avoidance of activities. The uncharacteristic irritability often has its basis in the PTSD client's perceived inability to perform a previously valued role, but this frustration is often expressed in the context of very minor hassles, e.g.

one's partner forgetting to buy bread. The overreaction to minor inconveniences begets an overreaction from the partner, and escalates into arguments. These conflicts are rarely resolved because they are not really about the ostensible subject matter. Over time, partners often cope by distancing themselves from each other. In turn this enhances the PTSD client's feeling that 'Nobody understands' and sometimes leads to taking solace in drink or drugs – with the partner increasingly looking to other relationships for support.

A particular problem is posed by the emotional numbness or emptiness of the PTSD client. Because many PTSD clients are leading a hermit-like existence, making excuses to avoid previous friends and family, they can easily conclude that their lack of a positive emotional response to their partner is a sign that they are no longer in love with their partner. These feelings may become the client's guilty secret, resulting in debilitation or, if expressed, leading to further estrangement from the partner. An additional source of strain is that the PTSD client is spending more time with their partner since the trauma, but is almost wholly inactive, to the former's chagrin or annoyance. It is therefore necessary to help the PTSD client elaborate clear and manageable life goals.

It is usually a good sign of progress in PTSD clients if they become able to talk with their partner or significant other about the trauma. The verbalizing of the trauma requires a labelling of confusing emotions but the client thereby attains a measure of control. (In cases where the PTSD client is unable to write about the trauma this can be used as a substitute.) But communication between the PTSD client and partner is often impeded by the former's insistence that the latter completely comprehend their trauma, and as soon as it becomes apparent that there is less than total understanding communication is halted. This can be particularly frustrating to a partner who believes that hitherto they had good communication. Part of these sessions should be devoted to encouraging group members to talk about the trauma to their partner for just a couple of minutes each day. It has to be stressed that their partner will only accept discussion of the trauma for a limited period each day, because to do otherwise would represent a failure to contextualize the experience, that is, it would relegate in importance all their joint, positive, pre-trauma interactions, such as cycling with their children in the local park. The emphasis should be on partners' committing themselves to trying to understand each other, rather than expecting instant attainment of that understanding.

Reconnection is also a major issue for single PTSD clients who may have been physically scarred by their trauma or lost a limb. Usually there is at most one member in a PTSD group for whom adapting to disfigurement or disability is a major issue and it is not therefore easy or appropriate to tackle it in the group. These aspects are often better addressed in an interpolated individual session. On the one hand these clients often desperately want to be in a relationship where they are special to someone, but the thought of rejection is terrifying and the prospect of the discovery of their scarring in a sexual relationship mortifying. It is useful to give such clients the last two chapters of Simon Weston's autobiography, *Walking Tall* (Weston, 1989). He was badly facially disfigured in the Falklands War, and the final chapters 'Looking Back' and 'Looking On', provide a commendable model of successful adaptation. For example, he reframes the concerns of many unattached people with such disabilities about whether they will meet someone special, by advising that at least if they do meet such a person they will know that it is not a superficial relationship and will last.

Not only PTSD clients with disabilities or disfigurements but virtually all PTSD clients have to establish new goals. Often a major obstacle to the elaboration and pursuit of a new goal is the client's belief that they should not have to redirect their energies, they have been the hapless victims of fate. The group leader's task is to acknowledge these feelings, i.e. help the client say 'Yes' to them, and then to ask pragmatically 'But does it work, saying that it's not fair?' It is recommended that clients are asked to construct a 'mental video' of themselves saying 'It's all not fair' and then to decide whether the watching of such a video is helpful in the long term.

Clients can be particularly reluctant to change track if their pre-trauma role was overvalued, i.e. the role was perceived as the sole gateway to self-efficacy – a sense of achievement and pleasure. In the work context such clients can be introduced to the notion that perhaps they were addicted to their organization, i.e. they behaved as if there was no life beyond the organization, and that therapy is partly about weaning them off their employer, with associated withdrawal symptoms. Possible new goals should be tackled in an experimental fashion, adopting a 'you don't know until you try' approach. Because the average PTSD client is moderately depressed it is important that any goal is broken down into small manageable steps, with breaks in between before progressing to the next sub-goal.

Sessions seven to nine: Understanding the information conveyed by emotions, errors of interpretation and the challenging of safety beliefs

The previous sessions have focused on PTSD clients reconnecting with others. One of the hidden obstacles to this is often the client's lack of understanding of their own emotional response. For example, emotional numbness is a common symptom of PTSD, yet few clients directly attribute this to their trauma. Because their lives typically become circumscribed they can easily connect this lack of affect to their partner, concluding that they are no longer in love with them, leading to the break-down of probably their most salient relationship. More generally, the PTSD client attempts to justify their emotional state in terms of something in the present; thus their fear response might be justified by news of some horror in the media.

There is a variety of cognitive processes that can be used to justify a sense of continuing threat and these are examined in these sessions. Box 6.5 (from Scott and Stradling, 1992, p. 43) lists some typical errors of information-processing post trauma, and these same processes can be operative in the interpretation of the trauma itself.

Thus the client justifying their fearfulness in terms of a news item in the media would be using a mental filter. The leaders should discuss each of these errors of processing, inviting group members to volunteer examples, and write down ones pertinent to themselves. There are no watertight distinctions between the ten thought processes, and any one client is likely to habitually use a particular two or three. Once clients become aware of their propensity for specific errors, they can use them as an immediate fault-finding list to help them stand back and critically assess their distress at any point in time. For homework, group members are asked to monitor their mood, noting the time, place and context of any down-turn in mood, then to perform a slow motion 'action replay' of the changes, scrutinizing them for any errors of processing, then to write down a more realistic way of thinking about the situation.

Box 6.5 *Errors of Information Processing in PTSD*

ERRORS OF INFORMATION PROCESSING IN PTSD

1. *All or nothing thinking.* Everything is seen in extreme terms, for example 'I am either in control of what's happening to me or I am not'.
2. *Over-generalization.* Expecting a uniform response from a category of people because of the misdeeds of a member, for example 'All men are potential rapists'.
3. *Mental filter.* Seizing on a negative fragment of a situation and dwelling on it, for example 'I could have been killed in that encounter'.
4. *Automatic discounting.* Brushing aside the positive aspects of what was achieved in a trauma, for example 'I was only doing my duty in saving the child'.
5. *Jumping to conclusions.* Assuming that it is known what others think, for example 'They all think I should be over it now, it was six months ago after all'.
6. *Magnification and minimization.* Magnification of shortcomings and mini-mization of strengths, for example 'Since the trauma I am so irritable with the family and just about manage to keep going to work'.
7. *Emotional reasoning.* Focusing on emotional state to draw conclusions about oneself, for example 'Since it happened, I am frightened of my own shadow, I guess I am just a wimp'.
8. *'Should' statements.* Inappropriate use of moral imperatives – 'shoulds', 'musts', 'haves', and 'oughts' – for example 'It's ridiculous that since the attack I now have to take my daughter shopping with me. I should be able to go by myself.'
9. *Labelling and mislabelling.* For example 'I used to think of myself as a strong person. I could handle anything, but since it happened I am just weak.'
10. *Personalization.* Assuming that because something went wrong it must be your fault. 'I keep going over my handling of the situation. I must have made a mistake somewhere for the child to have died.'

The key cognitive shift sought in these sessions is to have the client attribute their negative emotions to the past rather than the present. This can be illustrated to group members by referring to the film *Ryan's Daughter* in which a soldier is on leave from the battles in the trenches of the First World War. He goes into a pub in an idyllic little village in the West of Ireland and stands at the bar. The pub is empty except for a barmaid collecting glasses. She drops the tray with a crash and he curls up in a ball on the floor, experiencing intense flashbacks of being back in the trenches. As time goes on he is better able to check his fear reaction, reminding himself that he is in the West of Ireland. Implicitly he was putting a particular time and place label on his uncomfortable 'gut reactions'. Successful processing of emotional information requires that the client learn to stop and think through the meaning of an emotion rather than engage in a 'knee-jerk' reflex reaction.

Simply making PTSD clients aware that they are getting faulty signals, 'false alarms', from their body is of itself insufficient for a re-engagement in pre-trauma-like activities; they have to be encouraged to collect data that would contradict the messages from their body. An analogy can help make this point.

Leader	If you were in a friend's car and you noticed that the fuel gauge was indicating empty, you would probably be alarmed. If your friend said 'It is probably a faulty gauge', this would probably not reassure you. What would really convince you that it was a faulty gauge would be if you then drove a great distance without any problems. To reach the parts that matter you need action.

For homework clients are asked to challenge safety beliefs that they have been operating on since the trauma e.g., 'I am only safe if I go to the pub when it is empty.' These beliefs should be explicated in the sessions and the actions that would constitute a contradiction of them agreed for practice.

Sarah	I burst out crying for no reason at work. I feel stupid, the smallest hassle sets me off.
Leader	Does that happen at home?
Sarah	No, if I am at home and have got my family around me I am fine, but outside I am struggling. The other day my husband could not pick me up from work and he arranged for my daughter to collect me. She was fifteen minutes late and I was in an awful state when she arrived.
Leader	You play 'horror videos' when you are anywhere other than home?
Sarah	When I rang home and did not get any answer I was beside myself.
Co-leader	What was in your horror movie?
Sarah	I thought 'Something's happened to my husband, nobody's coming for me, I am trapped.'

Leader	It is in just those situations when you are getting agitated because of the 'video' you have been watching that we want you to shout 'Stop! Think!' (Writing on a whiteboard)
	1. What is my problem, exactly? E.g. 'I want to get home'.
	2. What are the options?
	    (a) wait another ten minutes
	    (b) ring for a taxi
	    (c) ring a friend
	    (d) try walking home, etc.
	3. Choose an option.
	4. See how the option works out and if necessary go back to the 'menu' at (2).
	This Stop! Think! problem-solving procedure means that you sort things out rather than let your mind go dancing.

Mary	It all sounds so simple sitting here but when it happens to you . . .
Co-leader	Some people find it helps to carry around a reminder with them because you can easily be caught off guard e.g., a piece of card in your purse that has 'Stop!' on one side and 'Think!' on the other. Doing this can help you ignore the false alarms in your nervous system.
John	I think it is these damn false alarms that stop me getting to sleep.
Co-leader	Override the alarms by putting a favourite music tape on a portable cassette player when you go to bed. As your mind races increase the volume of the tape and reduce the volume as you relax. If you are not asleep by the end of the tape calmly get up, do not get angry with the alarms – that makes it worse. If you keep your cool your body will not let you go without the sleep that you need. Just go back to bed when you feel tired.

The core task in these sessions has been to help the PTSD client label and understand their emotional state and to view this formulation as a statement about a particular past experience rather than one carrying any implications for current interactions and engagement with life.

At the ninth session, for homework clients are asked to 'complete their story' by writing about how they could realistically move forward and what pitfalls might befall them.

Session ten: Review and relapse prevention

The final session begins with group members discussing their hypothesized endings to their story and the problems that they may encounter. The rationale for this is that if clients construct and become familiar with a viable and adaptive 'video' of their future then they are likely to be sufficiently motivated to make it happen. The 'future video' should ideally represent a continuity from pre-trauma experiences, so that the basic personality and identity is still intact. Nevertheless, some changes are inevitable, as is evident in the following exchange.

Sarah	I have written that I probably will not be working in the shop, in the long run – another branch was robbed during the week. But I can see myself getting involved when the new grandchild arrives, as my daughter is only taking maternity leave. I am actually looking forward to that. I have started going out locally. I am determined to get myself right for when this baby arrives and it could well come on the anniversary of the robbery!
Co-leader	That is a great way of seeing that your assailant does not have the last word on what that week or month means to you.
Leader	I think that is one of the main messages that we have been trying to get over in the programme: your trauma is not fixed in a tablet of stone, you really can change how it figures in your mind.
Mary	But there are some things that you can't change. It's five years since the incident now and the legal side is still not sorted. Every time I get a solicitor's letter I go sick, the thought of appearing in Court kills me, all I want is an apology. I am not really interested in the money, I just want someone to say 'Sorry'. Court dates keep getting changed for stupid reasons. I don't know whether I am pleased or vexed.

Leader	Is the prospect of Court stopping you getting on with your life, Mary?
Mary	Yes, with more letters of late I feel in limbo.
Leader	Sounds like you are expecting 'understanding' from the Court and legal process. But your opposition is not a person, it is an organization (the insurers of a hotel where Mary was caught in a fire) who will be battling against you; people in your position do not end up feeling 'understood'. The legal process simply puts into monetary terms your distress. It is always 'cold'.
Mary	I wonder why I bother!
Sarah	If you did not you would kick yourself.
Mary	That's probably true.
Co-leader	Maybe, Mary, if you can accept that understanding from the legal process is not on, you can alter the status of the proceedings in your mind, crossing the legal bridges when you come to them. It would be sad if you stopped yourself making the most of each day whilst you waited for a legal conclusion only to find that nobody actually says 'Sorry' anyway.
Mary	I had to see the psychiatrist for the insurers again last week, and he kept going on and on about my brother's death twelve months before the fire. I told him I was on tablets for a couple of months after Keith but he went on and on. I said he was upsetting me but he said that he was only doing what would be done in Court.
Leader	I am afraid, Mary, that they will probably try to argue that your distress is due largely to your brother's death and not the fire.
Mary	That's a disgrace!
Co-leader	You have to see it just as an attempt of the other side to avoid parting with money. It is nothing to do with you personally because they do not know you.
Mary	So what you're saying is that I am better seeing the whole legal thing as a side issue about money?
Co-leader	That's about it. Place it in the background of your life, not the foreground. Deal with it when you have to – it will just be two or three probably unpleasant days in your life. Put the Court appearance into context the way you have the fire itself.
Mary	I think I might need to give you a ring at the time.
Co-leader	That's fine.

Each client will have their own possible relapse precipitants. Using the problem-solving procedure described in Sessions Seven to Nine, ways of coping with these should be elaborated. One option to be considered is further contact with the group leaders or with other group members. It is important to stress that it is unrealistic to expect that certain situations will not crop up which will knock them 'off balance' but that using the coping strategies taught in the course and with the support of fellow participants they will 'regain their balance', they will not be 'knocked over', much less 'knocked out'. The main message to be conveyed is that it is anticipated that they will be 'copers' in difficult times rather than 'masters', thus avoiding the tyranny of unrealistic expectations. Finally the programme is audited by re-administration of the psychological tests for PTSD symptomatology (PENN, IES) and co-morbid depression (BDI).

REFERENCES

American Psychiatric Association (1980) *Diagnostic and Statistical Manual of Mental Disorders*. Washington, DC: American Psychiatric Association.

American Psychiatric Association (1994) *Diagnostic and Statistical Manual of Mental Disorders* (fourth edition). Washington, DC: American Psychiatric Association.

Beck, A.T., Ward, C.H., Mendelson, M., Mock, J. and Erbaugh, J. (1961) An inventory for measuring depression. *Archives of General Psychiatry*, **4**, 561–71.

Blake, D.D., Weathers, F.W., Nagy, L.M., Kaloupek, D.G., Klauminzer, G., Charney, D.S. and Keane, T.M. (1990) A clinician rating scale for assessing current and lifetime PTSD: The CAPS-1. *The Behaviour Therapist*, **13**, 187–8.

Blanchard, E.B., Hickling, E.J., Vollmer, A.J., Loos, W.R., Buckley, T.C. and Jaccard, J. (1995) Short term follow up of post-traumatic stress symptoms in motor accident victims. *Behaviour Research & Therapy*, **33**, 369–78.

Coren, S. (1988) Prediction of insomnia from arousability predisposition scores: scale development and cross-validation. *Behavior Research and Therapy*, **26**, 415–20.

Falsetti, S.A., Resnick, H.S., Resick, P.A. and Kilpatrick, D.G. (1993) The Modified PTSD Symptom Scale: A brief self report measure of PTSD. *The Behaviour Therapist*, **17**, 161–2.

Foa, G.B., and Kozak, M.J. (1986) Emotional processing of fear: exposure to corrective information. *Psychological Bulletin*, **99**, 20–35.

Hammarberg, M. (1992) PENN inventory for posttraumatic stress disorder: Psychometric properties. *Psychological Assessment*, **4**, 67–76.

Horowitz, M.J., Wilner, N. and Alvarez, W. (1979) Impact of Event Scale: A measure of subjective distress. *Psychomatic Medicine*, **41**, 209–18.

Kenardy, J.A., Webster, R.A., Lewin, T.J., Carr, V.J., Hazell, P.L. and Karter, G.L. (1996) Stress debriefing and patterns of recovery following a natural disaster. *Journal of Traumatic Stress*, **9**, 37–50.

Kessler, R.C., Sonnega, A., Bromet, E., Highes, M. and Nelson, C.B. (1996) PTSD in the National Comorbidity Study. *Archives of General Psychiatry*, **32**, 1048–60.

Meichenbaum, D. (1985) *Stress Inoculation Training*. New York: Pergamon Press.

Ochberg, F.M. (1996) The counting method for ameliorating traumatic memories. *Journal of Traumatic Stress*, **9**, 866–73.

Rothbaum, B.O., Foa, E.B., Riggs, D.S., Murdock, T. and Walsh, W. (1992) A prospective examination of PTSD in rape victims. *Journal of Traumatic Stress*, **5**, 455–75.

Scott, M.J. and Stradling, S.G. (1992). *Counselling for Post-Traumatic Stress Disorder*. London: Sage Publications.

Scott, M.J., Stradling, S.G. and Lee, S. (1997) The utility and accuracy of three self-report measures of posttraumatic stress disorder. Presented at ISTSS Annual Conference Montreal, November 1997.

Trimble, M. (1985) Post-traumatic stress disorder. History of a concept. In C. Figley (ed.), *Trauma and Its Wake*. New York: Brunner Mazel.

van der Kolk, B.A. (1996) The body keeps the score. Approaches to the psychobiology of PTSD. In B.A. van der Kolk, A.C. Mcfarlane and L. Weisaeth (eds), *Traumatic Stress*. New York: Guilford Press.

Weston, S. (1989) *Walking Tall*. London: Bloomsbury Publishing.

CHAPTER 7

Letter Writing, Audiotaping and Videotaping as Therapeutic Tools: Use of 'Healing' Metaphors

Donald Meichenbaum

Give sorrow words: the grief that does not speak
whispers the o'er-fraught heart, and bids it break.
William Shakespeare, Macbeth

What cannot be talked about can also not be put to rest; and if it is not,
the wounds continue to fester from generation to generation.
(Bettelheim, 1984; 166)

WHY DOES TALKING/WRITING ABOUT TRAUMATIC STRESS HELP?

As Shakespeare and Bettelheim observe, having traumatized individuals put into words, either orally or in written form, their experiences is a critical feature of the 'healing' process. This hypothesis was tested in a series of studies by Pennebaker and his colleagues. The Pennebaker programme of studies indicated that having individuals, such as Holocaust survivors, adults who have been terminated from their job, and freshman college students who are adjusting to a new setting, each write about their respective experiences has resulted in improved psychological and physical well-being. More specifically, Pennebaker has reported that those subjects who had an opportunity to write or talk about upsetting events improved their long-term immune functioning, lowered their autonomic nervous system activity, reduced visits to their physician, and evidenced improvement on self-reports of adjustment (Pennebaker and Beall, 1986).[1]

Harvey *et al.* (1991) have described how *account-making* about severe stress (e.g. discussing sexual assault experience) facilitates coping and adjustment. Accounts are people's story-like construction of events. Victims/survivors who provide well-developed accounts are more likely to develop a perspective on events, become more hopeful about the future, and develop closure regarding stressors. When people fail to talk about a traumatic experience they tend to live with it, dream about it, and ruminate about it, in an unresolved manner. This repetitive or recurrent process provokes higher arousal levels (resting autonomic levels), higher depression and illness rates. By putting these images and their accompanying emotions into language, they become more organized, understood and resolved. This is illustrated by a study of incest victims by Silver *et al.* (1983). Those women who were able to relate and make sense of their traumatic experience reported less psychological distress, better social adaptation, higher levels of self-esteem and greater resolution of the experience.

While it is *not* clear exactly what features of the writing and talking processes contributed to adjustment, a number of hypotheses have been offered to explain these changes. Traumatic events can (a) provoke an increased number of intrusive, fragmented and disorganized thoughts about the upheaval as distressed individuals tend to often think about them for an inordinate amount of time (Horowitz, 1976); and (b) significantly alter or 'shatter' basic core beliefs about trust, intimacy, esteem, control and safety (Janoff-Bulman, 1992; McCann and Pearlman, 1990).

Pennebaker and others have demonstrated that writing or speaking about the upheaval can clearly affect the ways people think about the events over substantial periods of time. More specifically, a number of investigators have proposed that writing and talking about distressing events can:

(1)   facilitate the expression and labelling of feelings;
(2)   make the thoughts and feelings about the event more organized (i.e., since language is both more structured and social, talking and writing forces one's thoughts to be implicitly more integrated, less fragmented, leading to a more coherent explanation and an increased likelihood of accepting unchangeable aspects of the situation);
(3)   influence the accessibility of the thoughts and feelings (i.e., not being as preoccupied as a result of putting their stories into words) and solicit feedback from others;
(4)   foster some insight and reframing about their predicament and reach some degree of acceptance about themselves and closure about their situation;
(5)   provide an opportunity to explore the meaning of events and reconsider his or her reactions; draw connections between past events and present circumstance;
(6)   foster new perspectives and creative problem-solving.

Pennebaker concluded, 'Failure to translate upsetting experiences into language [or some other form of expression] can result in psychological conflict and stress-related health problems' (p. 21). The strategy of having clients who have been traumatized put into words their experiences has been embraced by most therapists who work with PTSD clients. This is illustrated in the heavy emphasis placed on encouraging clients (1) to describe their traumatic experiences; (2) to audiotape sessions, and subsequently, to listen to them; (3) to write letters, keep journals, offer testimonies, and the like. As we will consider, such letter writing may take various forms (as described below). These descriptive accounts may be offered in individual, group and family therapy, in debriefing sessions, and in informal social support settings. Note, there are *cultural differences* in how readily acceptable it is to 'share' descriptions and feelings about traumatic events with others.

If one accepts the conceptual framework that the nature of the narrative that an individual offers or 'scripts' both contributes to and reflects the level of adjustment, then a promising way to influence and alter the client's 'story' is to employ letter writing and audiotaping (even though the letters may never be sent). A number of clinicians have used these 'reauthoring' procedures in a creative fashion to help clients change their narrative accounts (see Brandt, 1989; Capacchione, 1979; Dolan, 1991; Epston *et al.*, 1992; Friedman, 1992; Harvey *et al.*, 1991; Herman, 1992; Meichenbaum and Fitzpatrick, 1993; O'Hanlon, 1992; White and Epston, 1990; Zaidi, 1994). The various ways that letter writing and audiotaping have been used include:

1. having the therapist write a letter to the client sharing his or her observations;
2. having the therapist write a report to the referring physician (agency) and then review the letter with the client. Ask for the client's input and feedback. Ask the client to co-sign the report and ask the client if he or she would like a copy of the letter for his or her records. The letter should incorporate the guidelines included in this section.
3. having the client write a letter to another person (relative, spouse, and so forth);
4. having the client write a 'rainy day' letter, namely, have the client write a letter to oneself when he or she is feeling strong and hopeful indicating strengths and 'signs of recovery'. The client can be asked to describe him- or herself sympathetically in the third person (Kelly, 1955). The letter can be read when the client feels the need. (Note, the notion of 'rainy days' needs to be introduced carefully. Some clients do *not* like the notion of future 'bad days'. Moreover, when clients 'feel down' they prefer to remind themselves that they have survived other bad days and feel they are in no mood to read about positive attributes. Once again, the therapeutic rule should be to collaborate with clients in considering which form of letter writing would be most helpful.)
5. having the client write a letter 'from the future', namely, write a friend or therapist 'as if' several years have passed. Write the letter 'as if' the positive events that the client would like to have happen (e.g. experiences in relationship, job, school, etc.) have indeed happened;
6. having the client write a letter of disclosure and personal strengths to a supportive other (e.g. family member);
7. having the client write a letter *from* a real or imaginary supportive other, specifying advice that he or she might have offered (e.g. write a letter from a wise older person, a therapist, a popular figure);
8. having the client write a letter 'as if' the client were someone else (*à la* George Kelly's fixed-role therapy) or communicate with a 'future self' who is benevolent, strong and wise;
9. having clients write a letter to themselves as 'an abused child' in order to

combat the sense of culpability and to underscore what the child did to survive. Client reads this letter to the group (Zaidi, 1994).

10. having the client write a letter to the perpetrator or abuser or to anyone else the client feels would be important to talk to more openly and honestly about the traumatic events. Client reads the letter to his or her therapy group. (*See guidelines below for writing letters to perpetrators.*)

11. having the client write a letter (or keep a journal) of what his or her experiences were during and after the traumatic event (e.g. kidnapping). The client may also ask family members to write their experiences during and after the trauma, as well. Jay (1994) describes how some families developed a ritual; namely, each year, on the anniversary of the traumatic event, the family read their recollections together. This annual ritual permitted the victimized individual and the family members to acknowledge both the trauma and their survival.

12. Holocaust survivors have made video testimonials conveying their memory of events in order to leave a legacy behind. Healing through sharing (Danieli, 1994).

13. torture victims have written 'testimonies' of atrocities. In the group, another member may be asked to read aloud the 'survivor's' account.

Dolan (1991) provides examples of how such letters can be written. The client is asked to write a letter *as if* one were an 'older, wiser self'.

Imagine that you have grown to be a healthy, wise older (woman, man) and you are looking back on this period of your life. What do you think that this older, wiser you would suggest to you to help you get through this current phase of your life? What would she or he tell you to remember? What would she or he suggest that would be most useful in helping you heal from the past? What would she or he say to comfort you? And does she or he have any advice about how therapy could be most useful and helpful? (p. 36).

Or the client can consider writing the letter from the viewpoint of a supportive, but deceased wise relative or friend; or the client can create a supportive other. Dolan suggests that the therapist ask the client what difference this supportive person has made in the past, even if that person did not know what the client was struggling with. The client is asked to imagine what this person would say, and then write a letter or make an audiotape describing the client's strengths that would be highlighted, and indicate the advice that would be offered.

If therapy is conducted on a group basis such letters can be read to the group. Also, in therapy the client can be asked to report (1) how he or she felt at the time of the trauma (e.g. rape); (2) how he or she felt when writing about it, and (3) how he or she feels about it now that he or she has read it to the group. These questions 'pull for' the client gaining some distance and perspective on changes in feelings since the traumatic incident.

Letters to the perpetrator (e.g. in the case of child sexual abuse) present specific 'healing' opportunities, but also possible dangers. Once again, there have been many clinical suggestions as to how such letters should be written. These letters are usually *not* mailed. For example, Dolan suggests that a series of letters may be written including:

1. an initial letter providing a detailed description of the abuse, conveying feelings about the abuse, efforts at coping, and any desire for retribution;
2. a second letter indicating what the perpetrator might write including what has been said during past confrontations, also covering the client's fears about what may occur;
3. a third letter indicating what the client would like the perpetrator to say, including the perpetrator taking responsibility for the abuse and expressing a desire to make amends. 'This is the letter the client needs, but has not received (and is unlikely to receive).'
4. after an interval of several months (e.g. three months) the client in collaboration with the therapist (and perhaps, significant others) can decide if the letter should be sent. Any decision about confronting the perpetrator needs to be weighed carefully and collaboratively with the client. As noted in Section I on the discussion of incest victims, *great caution is needed when conducting such 'family of origin' work.*

NOTES

1 See Clark (1993) for a discussion of the relative merits of writing versus talking about distressing events, and Murray and Segal (1994) for a discussion of how inviting clients to write about their traumatic events can be incorporated into the psychotherapy process (e.g. as implemented in *Cognitive Processing Therapy* by Calhoun and Resick, 1993).

REFERENCES

Bettelheim, B. (1984) Afterword. In C. Vegh, *I Didn't Say Good-bye*. New York: E.P. Dutton.

Brandt, L.A. (1989) A short term group therapy model for treatment of adult female survivors of childhood incest. *Group*, 18, 74–82.

Calhoun, K.S. and Resick, P.A. (1993) Posttraumatic stress disorder. In D. Barlow (ed.), *Clinical Handbook of Psychological Disorders*. New York: Guilford Press.

Capacchione, L. (1979) *The Creative Journal: The Art of Finding Yourself*. Athens, OH: Ohio University/Swallow Press.

Clark, L.F. (1993) Stress and cognitive-conversational benefits of social interaction. *Journal of Social & Clinical Psychology*, 12, 25–55.

Danieli, Y. (1994) As survivors age: Part II. *NCP Clinical Quarterly*, 4, 20–4.

Dolan, Y.M. (1991) *Resolving Sexual Abuse: Solution Found Therapy and Ericksonian Hypnosis for Adult Survivors*. New York: W.W. Norton.

Epston, D., White, M. and Murray, K. (1992) A proposal for re-authorising therapy: Rosie's revisioning of her life and a commentary. In S. McNamnee and K.J. Gergen (eds), *Therapy as Social Construction*. Newbury Park, CA: Sage.

Friedman, S. (1992) Constructing solutions. In S.H. Budman and M.F. Hoyt (eds), *The First Session in Brief Therapy*. New York: Guilford Press.

Harvey, J.H., Orbuch, T.L., Chwalisz, K.D. and Garwood, G. (1991) Coping with sexual assault: the role of account making and confiding. *Journal of Traumatic Stress*, **4**, 515–32.

Herman, J.L. (1992) *Trauma and Recovery*. New York: Basic Books.

Horowitz, M.J. and Wilner, N.R. (1976) Stress films, emotion and cognitive response. *Archives of General Psychiatry*, **33**, 1339–44.

Janoff-Bulman, R. (1992) *Shattered Assumptions: Towards a New Psychology of Trauma*. New York: Free Press.

Jay, J. (1994) Walls for wailing. *Common Boundary*, May/June, 30–5.

Kelly, G.A. (1955) *The Psychology of Personal Constructs*. New York: Norton.

McCann, I.L. and Pearlman, L.A. (1990) *Psychological Trauma and the Adult Survivor: Theory, Therapy and Transformation*. New York: Brunner/Mazel.

Meichenbaum, D. and Fitzpatrick, D. (1993) A constructivist narrative perspective on stress and coping. Stress inoculation applications. In L. Goldberger and S. Breznitz (eds), *Handbook of Stress: Theoretical and Clinical Aspects* (second edition). New York: Free Press.

Murray, E.J. and Segal, D.L. (1994) Emotional processing in vocal and written expression of feelings about traumatic experiences. *Journal of Traumatic Stress*, **7**, 391–405.

O'Hanlon, W.H. (1992) History becomes her story. Collaborative solution-orientated therapy of the after effects of sexual abuse. In S. McNamnee and K.J. Gergen (eds), *Therapy as Social Construction*. Newbury Park, CA: Sage.

Pennebaker, J.W. (1997) Opening up: The healing power of Expressing Emotions. New York: Guilford Press.

Pennebaker, J.W. and Beall, S. (1986) Confronting a traumatic event. Toward an understanding of inhibition and disease. *Journal of Abnormal Psychology*, **95**, 274–86.

Silver, R.L., Boon, C. and Stones, M.H. (1983) Searching for meaning in misfortune: Making sense of incest. *Journal of Social Issues*, **39**, 81–102.

White, M. and Epston, D. (1990) *Narrative Means to Therapeutic Ends*. New York: Norton.

Zaidi, L.Y. (1994) Group treatment of adult male inpatients abused as children. *Journal of Traumatic Stress*, **7**, 719–28.

The *Clinical Handbook on PTSD* can be ordered from Dr Meichenbaum. Send a cheque for $60 US Funds on a US Bank or an International Money Order made out to Don Meichenbaum. Mail to: Dr Donald Meichenbaum, University of Waterloo, Psychology Department, Waterloo, Ontario, Canada N2L 3G1. Upon receipt of payment, a book will be shipped.

CHAPTER 8

What Can Be Done to Help Clients with PTSD and DES?

Donald Meichenbaum

Before we consider a number of specific intervention procedures it is helpful to consider some general treatment guidelines that emerge across a variety of diverse treatment approaches. In this Chapter, I will outline the general treatment objectives[1] and the rationale for each. Although these clinical procedures are outlined in a sequential fashion, they may often be *implemented concurrently*. For example, while the therapist is addressing the client's presenting symptoms of hyperarousal, insomnia, anger control, depression or addictive behaviour, the therapist may also spend time on helping the client 'restructure' his or her 'story', and also re-establish relationships. These guidelines should *not* be seen as a lock-step prescription, but rather a framework to be followed *in a flexible fashion*, depending upon the client's needs and treatment goals.

As Susan Solomon (1994: 20) has observed: 'PTSD is a complex disorder, highly resistant to cure by any of the treatment modalities available to date. The development of new modes of intervention is called for.' *The present treatment guidelines provide an integrative cognitive-behavioural treatment approach that derives from a constructive narrative perspective.* The treatment approach can be viewed as consisting of *five phases*, each with their own treatment goals.

PHASE I – INTRODUCTORY PHASE

The treatment goals are to:

1. establish a therapeutic relationship or 'alliance',[2]
2. encourage the client to share his or her 'story' at his or her own pace; allow for the expression of feelings that should be 'validated'; collaboratively establish treatment goals;
3. ensure the client's safety and address practical needs first; recognize the need for rest and respite in a safe environment;
4. conduct assessments – both psychological and medical; assess the client's strengths;[3]

5. educate the client about the nature of PTSD and accompanying sequelae;
6. validate and help the client reframe his or her reactions, and engender 'hope';
7. consider the treatment options collaboratively with the client, namely individual, group, couples, family, day or inpatient treatment,[4] and examine specific treatment formats designed to address the client's problems of co-morbidity.

PHASE II – ADDRESS THE CLIENT'S PRESENTING SYMPTOMS AND SIGNS OF CO-MORBIDITY

The treatment goals are to:

1. help stabilize the client's clinical picture, reduce symptoms and provide relief;
2. teach coping skills to address the specific symptom, for example, directly treat flashbacks, intrusive ruminations, hyperarousal, irritability, avoidance, insomnia; assist client in affect modulation and emotional regulation so he or she does *not* fluctuate between numbing and withdrawal and hypervigilance and overarousal. Keep in mind, however, that it is possible that PTSD symptomatology can be reduced, but the client can still have a number of life adjustment problems.
3. check to determine if psychotropic medication[5] is indicated; provide adherence counselling for prescribed medication;
4. address the clinical picture of co-morbidity or coexisting disorders (e.g. depression, panic attacks, anger control problems, addictive behaviours, interpersonal and sexual difficulties, by such procedures as panic-control training, stress-inoculation training, relapse prevention training, cognitive therapy);
5. ensure the client's safety in terms of addressing the dangers of 'stigmatization', 'revictimization' and 'secondary victimization' (e.g. address issues that might arise from dealing with the legal and medical systems).

PHASE III – HELP THE CLIENT TO RESTRUCTURE HIS OR HER STORY AND TRANSFORM TRAUMATIC MEMORY, SHIFT FROM 'VICTIM' ROLE TO 'SURVIVOR' AND 'THRIVER' ROLES

The treatment goals are to:

1. help the client retell his or her story (re-experience, recollect the trauma in the 'here and now') and 'revise' the account in a way that leads to 'integration' and 'a sense of mastery', as well as provide an opportunity to 'find' meaning; enable the client to re-experience the trauma memories with a relatively high degree of voluntary control, evidencing a sense of mastery over intrusive recollections and the ability to tolerate discomfort.
2. re-expose the client to traumatic cues in a structured and supportive manner (e.g. use direct therapy exposure, various guided imagery procedures, hypnotic induction procedures, offering testimony, graded *in vivo* behavioural re-exposure);

3.   address the client's 'shattered' beliefs and resultant intra- and interpersonal difficulties (e.g. feelings of guilt, self-blame, rage/anger, grief/sadness,[6] helplessness, hopelessness, victimization) by means of cognitive restructuring procedures, problem-solving, letter-writing, 'journalling', and client self-selected ways of expression – artistic, engaging in a ritual, undertaking a 'mission';

4.   examine the potential of personal growth that can emerge from traumatic events (move from 'victim' to 'survivor' to 'thriver'); shift time orientation from the past to the present and future; provide opportunities for the client to regain 'self-esteem' and 'trust' in others and self; foster social relationships rather than social withdrawal and detachment; help client establish a more satisfactory lifestyle and develop and strengthen social supports;

5.   help the client mobilize own resources such as implicit belief systems (e.g. religious and philosophical belief systems); have clients consider whether engaging in a restorative or reparative individually or group-initiated activity (ritual) would be helpful (e.g. Native-American Indian purification sweat lodge ceremony; revisit the site of victimization; engage in memorial service; help others); help the client develop a sense of being able to build upon the experience and to develop a future sense of goals.

Note: The therapist should *not* try to provide meaning, but the meaning should come from the client.

PHASE IV – HELP THE CLIENT TO RECONNECT WITH OTHERS AND RESTORE FAMILIAL, SOCIAL AND OCCUPATIONAL FUNCTIONING

The treatment goals are to:

1.   re-establish relationship with significant others and work on client's interpersonal goals (may involve significant others in treatment or have the client participate in group sessions and group rituals and activities);

2.   address interpersonal difficulties and issues such as intimacy, trust, sexual difficulties – may involve couples sex therapy;

3.   address the possibility of 'revictimization' by employing cognitive restructuring and interpersonal problem-solving procedures;

4.   address issues of 'reparation' and family of origin issues which may take the form of a 'symbolic' 'metaphoric' 'coming to terms', rather than direct confrontation; address the issue of the 'impossibility of getting even' and the 'psychic costs' of being preoccupied with 'revenge'; such 'reparation' work may contribute to feelings of resolution;

5.   explore with the client the value of undertaking *restorative* attempts of rewriting his or her 'narrative'; the form this may take should come from the client (e.g. letter writing, soldier who killed his buddy in friendly fire may decide to visit his buddy's family, may visit grave site, may 'bear witness', and the like);

6.   empower and enable the client by encouraging and helping the client to arrange

to *act as a 'helper'* for others; nurture 'connectedness' to others by helping the client 'find a mission', if he or she wants; for example, this may take the form of trying to raise public awareness, help other victims, do preventative work; encourage reengaging activities; provide opportunity for the client to reassess his or her priorities and life goals.

Note: The therapist should hold a broad definition of what constitutes 'healing activities'.
The actual time in psychotherapy should be viewed as only one part of the healing process. It is a 'catalytic time' designed to help clients undertake 'reparative work' and to perform 'personal experiments' *in vivo*. The therapist reviews with the client the consequences ('results', 'data') from such personal experiments and the lessons learned. Some of these personal experiments may be conducted in the therapy session in the form of examining issues that arise between the client and the therapist and in the form of behavioural rehearsal. Most personal experiments will occur *in vivo* in the form of the client undertaking 'homework'.

PHASE V – TERMINATION PHASE

The treatment goals are to:

1. Bolster the client's self-confidence, sense of competence and self-efficacy; ensure that the client documents and 'takes credit' for accomplishments; while *self-attribution* process takes place throughout treatment, it receives special attention in the termination phase;
2. discuss the *'recovery work'* that lies ahead;
3. discuss *relapse prevention* efforts – client is taught ways to anticipate, accept and cope with possible lapses, setbacks and re-experiences; discuss that PTSD symptoms may reoccur when the client is stressed or under specific conditions (e.g. anniversary date);
4. arrange for *booster-sessions*, follow-through sessions, and *'pulsed' sessions* (provide follow-up sessions at critical junctures such as court appearance); include *follow-up assessments*.

In summary, it is important to consider how any specific treatment procedure (e.g. pharmacological interventions, direct therapy exposure, stress inoculation training, hypnosis, cognitive restructuring, couples or group therapy) is *embedded in an overall treatment package*. As outlined, the initial assessment and termination phases, the extra-therapeutic activities, each constitute critical features of treatment. Thus, when clinical investigators examine the relative effectiveness of a specific treatment approach, one should keep in mind the overall therapeutic regimen in which it is situated. This is true of all therapeutic relationships, but especially is the case in working with clients who have been victimized. In fact, the quality of the client–therapist relationship by the third session has been found to be one of the best predictors of treatment outcome for all modes of psychotherapy (see Meichenbaum and Turk, 1987).

But what can the therapist do to enhance such an 'alliance'? Some suggestions come from a study by Hamilton and Coates (1993) who asked abused women to describe which health–care providers they found 'most helpful' and those they found 'least helpful'. The women reported that the *helpful therapist:*

a) listened respectfully and took me seriously;
b) believed my 'story';
c) helped me to see if I was still in danger and explored with me how I could deal with this;
d) let me know I am not alone;
e) helped me see my strengths;
f) helped me understand the impact of traumatic events on myself and on others;
g) helped me plan for change.

In contrast, the unhelpful therapist:

a) did *not* listen, did *not* have an accepting attitude;
b) questioned my 'story';
c) dismissed, or minimized, the seriousness of my situation and the importance of the problem;
d) gave advice that I did *not* wish to receive;
e) blamed or criticized me.

In addition, there is also a need for the therapist to empower and enable *clients* so they *have choices* in terms of the material to be covered, the pace of disclosure, and the options for action.

THE VALUE OF HAVING CLIENTS TELL THEIR STORIES: WITH SOME CAUTIONARY OBSERVATIONS

Common to many forms of intervention with traumatized individuals is the practice of providing them with an opportunity to tell their stories. Whether it is in the form of a clinical interview, or more explicit retelling in the context of guided imagery procedures, therapists have embraced the principle that 'healing' is enhanced by helping clients to translate and transform their highly emotional, often fragmented, 'fixated', indelible images, and, sometimes, contradictory accounts into more coherent narrative accounts. As Herman (1992a: 179) describes in citing an incest survivor, 'Keep encouraging people to talk, even if it's very painful to watch them. It takes a long time to believe. The more I talk about it, the more I have confidence that it happened; the more I can integrate it.'

But great caution is required before therapists impose this therapeutic dictum to self-disclose on all traumatized clients. Some clients do *not* wish to 'stir up' old memories. Some clients do *not* wish to self-disclose. Should therapists respect the client's decision in this area? Is self-disclosure a necessary condition for change? Can self-disclosure ever make things worse? For instance, in examining such questions Clark (1993: 48) observed,

In the act of conversing, individuals construe meaning. They create a framework of reactions to it, that may previously have been lacking . . . However, there are also conditions under which, far from being helpful, *conversational interaction may actually hamper coping* . . . Conversations that reinforce the idea of trying harder (problem solving) may be *less helpful* than those that suggest a re-examination of one's abilities (accepting). Once the individual accepts his/her limitations, problem solving can be used to consider new options.

Thus, it is being proposed that it is *not* the opportunity for self-disclosure per se, but the type of therapeutic reaction to such disclosures that may prove critical. Moreover, not all clients respond favourably to the opportunity to retell their stories as evident in the following client's reactions. She observed:

I don't believe in let-it-all-hang-out, or it'll-feel-better-when-you-get-it-out mentality. In my experience it only makes it worse, because the session ends and I'm left with it. And no one's there when I relive it, or dream about it, or stay awake for hours thinking about it. If I have to tell my story, why not suggest I tell it in the third person so I can distance myself from it, while I tell it. It seems like it's a benefit for the therapist to have the story told. I am not so sure how much it does for me.

It is also important to keep cultural differences in mind. Members of some cultural groups (e.g. from South-East Asia) who have been traumatized prefer to focus on 'here and now' problems, rather than reconsider the past. Similarly, there is some suggestion in the CISD literature that some individuals may 'get worse' by participating in self-disclosure debriefing groups.

What is the treatment guideline that follows from this discussion? Well, like most areas of the treatment of PTSD, there are no simple answers. For many clients, soliciting their accounts and helping them to 'transform' their 'stories' will prove therapeutic. But, such self-disclosure may also prove to be unhelpful for some. Perhaps the best advice is to explore these issues with your clients and to allow the client *gradually* to recollect and re-experience the trauma in what Scurfield (1985) calls 'tolerable doses of awareness'.

AN EMPHASIS SHOULD BE PLACED ON THE CONSTRUCTIVE RATHER THAN ONLY ON THE RESTORATIVE

The treatment goal should *not* be merely to return the client to the level of functioning prior to the traumatizing experience. As Turnbull (1994) observes, the aim of treatment 'is not to ignore the very real potential for personal growth afforded by the disruption of the pre-existing schematic model of the world and the need to build a new one' (p. 7). In terms of a constructive narrative perspective, the exposure to traumatic events provides a unique opportunity to achieve 'positive growth'. *There is a need for the therapist not to hold a pathological bias, but instead to be sensitive to the client's strengths and resources and to listen actively to how the client changes his or her narrative in an adaptive fashion over the course of treatment.* For example, consider the following 'restorative' features of the client's new narrative that emerged over the course of treatment

- 'I'm *not* so hard on myself these days.'
- 'I can notice, catch myself; refocus on the present.'
- 'I can share with others.'
- 'I am starting to get bored with the story of X.'
- 'My memories do not go away, but they are losing their gripping quality.'
- 'My memories are no longer able to stop me in my tracks. I have control (authority) over them now.'
- 'My memories no longer make me feel undone.'
- 'I have choices now; I can choose to leave it if I want to.'
- 'I can bear the pain of what happened.'
- 'I can celebrate life now (join life, write a new chapter, rescript my life, take charge).'
- 'I have learned to cherish laughter.'
- 'The pain of what happened has immunized me against the most petty hurts.'
- 'I focus on the present and the future and leave the past in the past.'
- 'I am stronger because of what happened to me.'
- 'I can make a gift of what happened to me to others.'
- 'Life has new meaning for me.'

This array of client statements indicates that they can move beyond just merely coping with the aftermath of trauma to achieve a new and higher plateau of adjustment. In short, the goal of treatment is to help clients, not only improve their behaviour, but to also change the 'story' they tell to themselves and to others.

NOTES

1 Herman (1992b) has proposed that the treatment of traumatized clients can be viewed as consisting of (1) establishing safety, (2) restructuring the trauma story, and (3) restoring connectedness between the survivor and the community. The present analysis builds upon and elaborates on the Herman model. (For other descriptive accounts of treatment protocols for PTSD clients see Brom *et al.*, 1989; Marmar and Horowitz, 1988; Schwarz and Prout, 1991.) No matter what the form of intervention, it appears that *the earlier the intervention the better the outcome*. Early intervention reduces the likelihood of disruptive behavioural patterns becoming entrenched.

2 McFarlane (1995) observes that trust is an essential feature of the therapeutic alliance with traumatized clients. The client must feel secure and confident that the therapist is genuine, empathetic and warm, and that the therapist can also cope with bearing witness to the trauma and understanding its significance (p. 402).

3 Caution is required in assessing the client's strengths. As one client observed: 'I recently went to see a therapist and I know she means well, but she kept asking me, 'What would need to happen for you to feel better?', and she also tried to 'tap my strengths'. On the surface these are reasonable questions. But I didn't know the answers and in the asking somehow I felt she had *not* been hearing what I had been telling her. She didn't help me find the triggers or what I could do about them'.

The caution is *not* to pursue the client's strengths before hearing the client's narrative account. Once again, it is not the clinical procedure, but the timing that proves critical.

4 The decision to have clients participate in individual, group, couples, family, day, inpatient treatment, or some combination of these interventions, has *not* been systematically examined. In fact, we don't know which form of individual, group, or family-based intervention is best for which type of traumatized client. The severity of the client's distress (risk to self and others); the nature of the client's presenting problems (e.g. whether it involves significant others as in the form of intimacy and sexual problems); whether it involves co-morbidity; the impact of the trauma on the family members; the nature of the social supports; and the like – each can influence the treatment decision-making process. In general, clinicians seem to operate with implicit algorithms that they use in suggesting treatment alternatives. *It is critical to examine the pros and cons of the different treatment options in a collaborative fashion with the client.*

5 The complexity of the PTSD and DES populations underscore the need for a *bio-psycho-social* integrative treatment approach.

6 Scurfield (1985) observes that focusing on the client's initial reactions of rage and anger invariably uncovers the client's feelings of grief and sadness.

REFERENCES

Brom, D., Kleber, R.J. and Defares, P.B. (1989) Brief psychotherapy for post-traumatic stress disorders. *Journal of Counseling and Clinical Psychology*, **57**, 607–12.

Clark, L.F. (1993) Stress and cognitive-conversational benefits of social interaction. *Journal of Social and Clinical Psychology*, **12**, 25–55.

Hamilton, B. and Coates, J. (1993) Perceived helplessness and use of professional services by abused women. *Journal of Family Violence*, **8**, 313–24.

Herman, J.L. (1992a) *Trauma and Recovery*. New York: Basic Books.

Herman, J.L. (1992b) Complex PTSD: A syndrome in survivors of prolonged and repeated trauma. *Journal of Traumatic Stress*, **5**, 377–91.

McFarlane, A.C. (1995) Helping victims of disasters. In J.R. Freddy and S.E. Hobfoll (eds), *Traumatic Stress: From Theory to Practice*. New York: Plenum Press.

Marmar, C.R. and Horowitz, M.J. (1988) Diagnosis and phase orientated treatment of post-traumatic stress disorder. In J. Wilson, Z. Havel and B. Kahana (eds), *Human Adaptation to Extreme Stress: From the Holocaust to Vietnam*. New York: Plenum Press.

Meichenbaum, D. and Turk, D. (1987) *Facilitating Treatment Adherence: A Practitioner's Guidebook*. New York: Plenum Press.

Schwarz, R.A. and Prout, M.F. (1991) Integrative approaches in treatment of post-traumatic stress disorder. *Psychotherapy*, **28**, 364–73.

Scurfield, R.M. (1985) Post-trauma stress assessment and treatment: Overview and formulation. In C.R. Figley (ed.), *Trauma and Its Wake: The Study and Treatment of Post-traumatic Stress Disorder*. New York: Brunner/Mazel.

Solomon, S.D. and Smith, E.M. (1994) Social support and perceived control as moderators of responses to dioxin and flood exposure. In R. Ursano *et al.* (eds), *Trauma and Disaster*. New York: Cambridge University Press.

Turnbull, G.J. (1994) Acute treatments. In B. van der Kolk, S.M. Farlane and L Weisaeth (eds), *PTSD Handbook*. New York: Guilford Press.

The *Clinical Handbook on PTSD* can be ordered from Dr Meichenbaum. Send a cheque for $60 US Funds on a US Bank or an International Money Order made out to Don Meichenbaum. Mail to: Dr Donald Meichenbaum, University of Waterloo, Psychology Department, Waterloo, Ontario, Canada N2L 3G1. Upon receipt of payment, a book will be shipped.

CHAPTER 9

Expressive Art as a Form of Prevention and Treatment of PTSD with Children

Donald Meichenbaum

Art is a process of self-healing.
Art helps the chaos inside come out in a creative form.
Golub, 1994: p 33

I have taken the liberty of sharing several 'stops' in my journey consulting on the topics of stress and coping. One of the more memorable was an invitation to visit the Stress Centre at the University of Haifa, in Israel. This picturesque campus overlooks the nearby mountainside. The meeting room in which I was to present had a magnificent vista, but it was what was inside the room that most moved me. Whatever comments on stress and coping that I had to offer were 'dwarfed' by the art that hung about the room. These were sketches and paintings created by concentration camp inmates while they had been in the camps. Most of these artists did not survive the Holocaust. Their images, their symbols, their pictures, captured, more poignantly, the content of what I had planned to present. Golub (1994) has described and reviewed a number of books of children's images of trauma. She notes that 'making art makes whole what has been shattered', especially when expressed by children. This premise has been central to several of the projects to be described.

The therapeutic aspects of expressive art forms, and of the creative process, have long been recognized, but only of late have they been systematically studied. Many diverse art forms have been used with individuals who have experienced traumatic events, including drawing, painting, music expression, poetry, journal-writing, writing essays, story-telling, drama, movement, dance, pantomime, sculpture, ritual, sand play, and the collection of objects of remembrance[1] in the form of a personal collage (Kazanis, 1991). These expressive works help individuals transform their emotional pain, internal conflicts and feelings into words and other forms of expression. For example, by asking individuals who have experienced traumatic events to draw what they are feeling, by asking them to use self-selected objects of remembrance to artistically create their own 'small altars', Kazanis (1991) was able to help them on their 'personal journey of healing' and their 'ceremonies of transition and completion'. As we will see, art forms not only serve as outlets for expression and transformation, they also provide metaphoric means of creating new narratives. Perhaps this is most evident in the most ambitious structured art therapeutic programme by Dr Arpad Barath with children in war-torn Bosnia and in the expressive art therapy programme 'Art from Ashes' by Zelmut and Metrick, who worked with school children in Oakland, California, after the devastating fires of October 1991, as well as some of the other child and adolescent-based interventions.

HELPING THE CHILDREN IN BOSNIA

Dr Arpad Barath, who is at the University of Zagreb Medical School in the Department of Health Psychology, is the director of an extensive prevention and intervention programme to decrease PTSD among schoolchildren in Croatia. The programme has reached 40,000 children between the ages of 6 and 14, has involved 1,000 teachers and 40 school psychologists. More than 100 teams consisting of a psychologist and an art teacher have worked together in local schools to provide art expressive therapy, to undertake screening for PTSD and to produce educational materials (handouts, audiotapes, worksheets), as well as training.

The need for such a programme is quite evident when we learn that the war in Croatia has created 2 to 3 million refugees, 55% of whom are children and adolescents. The death toll has been estimated at 150,000 and those who survive have witnessed the horrendous sights of war and have felt direct threats to their lives. Barath reports that 35% of the children experience severe forms of PTSD. More girls than boys report the negative psychological after-effects of war that include general fear and anxiety, worry about family members, separation anxiety, depression over losses. Bloch (1993) reports that the Barath art-structured programme significantly reduced children's scores on standardized measures of PTSD (N = 5823), relative to their pre-intervention levels and relative to control groups.

The structured art programme called 'Images of my childhood in Croatia since 1991' moves each child through seven expressive stages of images of life before war, through feelings of fear and anger felt during the war, and finally, through stages expressing hope, love, and 'messages to the world'. In order to help the children overcome fear and their sense of powerlessness and to nurture feelings and beliefs in the future, the programme uses painting, poetry and music as expressive forms. More specifically, the seven thematic expressive stages included:

1. memories – paths to my childhood;
2. time – what happened to me since the summer of 1991?
3. space – where I am now?
4. fear – what I am afraid of and how?
5. war – what colour, touch and smell is the war?
6. peace – if I were a white dove . . .
7. love – if I were a magician . . .

For each thematic topic the children were exposed to a relevant piece of music, a form of art (e.g., Picasso's *Guernica* when the topic of war was introduced), and a guided visualization activity that included a prepared audiotaped exercise. Interestingly, the children's poetry and art works from this Croatia project have toured the US (Cincinnati, Philadelphia and other cities). Inquiries about the Croatia Project can be directed to Dr Ellen Bloch (515–221–8545) (Also see Bloch, 1993).

Shaw and Harris (1994) describe an intervention programme for 'children of war and children at war: child victims of terrorism in Mozambique'. In the context of an overall intervention regimen, they describe how expressive forms of art can be used therapeutically. They asked children to draw pictures of the 'worst moment', of the moment when they were freed from captivity, and 'what you would like to be in the future'.

HELPING THE CHILDREN IN THE OAKLAND FIRESTORM

A somewhat different form of expressive arts therapy was developed by Zelmut and Metrick (1992) whose 'Art from Ashes' project consisted of eight to ten weekly sessions of approximately sixty minutes each, that combined the talents of psychologists, artists and teachers. Through a variety of creative expressive activities the children who had to deal with the massive Oakland firestorm were invited to participate in school in group and individual art projects that provided an opportunity and outlet to get 'in touch' with their feelings of anxiety and fear and to do so in a supportive environment that nurtured co-operation and a sense of mastery. Illustrative projects included the following (see Zelmut and Metrick, 1992, for information on how to obtain more detail on the *Art from Ashes* guidebook):

1. Create a 'this is me' collage – cover before and after traumatic event. Create a collage of positive and negative consequences of the trauma.
2. Use of creative art to honour animals and pets that were lost in the fire.
3. Draw pictures of the fire, what happened now, and make cardboard shields as means of expressing control. (Use symbol of the phoenix as the bird who rose from the ashes.) The teacher also asked children to draw pictures of what they had learned, what they could do to feel better and safer, what they could do to be better prepared for future stressors, how they have changed.
4. Paint time lines of their lives to put the episode of the firestorm in perspective.
5. Read stories that are illustrative of coping (e.g. the Winnie the Pooh story which conveys that each ending is just another beginning) and that convey a sense of moving forward.[2]
6. Journal-making, puppet-making and doll-making. The doll-making came from the Guatemalan custom of using a tiny 'worry' doll to whom one turned over one's concerns and burdens.
7. Use 'safe-place' imagery and meditation – an imaginary safe place to which the child could enter. The child could invite a special protector or guardian angel to enter this place with the child and answer any questions or protect him or her.

At the end of the art projects the children had an art display for the other students, teachers and parents, so this became a 'healing ritual' of 'authentic' products.

HELPING THE CHILDREN OF THE LOMA PRIETA EARTHQUAKE

Spoffard and his colleagues (1992) have described a school intervention programme that serviced 25,000 individuals over a 16-month period following the Loma Prieta earthquake (October 1989) in Santa Cruz, California. A detailed handout describing the programme is available.[3] Their programme includes the use of children's art work, children group meetings, parent drop-in, and other activities. Consistent with the suggestions offered by other clinicians, Spoffard *et al.* employed the children's 'art work' as a way of nurturing a sense of their 'personal empowerment'. Following their initial expression of art that reflected what they had experienced, the children were encouraged to:

1. Draw themselves as being *more prepared* for another earthquake.
2. Share (tell) the group of fellow students about their picture. Children were also encouraged to take their picture home to share with family members. An art display was set up.
3. The art work was used as a *catalyst for discussion*. For example: 'Share one thing each child could do to prepare for any future earthquakes (aftershocks).' 'What is something positive that the child has learned about him/herself?' 'What was a favourite thing that you were glad was OK?' 'How did your pet respond?' 'What could the child do to comfort his or her pet (or younger sibling) should there be another tremor?' Put each child in a 'helper' role.

In a psychotherapeutic setting a number of clinicians have described how expressive forms can be used with children who have been traumatized. For example, Rhoe and Lynn (1991) have described how storytelling, imagination and fantasy can be used to help children who have been sexually abused. They ask the child his or her favourite tale, story character, and/or superhero. They then ask the child to build a 'safe place' in his or her fantasy and to fill it with the trappings or creatures that can help protect him or her. The child is asked how he or she can feel even better or safer in this place. For example, add a gate, use magic words, make special wishes, use certain coping responses (e.g., relaxation responses, things to say to him- or herself). They supplement this imagery procedure with storytelling. Brooks (1981) uses storytelling with creative characters to help traumatized children. The metaphorical stories usually include a representative of the child (e.g. an angry tornado, a hurt puppy), a representative of the therapist (e.g. a wise owl, a teacher, a detective), a representative of a moderator (e.g. a newscaster who interviews both parties and elucidates issues). The stories are usually *brief* and linked to the child's real life situation. This storytelling approach is to be contrasted with the lengthy and somewhat complex metaphorical stories offered by Davis (1990). Whatever the nature of the metaphorical stories used with children, the critical feature is the ability of the child to *generalize* what is learned in the story to his or her outside real-life situations. Deblinger *et al.* (1990) and Ruma (1994) have described how *cognitive-behavioural play therapy* can be used successfully with victimized children.

HELPING THE CHILDREN OF AN ITALIAN EARTHQUAKE

Galante and Foa (1986) used a 7-session school-based small group intervention for children in grades 1–4 following an earthquake. Each session had a cognitive, emotional and activity component (e.g. drawing pictures while listening or role playing). Children could express fears freely and 'irrational' fears and misinformation could be corrected. Various coping skills were practised.

NOTES

1 Kazanis (1991) reminds us of the many moving personal remembrances that have been left at the Vietnam Memorial in Washington, each with its own poignant and highly idiosyncratic personal meaning. Why do such commemorative behaviours aid 'healing'?
2 An illustration of this process was evident when I visited the public school in LaGuna Beach, California where they had experienced the devastating fires due to arson. The children had placed a large sign at the entrance that said, 'You can't have a rainbow unless you first have a storm.'
3 Spoffard, C.J. (1992) *School intervention following a critical incident.* Available from Community Mental Health Services, Project COPE, P.O. Box 962, 1060 Emeline Ave., Santa Cruz, CA, 95062.

REFERENCES

Bloch, E.L. (1993) Psychologists in Croatia work to ease trauma among young war victims. *Psychology International,* Summer. (Published by APA.) (Enquiries about the Croatian Project can be directed to Dr Ellin Bloch, Center for Traumatic Information and Education (CTTE), PO Box 55409, Cincinnati, Ohio 4525–0409 (tel. 513–321–4667) or from CTIE, 2522 Highland Avenue, Cincinnati, Ohio 45219 (tel. 513–221–8545, fax 513–321–8405).)

Brooks, R. (1981) Creative characters: A technique in child therapy. *Psychotherapy,* 18, 131–9.

Davis, N. (1990) *Once Upon a Time . . .: Therapeutic Stories to Heal Abused Children.* Published by Psychological Associates of Oxon Hill, 6178 Oxon Hill Road, Suite 306, Oxon Hill, Maryland 20745 (tel. 301–567–9297).

Deblinger, E., McLeer, S.V. and Henry, D. (1990) Cognitive-behavioural treatment of sexually abused children suffering post-traumatic stress: Preliminary findings. *Journal of American Academy of Child and Adolescent Psychiatry,* 29, 747–52.

Galante, R. and Foa, D. (1986) An epidemiological study of psychic trauma and treatment effectiveness for children after a natural disaster. *Journal of American Academy of Clinical Psychiatry,* 25, 357–63.

Golub, D. (1994) Special media review: Children's images of trauma. *Journal of Traumatic Stress,* 7, 329–33.

Kazanis, B. (1991) Finding and respecting our own way of grieving. *Creation Spirituality* (November/December), 42–3.

Rhoe, J.W. and Lynn, S.J. (1991) Storytelling, hypnosis and the treatment of sexually abused children. *International Journal of Clinical and Experimental Hypnosis,* 39, 198–214.

Ruma, C.D. (1994) Cognitive-behavioural play therapy with sexually abused children. *Journal of Child Sexual Abuse,* 3, 79–91.

Shaw, J.A. and Harris, J.J. (1994) Children of war and children at war: Child victims of terrorism in Mozambique. In R. Ursano *et al.* (eds), *Trauma and Disaster.* New York: Cambridge University Press.

Spoffard, C.J. (1992) *School Interventions Following a Critical Incident*. Santa Cruz, CA: Community Mental Health Services.

Zelmut, D. and Metrick, S. (1992) *Art from Ashes*. Available from Bay Area Arts Relief Project, c/o Cultural Arts Division, 474 14th Street, Suite 1130, Oakland, California, 94612.

The *Clinical Handbook on PTSD* can be ordered from Dr Meichenbaum. Send a cheque for $60 US Funds on a US Bank or an International Money Order made out to Don Meichenbaum. Mail to: Dr Donald Meichenbaum, University of Waterloo, Psychology Department, Waterloo, Ontario, Canada N2L 3G1. Upon receipt of payment, a book will be shipped.

CHAPTER 10

Helping the Helpers

Donald Meichenbaum

> I love my work but lately I find it contaminating my personal life. I have nightmares about the horrible things I hear about from clients, my sex life has deteriorated, I'm irritable and distractible, I'm afraid for my kids and tend to over-protect them, and I don't trust anybody anymore. I don't know what is happening to me.
>
> A therapist (as cited by Courtois, 1993: 8)

Working with clients who are 'in crisis', who have been traumatized, who have experienced human-induced victimization (e.g. family violence, war, torture, criminal assault, sexual violation), as well as horrific natural disasters, can have a 'traumatizing' impact on 'helpers'. The emotional and personal demands, as well as the technical challenges of this work, can lead to what has been called 'burnout' (Maslach and Jackson, 1981), 'compassion fatigue' (Figley)[1] and 'vicarious traumatization' (McCann and Pearlman). A number of authors (Chu, 1990; Courtois, 1993; Danieli, 1988; Haley, 1974) have discussed the impact on the therapist of working with 'traumatized' clients. Agger and Jensen (1994) have described distressed therapists as 'wounded healers'. (See the National Center for PTSD *Clinical Newsletter*, Spring, 1993 issue for a discussion, as well.) Straker and Moosa (1994) have discussed the stress on psychotherapists of working with traumatized clients in a country with continuing conflict and political repression.

Wilson and Lindy (1994) have described two major types of emotional strain experienced by therapists who work with traumatized clients. Under the heading of 'countertransference', they describe two types of therapist tendencies: Type I they characterize as the therapist's tendency to *avoid* and engage in *empathetic withdrawal*. Type II is the therapist's tendency to *overidentify* and engage in *empathetic enmeshment*.

The recognition of the potential negative impact of working with traumatized individuals is not limited to psychotherapists. It has long been recognized by those who work with emergency workers, firefighters, police personnel, and body handlers (e.g., see McCann *et al.*, 1988; Medeiros and Prochaska, 1988; Mitchell, 1985; Raphael *et al.*, 1983, 1984). For example, Raphael and Wilson (1994) review the literature that indicates between 20 per cent and 80 per cent of rescue workers have shown symptoms of prolonged stress response. They provide an analysis of the major themes common to rescue work. These themes that contribute to such stress reactions include:

1. force and destruction involved;
2. confrontation with death (massive, gruesome and mutilating death);
3. feelings of hopelessness ('helplessness of humanity');
4. feelings of anger (anger that more was not done, as well as sometimes being the recipient of anger from survivors);
5. significant loss and accompanying grief ('identification sympathy');
6. attachment and relationships ('strong bonds') that develop among rescue team members;
7. elation or 'feelings of triumph' among some rescue workers;
8. survivor guilt ('not do more');
9. voyeurism.

Our focus here is on psychotherapists and counsellors who work with 'victimized' clients or the 'survivors' of traumatic events. What can 'helpers' do to protect themselves from the stress that 'comes with the territory' of working with such challenging clinical populations? A number of suggestions have been offered in the literature and from the group of diverse therapists with whom I have had the privilege of working.

1. *Recognize that 'vicarious traumatization', as well as potential 'secondary victimization' are highly likely* in working with PTSD population. As Pearlman and Saakvitre (1994) have explained, 'vicarious traumatization' can result from the cumulative impact of trauma work and be evident in the form of 'depression, despair, cynicism, alienation, psychological and physical symptoms, withdrawal, and a heightened sense of vulnerability'. Listening to descriptions of 'horrific tales' can take a toll. The 'secondary victimization' that many health-care providers experience compounds this situation. There is the 'danger' that counsellors who work with 'traumatized' clients may come to feel isolated, distinct and rejected from other health-care providers. For example, questions may be raised by others, either surreptitiously or explicitly, as to whether the therapist may be inadvertently, unwittingly, and unknowingly, iatrogenically suggesting to his or her clients that they may have been victimized or abused. Such insinuations are especially stressful and threatening to therapists since there is the possibility of legal suits against therapists by clients and their family members who may retract their stories of abuse and charge their therapist as the 'cause' of their accounts of abuse. As noted, at the meeting of the False Memory Syndrome Foundation, workshops were offered to clients, family members and lawyers on how to represent 'retractors' in court and how to sue therapists.

2. In order to cope with such distress therapists need to engage in *personal, professional and organizational* activities. (See Pearlman and Saakvitre, 1994; Raphael *et al.*, 1983–1984 for a more complete account of possible activities, and Danieli (1994) for a series of exercises that therapists can engage in to deal with vicarious traumatization.) At this point I will enumerate a number of specific suggestions.

PERSONAL INTERVENTIONS

A. The therapist should recognize emotional, cognitive and physical signs of incipient stress reactions in self and in colleagues (increased self-awareness).

B. The therapist should *not* delimit clinical practice to PTSD clients only; balance victim and non-victim caseloads.

C. Limit overall caseload. Monitor caseload in terms of size and number of trauma cases.

D. Engage in self-care behaviours (e.g. relaxation activities of leaving work at work, vacations, exercise, 'soothing' activities like a massage).

E. Recognize that you are not alone in facing the stress of working with traumatized clients ('normalize' your reactions).

F. Engage in 'healing activities' and in activities that renew meaning of life, both in therapy and out of therapy settings. Some therapists report bringing into their offices 'signs of life and hope' such as plants and pictures that remind them of beauty and rebirth. Ensure physical and mental well-being (nutrition, sleep, relaxation, activity, creative expression, humour). Replenish!

G. Adopt a philosophical or religious outlook and remind yourself that you cannot take responsibility for the client's 'healing', but rather should act as a 'midwife on the client's journey toward healing'. Recognize limitations! Remind yourself of the 'healthy' parts of the client's story.[2]

H. Share your reactions with the client. As one astute clinician noted, 'Sometimes I tell my clients that there is a part of me that does *not* want to hear such horrific things, but there is another part of me that says we must continue because it is important, and doing so is part of the healing process. But I would not be honest with you (the client), if I did not comment that no one should have suffered, nor endured, what you have experienced. I am heartened by your willingness and ability, your courage to share your story, as part of the healing process.' Such statements to clients can often foster a stronger therapeutic alliance, highlighting the therapist's empathy and humanity. Such statements also convey to the client that his or her reactions are not unique, nor are those of the therapist.

PROFESSIONAL INTERVENTIONS

A. Maintain collegial on-the-job support, thus limiting the sense of isolation. Use case consultation and supervision. Establish a 'buddy system'. Ensure that you have an opportunity to share your reactions with understanding and supportive others and obtain peer supervision. Use a team for support, join a study group, attend conferences. I have had an opportunity over the last year to listen to audiotapes of a group of clinicians (family physician, psychiatrists, social workers) who each work with traumatized clients. These monthly meetings have proven both supportive and instructive for the participants. As an invited consultant I have provided feedback on their reactions. This supervisory model has worked well.

B. Where indicated the counsellors can undergo debriefing. It is suggested that counsellors discuss together the cases that were seen; what each counsellor did; how they perceived their clients; what the experience was like for them; whether they 'identified' with the traumatic events that their clients experienced or with their clients? Sometimes, outside professional services are useful in helping conduct these group meetings. Such sessions may cover such topics as, What is it like working with 'traumatized' clients? What is most difficult or challenging? What is most rewarding? What do you need now? How can we be of help?

C. Yassen (1993) has described how a time-limited group approach can be used with clinicians who have a history of trauma. The group can help therapists deal with self-doubts, ways to manage their own memories and feelings that are elicited in treatment. The need for such preparatory groups is underscored by the observation that often peer counsellors are used. For instance, in the Veterans Centres, 60% of the counsellors in the Readjustment Services programme are combat veterans, having served in Vietnam. Catherall and Lane (1992) consider the potential advantages and disadvantages of using patient therapists.

D. Become knowledgeable about PTSD. Seek professional training. Obviously, your reading this book shows good judgement, and hopefully, it will prove helpful.

ORGANIZATIONAL INTERVENTIONS

A. Some therapists, like their clients, find a 'mission' in trying to find meaning. They work actively to change the circumstances that lead to 'victimization' or they work on alleviating the distress of survivors. This may be done at a local, national or organizational level. Legislative reform, social action.

B. Encourage your local, state and national organization to educate professionals and nonprofessionals about PTSD. Engage in preventative activities.

C. Join a network of others who work with a PTSD population.

NOTES

1 Figley (1994) has developed a questionnaire to assess 'Compassion fatigue' (Florida State University). Also see book on *Compassion Fatigue* edited by Figley (1995, Brunner/Mazel).

2 I recall having been asked to review a text on cognitive-behaviour therapy for a journal. In the book, someone observed that what impressed her most about cognitive-behaviour therapy was that the therapist never seemed to 'give up'. With this observation in mind, I have often wondered why it is that various forms of cognitive therapy seem to work so well with depressed clients (see Munoz *et al.*, 1994). My tongue-in-cheek answer is that cognitive-behavioural interventions 'work', in part, because they help to prevent depression in psychotherapists. No matter what the client tells the therapist, from a cognitive-behavioural perspective, the therapist recognizes that the client's narrative account is only 'part' of the story that is coloured by mood, current appraisal and social context. Another way to cope with the accounts of 'victimized' clients is to view such descriptions as a set of coping techniques that were at one time adaptive and functional, but are currently being overused or no longer needed. The current treatment need is to help the client feel safe enough and resilient in order to become 'unstuck', and discontinue what was needed in the past but is no longer needed at the present time, and to employ 'healthier' ways to achieve his or her goals.

REFERENCES

Agger, I. and Jensen, S.B. (1994) Determinant factors for countertransference reactions under state terrorism. In J.P. Wilson and J.D. Lindy (1994) *Countertransference in the Treatment of PTSD*. New York: Guilford Press.

Catherall, D.R. and Lane, C. (1992) Symbolic recognition: Ceremony and treatment of post-traumatic stress disorder. *Journal of Traumatic Stress*, **5**, 37–44.

Chu, J. (1990) Ten traps for therapists in the treatment of trauma survivors. *Dissociation*, **1**, 24–32.

Courtois, C.A. (1993) *Adult Survivors of Child Sexual Abuse*. Milwaukee: Families International.

Danieli, Y. (1988) Treating survivors and children of survivors of the Nazi Holocaust. In F.M. Ochberg (ed.), *Post-Traumatic Therapy and Victims of Violence*. New York: Brunner/Mazel.

Danieli, Y. (1994) As survivors age: Part II. In *NCP Clinical Quarterly*, **4**, 20–4.

Figley, C.R. (1994) Systematic post-traumatic stress disorder: Family treatment experiences and implications. In G. Everly and J. Lating (eds), *Post-Traumatic Stress*. New York: Plenum Press.

Haley, S. (1974) When the patient reports atrocities. *Archives of General Psychiatry*, **30**, 191–6.

McCann, I.L. and Pearlman, L.A. (1990a) Vicarious traumatisation: A framework for understanding the psychological effects of working with victims. *Journal of Traumatic Stress*, **3**, 131–49.

McCann, I.L., Sakyeim, D.K. and Abrahamson, D.J. (1988) Trauma and victimisation: A model of psychological adaption. *The Counseling Psychologist*, **16**, 531–94.

Maslach, C. and Jackson, S.E. (1981) Measurement of experienced burnout. *Journal of Occupational Behaviour*, **2**, pp. 99–113.

Medeiros, M.E. and Prochaska, J.O. (1988) Coping strategies that psychotherapists use in working with stressful clients. *Professional Psychology: Research and Practice*, **1**, 112–14.

Mitchell, J.T. (1985) Healing the helper. In NIMH (ed.), *Role Stressors and Supports for Emergency Workers*. Washington, DC: NIMH.

Munoz, R.F., Hollon, S.D., McGrath, E., Rehm, L. and van den Bos, G.R. (1994) On the AHCPR Depression in Primary Care Guidelines. *American Psychologist*, **49**, 42–61.

Pearlman, L.A. and Saakvitre, K.W. (1994) Treating vicarious traumatization in therapists of adult survivors of childhood sexual abuse. In C. Figley (ed.), *Trauma and Its Wake* (Vol 111). New York: Brunner/Mazel.

Raphael, B., Singre, B. *et al.* (1983–1984) Who helps the helpers? The effects of disaster on rescue workers. *Omega* **14** (1).

Raphael, B. and Wilson, J.P. (1994) When disaster strikes: Managing emotional reactions in rescue workers. In J.P. Wilson and J.D. Lindy (eds), *Countertransference in the Treatment of PTSD*. New York: Guilford Press.

Straker, G. and Moosa, F. (1994) Interacting with trauma survivors in contexts of continuing trauma. *Journal of Traumatic Stress*, **7**, 457–65.

Yassen, J. (1993) Groupwork with clinicians who have a history of trauma. *NCP Clinical Newsletter*, **3**, 10–11.

The *Clinical Handbook on PTSD* can be ordered from Dr Meichenbaum. Send a cheque for $60 US Funds on a US Bank or an International Money Order made out to Don Meichenbaum. Mail to: Dr Donald Meichenbaum, University of Waterloo, Psychology Department, Waterloo, Ontario, Canada N2L 3G1. Upon receipt of payment, a book will be shipped.

CHAPTER 11

The Counting Method for Ameliorating Traumatic Memories

Frank M. Ochberg

The Counting Method is a technique for modulating and mastering traumatic memories in which the therapist counts out loud to 100 while the client silently remembers a traumatic event. Immediately afterward, the recollection is reported, discussed and reframed. This method is briefly described and its use within the context of ongoing therapy is explained.

By definition, Post-traumatic Stress Disorder (PTSD) includes episodic re-experiencing of traumatic events, usually in the form of dysphoric memories. Because these memories are vivid, frightening and unexpected, they have secondary effects, causing sufferers to doubt their sanity, their progress in recovery, their fundamental sense of security. The original traumatic experience had elements of terror, horror, or helplessness. Persistent episodes of traumatic memory continue and compound those elements.

Several clinicians have developed, tested and promulgated therapies designed to prevent or ameliorate traumatic memory and associated dysphoria (Foa, Rothbaum, Riggs and Murdock, 1991; Keane, Fairbank, Caddell and Zimering, 1989; Richards, Lovell and Marks, 1994; Shapiro, 1989). The Counting Method is one such approach. Although the method has been disseminated through instructional videotape (Ochberg, 1993a) and subsequent reviews (Bell, 1995; Wilson, 1993), this is the first written description and guidelines.

RATIONALE AND EFFICACY

The Counting Method was developed for use in the context of Post-traumatic Therapy (Ochberg, 1988, 1991, 1993b) by a skilled clinician who provides a full range of restorative opportunities to a PTSD client. Post-traumatic Therapy is collegial, normalizing and individualized. Its eclectic approaches include education, holistic health, social support and search for meaning. The goal is a realistic, enhanced sense of self, rather than merely symptom reduction. Survivor rather than victim status ('I look back with sadness rather than hate, I look forward with hope rather than despair, I may never forget but I need not constantly remember. I *was* a victim. I *am* a survivor'; Ochberg, 1988, p. 17) is another way of summarizing the goal of Post-traumatic Therapy.

The Counting Method is one element of Post-traumatic Therapy that has been employed for nine years with several dozen clients by the author, colleagues and students. In most cases, clients reported reduction in the frequency and intensity of dysphoric intrusive recollections. For example, a 40-year-old teacher was tortured and raped eight years before beginning Post-traumatic Therapy. Her symptoms included panic attacks, depression, and Post-traumatic Stress Disorder. Medication relieved panic and elevated mood, but flashbacks and intrusive recollections persisted. The Counting Method, begun six months after the first encounter, and utilized on seven occasions, resulted in eventual elimination of traumatic memories, sustained at four-year follow-up.

No clients reported negative consequences attributable to the Counting Method. Approximately 80% reported improvement in the frequency and intensity of traumatic memory.

The Counting Method works, theoretically, in several ways. First, the traumatic memory is connected to the therapist's voice and to the experience of therapy. A terrifying, lonely piece of personal history is associated with the security, dignity and partnership of Post-traumatic Therapy. Future recollection, spontaneous or deliberate, may evoke aspects of therapist and therapy and therefore be less frightening and degrading.

Second, the memory is contained within an interval of 100 counts – less than two minutes. This means that a relatively brief dose of traumatic recollection is received. Moreover, some control over the initiation, continuation, and conclusion of that recollection is experienced. With practice and encouragement, the client determines the duration of a particular memory and feels less anxious about future episodes of spontaneous recall.

Third, the intensity of dysphoria is deliberately raised and lowered during the counting. This affords another dimension of mastery, dosing and titrating one's thoughts and feelings, leading to enhanced self-control.

Therefore, the Counting Method shares some elements of Shapiro's (1989) eye movement desensitization (pairing a therapist activity with the traumatic image), of desensitization (relaxation during remembering), and of flooding (tolerating intense affect). But scientific determination of the way the method works and how efficacious it is must await controlled outcome study. This research is under way (Johnson, Lubin, Morgan and Grillon, 1995), evaluating clients randomly assigned to therapists cross-trained in Foa's (1991) flooding technique, Shapiro's eye movement desensitization, and the Counting Method.

SUMMARY OF THE METHOD

Having established that specific traumatic memories are part of a PTSD syndrome, the clinician offers the client an opportunity to recall a memory while the clinician counts to 100. The client is asked not to speak during the counting. After the counting the client is encouraged to tell what has just been remembered. After that, clinician and client discuss, reframe and digest the traumatic memory and the way the memory was modulated during counting.

Scheduling a counting session

PTSD clients may come to therapy soon after a traumatic event or decades later. They may or may not have told details to others. The trauma may have been circumscribed, prolonged, or repetitive. Rapport and trust between client and therapist may develop quickly or slowly. Some clients are reluctant to reveal details; others are grateful for the first chance to vent. For these and other reasons, there are no firm guidelines for timing the first counting session. But it is often helpful to advise the client that the Counting Method is an option for some future date, and can be scheduled when client and therapist agree the timing is appropriate. This demonstrates respect for the power of the traumatic memory and gives control to the client. It allows, metaphorically, elective rather than emergency surgery. It suggests that other dimensions of the therapeutic alliance come before tackling a core problem.

Once therapist and client agree that Post-traumatic Therapy is under way, that progress is occurring, that the client feels less like a victim and more like a survivor, the Counting Method can be scheduled.

Preliminary discussions

Some clients are willing to plunge into the Counting Method with little preparation; others want to know exactly how and why the method works. Depending upon the needs of the client, the following points can be discussed:

Counting affords the client a relatively short interval (100 seconds), with a beginning, middle and end, in which deliberately to recall an intrusive recollection.

1. Silent recall allows privacy.
2. Hearing the therapist's voice links the painful past to the relatively secure present.
3. Feelings of terror, horror and helplessness may recur during counting, but they will be time limited and, most likely, modulated by connection to the therapist.
4. The traumatic memory itself may be modified. That, after all, is the ultimate objective. If and when the memory emerges spontaneously at some future time, it may be attenuated by the experience of the Counting Method. The client will associate the dignity and security of therapy with the intrusive recollection.

Most clients who accept the Counting Method appreciate these theoretical points. Many have additional, practical questions:

- Will I be able to drive home?
- How many sessions will I need?
- Must I remember every trauma and every moment?

The therapist can assume that memories evoked during counting will be no worse than spontaneous re-experiencing (however, occasional exceptions occur when forgotten images return). If flashbacks have been recent, vivid and overwhelming, a companion to drive the client home *is* advisable.

The method is different from flooding or extinction of anxiety, in that once a client experiences some mastery over the memory there may be no need for further counting sessions. The experience of connecting one significant portion of a bank of traumatic memories to the therapist's voice may generalize to all traumatic memories. Often, two or three sessions are sufficient.

The day of the Counting Method session

When feasible, the first session of counting should be scheduled at a convenient time for client and therapist – e.g. at the end of the day, allowing extra minutes for closure. Counting should commence early in the session, but not before a review of progress. This helps dispel anxiety and pessimism. The therapist should ask which traumatic event will be recalled when several have been implicated in the PTSD. The client should be told to try to fill the 100 seconds with that memory, letting the worst feelings crest as the counting goes through the 40s, 50s, and 60s, then coming out of the past and into the present as the counting proceeds through the 90s.

The therapist might say at the outset, 'Are you comfortable? Just gaze off; you needn't look at me. Let's begin. 1 ... 2 ... 3 ...'

During the counting

The therapist should keep an eye on the clock to maintain a steady rhythm of approximately one number per second. Precision is not necessary, but standardizing the tempo facilitates replication.

Observe the client closely. There may be tears, grimaces, shuddering, clenching of hands or defensive postures. Conversely, there may be no sign of distress, which may mean that traumatic memories were not recalled and the method did not elicit sufficient affect.

Try to count in a clear and friendly voice, a natural voice. The qualities of the therapist and the experience of therapy are transmitted in the counting. Although a recitation of digits is not particularly personal, the fact that the therapist's voice is heard concurrently with recollection of terrible reality brings treatment and trauma together.

At 93 or 94 the therapist can say 'Back here', to assist those clients who need such a reminder. While counting is not meant to be hypnotic, it has that effect in some cases. A partially dissociated client is helped by the suggestion to return to current reality.

After the counting

When clients succeed at the task, voluntarily recollecting a trauma during counting and, possibly, re-experiencing that trauma, they usually appear dazed, moved or transformed. They may not speak for a while. They may feel some sense of accomplishment, some relief, or some residual terror from the original event. They may have recalled aspects of the trauma that were forgotten or repressed (psychogenic amnesia). They may be embarrassed and unwilling to discuss recovered memories (rarely) or be excited by the chance to share a revelation (more common).

The therapist is advised to wait for clients to speak, but if they do not or if they change the subject, the therapist should ask, 'Can you describe what you just remembered?'

Usually, this will uncork the bottle and a detailed narrative will flow. But not always. There may not have been meaningful recollection. Or the recollection may have been too intense for retelling. When the latter is the case, the therapist can assist by asking, 'What did you recall when I was counting in the 20s and 30s?' If the narrative is fragmented, further probing by the numbers (e.g. 'Now, how about the 40s . . . the 50s . . . the 60s') can help elicit the whole recollection.

Verbatim note-taking during this phase is useful because it allows uninterrupted reporting by the client and captures the images for later discussion. It also allows time between the solitary act of private recall and the collaborative endeavour of redefining a piece of personal history.

This is a time when many clients appreciate seeing their clinicians taking notes. Eye contact is less important than obvious attention to those very details that have been haunting and disrupting the PTSD sufferer.

Reflection and closure

Finally, the therapist and client discuss what has just occurred. There are several therapeutic objectives and many strategic options at this point. The most important goal in the outpatient setting is to end the session on a positive note, with the client composed enough to leave the office and secure enough to continue therapy. This may require deflection from the trauma scene and concentration on positive performance: 'You did well. You remembered. You turned the tape on and you turned the tape off.' Or the therapist can ask about the method itself: 'Did 100 seem like enough time? Too much time? Did my counting help or distract?' This process discussion diminishes strong affect.

Time permitting, the objectives of abreaction, ventilation and full disclosure of hidden aspects of the trauma may be accomplished. While the Counting Method is not designed to resemble a sodium amytal interview, it may have certain similar benefits. That is, relaxation may elicit sensations, thoughts and feelings that were previously inaccessible. The therapist should allow these to emerge as long as they are tolerable, and should express interest in returning to them at a future time.

The central objective of fusing the traumatic memory and the therapeutic experience can be enhanced by explicit direction. For example, 'In the future, when you recall that awful night, you can remember how you turned off the tape at 94, how you heard the counting, how we revisited the scene together.'

But such explicit direction may be superfluous. Clients usually know when they have mastered and ameliorated their traumatic memories.

In those instances when the method clearly fails (usually because the client could not remember, or merely restated the story silently, without emotion), the therapist must determine whether to repeat the effort or abandon it. Again, this should be a collaborative decision, made after exploring the reasons for the failure. Obviously, it is best to suggest that the method failed, not the client.

Further sessions

The question of whether and when to schedule further Counting Method sessions can be delayed until a later time. The first session usually leaves the client with more than enough to digest.

Some traumatic memories are relatively short and specific. These require relatively few sessions. Some are varied, multidimensional, with multiple meanings for the client. For example, a woman who was raped recently and abused as a child may require sessions dealing with several discrete episodes. She may prefer to have these spaced months apart. A person held hostage for days may have many elements of a prolonged trauma that he or she wishes to remember during a half dozen counting sessions.

Those who experience some relief after counting, but have continuing flashbacks, may request Counting Method sessions dealing with the same memory. In sequential sessions they confront different issues and perfect their sense of control and their courage to remember voluntarily.

Clients may deliberately alter their memories, adding fantasies of successful resolution, or of turning the tables on their assailants. One woman changed her abuser into a cartoon figure who ran away.

Bearing these possibilities in mind, therapist and client may discuss the merits of further sessions, their timing and their intended consequences. Post-traumatic Therapy concludes when survivor status is achieved. Counting Method sessions are scheduled to help reach this overarching goal of therapy, and should not unnecessarily prolong the process.

In sum, the Counting Method is one technique that may help clients with PTSD reduce the debilitating effects of traumatic memories. It was developed with out-patients receiving Post-traumatic Therapy from an experienced clinician. More experience is needed before therapists can know when to expect success by using the method. Outcome research is under way to test the validity of the method as a clinical tool.

ACKNOWLEDGEMENTS

The author gratefully acknowledges the support of The Dart Foundation of Mason, Michigan, and the assistance of David Read Johnson and Hadar Lubin.

REFERENCES

Bell, J. (1995). Videotape review. *Journal of Traumatic Stress*, 8(1), 197–9.

Foa, E., Rothbaum, B., Riggs, D. and Murdock, T. (1991). Treatment of post-traumatic stress disorder in rape victims: A comparison between cognitive-behavioral procedures and counseling. *Journal of Consulting and Clinical Psychology*, 59, 715–23.

Johnson, D., Lubin, H., Morgan, A. and Grillon, C. (1995). *Brief Treatment for PTSD. Research Study in Progress.* Yale University Department of Psychiatry.

Keane, T., Fairbank, J., Caddell, J. and Zimering, R. (1989). Implosive (flooding) therapy reduces symptoms of PTSD in Vietnam combat veterans. *Behavior Therapy*, 20, 245–60.

Ochberg, F. (ed.) (1988). *Post-traumatic therapy and victims of violence.* New York: Brunner/Mazel.

Ochberg, F. (1991). Post-traumatic therapy. *Psychotherapy*, 28(1), 5–15.

Ochberg, F. (1993a). *Frank Ochberg on Post-Traumatic Therapy. The Counting Method.* Camden, ME: Varied Directions & Gift From Within, 1–800–888–5236.

Ochberg, F. (1993b). Post-traumatic therapy. In J.P. Wilson and B. Raphael (eds), *International Handbook of Traumatic Stress Syndromes* (pp. 773–83). New York: Plenum.

Richards, D., Lovell, K. and Marks, I. (1994). Post-traumatic stress disorder: Evaluation of a behavioral treatment program. *Journal of Traumatic Stress*, 7(4), 669–80.

Shapiro, F. (1989). Efficacy of the eye movement desensitization procedure in the treatment of traumatic memories. *Journal of Traumatic Stress*, 2, 199–233.

Wilson, J.P. (1993). Videotape review. *Psychotherapy*, 30(4), 705.

CHAPTER 12

Journeying with the Traumatized – the Hillsborough Disaster

Michael J. Scott

On Saturday 15 April 1989 it was a beautiful spring day at home in Liverpool. I had just returned from taking my son for a walk, intent on listening to the Liverpool versus Nottingham Forest FA Cup semi-final on Radio Merseyside. Initially there appeared to have been some crowd disturbance. Then the true horror unfolded – 96 victims eventually died. That weekend there was an eerie silence over the whole of Merseyside. I felt a sense of bewilderment, puzzlement at how one can go from the everyday joy of a football game to a literal hell. Such tragedies affect not only the victims themselves who are at the epicentre of the trauma but also the wider community. Many of the friends and families of victims who heard the tragedy unfolding on the media were themselves traumatized. Counsellors are part of the wider community and, though touched to some extent by the tragedy themselves, have the task of soothing survivors and their families and friends. Large-scale disasters bring home to the counsellor the social dimension of individual distress and serve to remind the professional of the possibility of working not only with the traumatized individual directly but also indirectly via other survivors, family and friends.

LISTENING TO THE VICTIMS

It is a matter of respect for the trauma victim that society listens to their tale. In the case of the Hillsborough disaster, Liverpool Football Club players made themselves available to survivors and church leaders organized special ecumenical services. Social Service departments, voluntary organizations and some employers made staff available to help victims. Listening to survivors over the past ten years there has been much praise for the services in the immediate aftermath of the Hillsborough disaster. Special mention has been made of the involvement of the Liverpool players, in particular of the ongoing involvement of John Aldridge, now manager of Tranmere Football Club. A Hillsborough Family Support Group was formed, and for many this has been a focus at times such as the anniversary of the disaster and for the sharing of experiences such as their encounters with the legal system.

The 'unaffected'

In routine clinical practice clients are referred to the counsellor precisely because they are thought to be suffering from PTSD. This can give the practitioner the mistaken impression that debility is an inevitable response to the trauma. However, seeing survivors of a large-scale disaster serves as a reminder that a PTSD-like response is by no means inevitable. There were some individuals I encountered for whom the tragedy was a positive turning point. For example Peter, whom I met some weeks after the disaster, changed his whole approach to life. Before the incident he had been a workaholic, to his wife's dismay working every weekend and neglecting their 7-year-old son. After Hillsborough he decided that he was no longer going to work weekends and would spend the time with his son, and to his surprise he discovered how much he enjoyed taking him out. There were others for whom the experience was not a positive one, yet they were unaffected. A week after Hillsborough I met Matt, who described driving home after the match in silence and feeling surprised when on the Sunday he realized he had actually been involved in the incident. He has shown no problems relating to Hillsborough over the past ten years. But of those that I have met, Peter and Matt were the exceptions. Most have struggled to varying degrees to adapt to the memory of the incident, and although many appear to have won the battle, some are still debilitated ten years after the event.

I discovered that a person's initial neutral response to the trauma did not necessarily represent how they were going to fare. Brian, whom I met about one week after Hillsborough, was very matter-of-fact about the trauma and I simply gave him my card to ring if necessary. He contacted me about six weeks later. He had functioned well in the interim, until seeing a roll-call of the dead in alphabetical order on the television, and then saying to himself 'I should have been between the letters X and Y', he became very distraught. His distress, however, was relatively short-lived and confined to being phobic about going into lifts in work.

The 'affected'

Clinically there is no clear dividing line between those unaffected and those affected by a trauma. It is probably more useful to introduce an additional category of a sub-threshold level of disorder. The usefulness of this categorization became apparent when I met Bill, who suffered from Post-traumatic Stress Disorder after Hillsborough. He had been at the game with his brother and nephew and they were together in Leppings Lane, the epicentre of the tragedy. His brother had been totally unaffected by the incident, and in Bill's view relished every opportunity to talk about the tragedy. By contrast, his nephew totally refused to talk about Hillsborough and had become uncharacteristically irritable. It seems likely that the latter had a sub-threshold or sub-syndromal level of PTSD.

Bill was first referred about six months after the tragedy. His graphic description of the horror is still etched upon my mind. He described how he realized he was standing on a body and looked down to see a man's blue face. Bill had also seen a child passed over the top of the crowd, and he noticed that he had defecated. He remembered that though he was preoccupied with saving his nephew, strangely uppermost in his mind was the thought that if he failed he would incur the great wrath of his own aged mother! Unfortunately Bill had to give up his job, because he could no longer bear to be in the confined space of a cab. He became a recluse and has only recently made some very tentative connections with old friends. But he is still unable to tolerate any crowds. During the Euro 96 competition he inadvertently strayed into a pub in which football supporters were watching a match on television, and he was upset for days after this reminder. Quite why Bill should have been so badly affected compared to other family members is unclear. What is clear, however, is that the trauma itself is not the only important feature of PTSD.

Social support can play an important role in recovery from PTSD, and typically it is partners who chiefly exercise this pivotal role. But if both partners have been severely traumatized they may be unable to provide the necessary support, or even worse have a negative effect on the other. Barrie was a paramedic and went to the match with his partner. He had gone on to the pitch to render what help he could and was distraught that he had been unable to revive a young boy. His trauma-related guilt was so great that he resorted to drink and refused to talk to his partner about the trauma. Since the incident she has experienced panic attacks and become increasingly agoraphobic. Their relationship deteriorated and she left him to live with her mother. Jill and Barrie exemplified the complexity of trauma responses and how PTSD is often only one of many issues to be addressed.

Many of the Hillsborough victims that I saw became involved in litigation and to varying degrees this constituted a re-traumatization. At its worst, experts for the defendants' insurers conducted wholly unstructured interviews that the clients experienced as interrogation, believing themselves not to have been believed. One client was so distressed by an interview that afterwards she simply sat down on the kerb outside and cried. To help protect clients against such interviews I have written a set of guidelines for the legal profession so that they can properly assess the conduct and professionalism of the expert psychologist or psychiatrist in cases of compensation (Scott, 1998). It is important that counsellors offer clients appropriate guidance if they are seeking litigation. Clients are understandably seeking justice, perhaps even relishing their 'day in court', but there is an emotional cost to litigation to be borne in mind – some of the compensation cases following major disasters can go on for many years, and eight to ten years is not unheard of. Many litigants are seeking primarily an apology, but these clients need to be made aware that the only person likely to be in court is an anonymous individual from the defendant's insurers who is unlikely to lose any sleep over the outcome. Litigation is primarily a way of translating personal distress into financial terms, so that even if there is a fairly reasonable outcome financially, it is still quite likely that the client's anger is not fully assuaged. This is not at all an argument against clients pursuing litigation but the counsellor is well placed to explain the emotional consequences.

FACILITATING ADAPTATION

In the wake of Hillsborough the intervention model adopted by professionals was largely one of crisis intervention. At that time there were no standardized treatment protocols for PTSD that were routinely available. About eighteen months after Hillsborough the extra professional resources deployed to help survivors were withdrawn.

This was clearly in part a cost-saving exercise on the part of the authorities, but it also reflected an inadequate understanding of the natural course of PTSD. There appeared to be little understanding that though most of those affected by the trauma would have recovered naturally within about eighteen months, a significant minority would continue to be debilitated in the long term, and this latter group were left without any specialist resources. The author's experience of referred patients and litigants is that probably no more than 15% of those with PTSD are currently treated with a standardized protocol for the condition. In part this reflects a shortage of professionals with the requisite expertise, but it also reflects a view often found in mental health services that, so long as the counsellor is able to form a relationship with the clients, nothing further is required. A number of studies have shown that treatment outcome is correlated with therapists' competency and protocol adherence (e.g. Frank *et al.*, 1991). It seems likely that of those with chronic PTSD following Hillsborough, only a small proportion have received adequate counselling.

The use of a standardized treatment protocol does not mean that the counsellor ignores the social factors acting on the individual. Rather, such interventions should nudge the clients along naturally occurring pathways of recovery. For example Simon was referred to me by his GP three years after Hillsborough. I took him through the protocol described in Scott and Stradling (1992), involving his girlfriend in the treatment. After about six sessions no progress was being made. Then Simon encountered his 17-year-old friend who had been at the match with him. The latter was very debilitated and Simon was deeply moved by his distress. Simon began insisting that the friend practise precisely the strategies that he himself had been told in counselling, and became angry when the friend resisted his advice. After this encounter Simon realized that he could not give such advice without taking it very seriously himself. He then made a very speedy and lasting recovery. It is not suggested that the protocol will be acceptable to every client – for example Barrie, the paramedic mentioned above with trauma-related guilt, was never able to focus on the detail of Hillsborough sufficiently, his drink problem and domestic difficulties conspiring against this.

CHRONIC ADAPTATION

For those still suffering PTSD ten years after Hillsborough, their most pressing concern is now not so much intrusive recollection of the tragedy but rather a sense of having been damaged, often expressed as 'I am not the same person'. They are conscious that they have developed an inability to connect with their friends, family and the wider society. In many cases they look back upon the rupturing of relationships and the steady development of a hermit-like existence. The survivors have undergone an enduring personality change. Just as it is very difficult for the counsellor to engage clients with a personality disorder in the therapeutic enterprise, it can be similarly problematic developing a therapeutic alliance with what appears to be a client with a post-traumatic personality disorder (PTPD). Clinically it may be necessary to address not the only the PTSD but also the PTPD.

GRIEF AND BEYOND

Counsellors, friends and family have an obvious role in helping the bereaved cope with their loss, but what was also needed following Hillsborough was for mental health professionals to assist those who had experienced a different form of bereavement – the annihilation of the personality of their loved ones. Often this was not appreciated, and counsellors' efforts were directed almost entirely at a trauma victim. In retrospect it might have been more beneficial to include routinely, with the client's permission, a relative or friend of the victim in at least the initial counselling session, and to make further provision for the latter as necessary. Increasing attention has rightly been paid to the needs of rescuers and professionals involved in trauma work counselling sessions, but how much greater are the needs of family members who are constantly with the trauma victim. This social dimension of the Hillsborough tragedy was graphically illustrated in the play *Guiding Star* which depicts a family virtually destroyed by the devastating impact of the tragedy on the father. Interestingly the play ends with the victim and his wife trying to reconstruct their life by returning to the spot where they had many happy times courting. This process of construction/resurrection is at the heart of the constructivist approach described in this volume by Donald Meichenbaum. It is a process exemplified by Trevor Hicks, the leader of the Hillsborough Family Support Group, who himself lost two daughters in the tragedy and who has since devoted himself to seeking justice for those affected. Clearly not everyone so deeply affected by tragedy would or should cope in this way, but psychological survival does depend on developing or finding some sort of meaning and it may be that some belief systems confer some protection against the long-term effects of the slings and arrows of outrageous fortune.

REFERENCES

Frank, E., Kupfer, D.J., Wagner, E.F., McEachrn, A.B., Cornes, C. (1991) Efficacy of interpersonal psychotherapy as a maintenance treatment of recurrent depression. *Archives of General Psychiatry*, **48**, 1053–59.

Scott, M.J. and Stradling, S.G. (1992) *Counselling for Post-traumatic Stress Disorder*. London: Sage Publications.

Scott, M.J. (1998) Stress and compensation. In A. McDonald and A. Georges (eds), *Industrial Diseases Litigation*. London: Sweet & Maxwell.

CHAPTER 13

Power Therapies, Miraculous Claims and the Cures that Fail

Gerald M. Rosen, Jeffrey M. Lohr, Richard J. McNally and James D. Herbert

Recent 'Power Therapies' claim near miraculous cures but fare less well under controlled testing. These developments recall for cognitive behaviour therapists the history of past 'cures' that temporarily induced high levels of expectancies, but failed the test of time.

Long before Frank (1961) wrote his classic text *Persuasion and Healing*, Walsh (1923) had reviewed the history of failed therapies and noted the role of patients' faith in treatment. In an earlier volume, Walsh (1912) observed how faddish techniques of the day often parallel the latest developments in science. Now, with the approach of a new millennium, it appears that Walsh's observations still hold true. In recent years, a number of techniques called 'Power Therapies' (Figley, 1997) have been promoted as rapid cures for Post-traumatic Stress Disorder, phobias, and an ever-widening array of clinical disorders. Developed in the United States, and now taught around the globe, the Power Therapies include Thought Field Therapy (TFT: Callahan, 1985); Eye Movement Desensitization and Reprocessing (EMDR: Shapiro, 1989, 1995); Trauma Incident Reduction (TIR: Gerbode, 1988); and Emotional Freedom Techniques (EFT: Craig, 1997). As predicted by Walsh (1912), the Power Therapies parallel current themes in science and society; they borrow computer terminology by speaking of 'accelerated information processing', and they appeal to popular alternative health care models with an emphasis on tapping 'energy points'.

The most widely known and studied of the Power Therapies is EMDR. This technique involves the waving of fingers in front of a patient's face, or alternate manoeuvres such as finger snapping, to alter neural connections between affect, cognition and memory. Although the face validity of this technique is questionable, and its theoretical explanation approaches the limits of neurobabble (Lohr, 1996; O'Donohue and Thorpe, 1996), EMDR has been taught to over 23,000 clinicians worldwide in the short span of eight years. Training in EMDR now requires a 'Level II' workshop for certification in the eye movement method (Rosen, 1996), despite several studies finding that eye movements add nothing to treatment outcome (see

Lohr, Tolin and Lilienfeld, in press). Studies on EMDR (see Lohr, Kleinknecht, Tolin and Barrett, 1995; Lohr *et al.*, in press) further show that effects of the technique are largely limited to verbal report indices, and are no greater than those achieved by already established exposure-based therapies.

The empirical status and theoretical justification for other Power Therapies are even weaker. For example, TFT has been aggressively disseminated in trade magazines and the popular press, yet outcome and process research on the technique is virtually non-existent (Hooke, in press). TIR and EFT fare no better, although great claims of extraordinary cures are made by proponents of these methods.

Critics of the Power Therapies have noted the obscure theoretical foundations of these interventions and the paucity of evidence supporting their efficacy; such observations fail to explain the widespread popularity these techniques hold among mental health professionals. It is here that historical and sociological perspectives may illuminate relevant factors. Indeed, one of us (McNally, in press) has documented no less than sixteen striking parallels between EMDR and Mesmerism, an eighteenth century psychosocial intervention heralded as a breakthrough treatment for a remarkable range of ailments. Comparative inspection of these two interventions suggests that ingeniously promoted 'miracle cures' are likely to share many properties. They are often established by charismatic individuals whose visionary perspective inspires the masses of practitioners who struggle to treat hitherto intractable problems. Promises of rapid cures for human misery excite the hopes of besieged therapists, and remoralize sufferers. Leaders of these movements portray themselves as outsiders marginalized by a moribund Establishment whose scientific scepticism is little more than self-interested intellectual insularity. Training in the revolutionary treatment is shrouded in mystery, and obtainable for a fee. Individuals initiated into the system receive diplomas signed by the leader, or other formal recognition of their status, and they are told not to divulge the powerful methods to outsiders. In all these respects, EMDR and Mesmerism share striking similarities. The history of Mesmerism also suggests that maintaining ideological conformity within the Power Therapy movement will be difficult. Apostates are likely to emerge, claiming to have discovered more powerful interventions than those advanced by the founders.

Historical lessons derived from past 'cures' that temporarily induced high levels of expectancies, but failed over time, argue for sceptical caution among today's cognitive-behaviour therapists. Current research shows there is little reason for therapists to wave fingers in front of their patients' eyes, nor is there support for them to engage in elaborate tapping rituals while holding the notion that such ministrations accelerate information-processing or rebalance body energy fields. Well-established cognitive and behavioural principles are more likely to serve patients' needs as we approach the next millennium.

REFERENCES

Callahan, R. (1985). *Five Minute Phobia Cure*. Wilmington, DE: Enterprise.

Craig, G. (Producer, 1997). *Six Days at the VA: Using Emotional Freedom Therapy* (videotape). Available from Gary Craig, 1102 Redwood Blvd, Novato, CA 94947, USA.

Figley, C. (1997, December). The active ingredients of the Power Therapies. Keynote presentation at

The Power Therapies: A conference for the integrative and innovative use of EMDR, TFT, EFT, advanced NLP, and TIR. Lakewood, Colorado.

Frank, J.D. (1961). *Persuasion and Healing*. Baltimore: Johns Hopkins Press.

Gerbode, F. (1988). *Beyond Psychology: An Introduction to Metapsychology*. Palo Alto, CA: IRM Press.

Hooke, W. (in press). A review of Thought Field Therapy. *Electronic Journal of Traumatology*, http://rddz.stjohns.edu/traum/

Lohr, J.M. (1996). Analysis by analogy for the mental health clinician (Review of Shapiro, 1995). *Contemporary Psychology*, **41**, 879–80.

Lohr, J.M., Kleinknecht, R.A., Tolin, D.F. and Barrett, R.H. (1995). The empirical status of the clinical application of Eye Movement Desensitization and Reprocessing. *Journal of Behaviour Therapy and Experimental Psychiatry*, **26**, 285–302.

Lohr, J.M., Tolin, D.F. and Lilienfeld, S.O. (in press). Efficacy of Eye Movement Desensitization and Reprocessing: Implications for behavior therapy. *Behavior Therapy*.

McNally, R.J. (in press). EMDR and Mesmerism: A comparative historical analysis. *Journal of Anxiety Disorders*.

O'Donohue, W.T. and Thorpe, S. (1996). EMDR as marginal science (review of Shapiro, 1995). *The Scientist Practitioner*, **5**, 17–19.

Rosen, G.M. (1996). Level II training for EMDR: One commentator's view. *Behavior Therapist*, **19**, 76–7.

Shapiro, F. (1989). Eye movement desensitization: A new treatment for post-traumatic stress disorder. *Journal of Behavior Therapy and Experimental Psychiatry*, **20**, 211–17.

Shapiro, F. (1995). *Eye Movement Desensitization and Reprocessing: Basic Principles, Protocols, and Procedures*. New York: Guilford Press.

Walsh, J.J. (1912). *Pyschotherapy*. New York: D. Appleton & Co.

Walsh, J.J. (1923). *Cures: The Story of the Cures that Fail*. New York: D. Appleton & Co.

Afterword

Michael J. Scott and Stephen Palmer

The strategies suggested in this reader are a guide to best practice, in that they are derived from the positive cognitive-behavioural, adult and child PTSD outcome studies, yet adapted for the constraints of routine clinical practice. The counsellor can be confident that they are offering the best available help by reflecting on the review of adult outcome studies conducted by Van Etten and Taylor (1998). These authors assessed the effectiveness of an intervention by subtracting the mean of a sample before from that after, and dividing by a measure of the overall spread of results (the pooled standard deviation) to give an effect size, termed Cohen's d.

There have now been thirteen studies involving some form of a cognitive-behaviour therapy in the treatment of Post-traumatic Stress Disorder, with assessment based on structured interviews. These have yielded an average effect size of 1.89. The next most effective intervention is the class of drugs that includes Prozac and Seroxat (SSRIs – selective serotonin reuptake inhibitors) with an effect size of 1.43 based on four studies. It seems possible, therefore, that a combination of cognitive-behaviour therapy and SSRIs may prove particularly effective. These drugs were developed as antidepressants and it may be that in the future drugs will be developed to take account of the specific neurochemistry of PTSD and will therefore be even more effective. Though cognitive-behaviour therapy might properly be regarded as the treatment of choice, examination of the studies shows that the proportion of patients that clinically significantly improved, i.e. improved more than two standard deviations on their pre-treatment score, was no greater than one-half to two-thirds (see Foa et al., 1991) and that doubtless even more efficacious treatments will be developed.

The results of a controlled trial are not necessarily wholly applicable to patients in routine clinical practice. Though exposure treatments have had a demonstrated efficacy in controlled trials, in routine practice the procedure is relatively rarely used. In part this may be because of practitioners' lack of skill and/or bias against the method. But Scott and Stradling (1997) have examined client-compliance with exposure treatment in routine clinical practice. In the first study involving fourteen clients only one completed an image habituation procedure for homework in the manner advocated by its originators. In the second (N = 37), only 57% complied with audiotape exposure treatment, and compliance was related to initial symptoms severity and to severity of co-morbid depression. Thus it is important to know not only how effective an intervention can be but also how useful it is at the 'coal-face'.

There have been eleven studies that examined eye-movement desensitization repro-cessing (EMDR), but the mean effect size was 0.69, substantially less than cognitive-behaviour therapy or SSRI's (Van Etten and Taylor, 1998). But when scores on self-report measures were used as the yardstick, cognitive-behaviour therapy and EMDR were comparable, with effect sizes of 1.27 and 1.24 respectively. Whilst Rosen *et al.* in this volume (see Chapter 13) have raised doubts about both the efficacy of the eye movement desensitization reprocessing and the theory behind it, it may still have a place in the therapeutic armamentarium – a technical eclecticism may be the most appropriate response.

Smyth (1994), while not subscribing to Shapiro's (1995) theoretical position on EMDR, has made a case for an eye movement technique as a way of simply facilitating exposure and as an anxiety management procedure. In essence he has the client imagine a trauma-related image or a panic-related scene that produces a modest distress that is a score of six or seven on a one-to-ten scale of subjective units of distress (SUDS). He then moves his finger about twelve inches from the client's face across the client's field of vision at the rate of about one movement per second, coming back to the same spot about 25 times. Clients are asked for a SUDS score after each set of 25 and for their experiences during it. The procedure is repeated until there is a reduction of the SUDS score to four or five. Once this has been achieved the patient is asked to imagine another moderately distressing trauma or panic and move their eyes quickly from one corner of the room to the other 25 times. Again there is discussion about the impact of this on anxiety levels and the sets are repeated until a significant reduction in SUDS. When the patient is able to do this they can move on to performing the same procedure with their eyes closed. In this way clients can be given a very portable anxiety management technique as well as being enabled to start to interact voluntarily with the trauma memory. The technique could be a useful adjunct to those strategies already described in this volume and represents another way of overcoming the problem of exposure therapy in everyday practice.

Currently there is as much controversy over debriefing as there is over EMDR. Kenardy *et al.* (1996) examined the effects of stress debriefing on the rate of recovery of 195 helpers following an earthquake. There was no evidence of an improved rate of recovery among those helpers who were debriefed. Bisson *et al.* (1997) conducted a randomized trial of psychological debriefing on 133 burn victims and found that 26% of those who had psychological debriefing had PTSD at thirteen months compared to 9% amongst those who were not debriefed. But the debriefing group did have higher initial questionnaire scores. Wessely, Rose and Bisson (1998) have conducted a review of brief psychological interventions for the treatment of immediate trauma-related symptoms and the prevention of PTSD, and concluded, 'One session of psychological debriefing after recent trauma does not reduce psychological distress or prevent the development of post-traumatic stress disorder'. But Mitchell and Everly (1998) have made the point that there is a great variation in the contents of debriefing and that there ought to be a specification of the debriefing before going on to examine its efficacy. They claim that when the debriefing involves Mitchell's specific group critical incident stress debriefing model (CISD) the resultant mean effect size (Cohen's d) was 0·86, across the five studies they considered. But only two of the five studies they cite have appeared in journals. Thus the jury is still out on the efficacy of debriefing. Nevertheless mental health workers are likely to continue to be asked to provide debriefings following trauma and in the light of the studies mentioned it is necessary to ensure that any elements that might be even remotely harmful to clients are removed. It is in this context that the 'Guidelines for Crisis Counselling' in this volume are presented. Mitchell and Everly (1998) have made the point that their critical incident stress debriefing (CISD) was never intended to stand alone but to be part of a critical incident stress management package (CISM), and that it is this package that should be evaluated. This same need for a comprehensive package of interventions following a disaster was echoed in this volume by Scott in his observations on counselling provision following the Hillsborough football disaster.

Outcome studies on treating children with PTSD have lagged behind those for adults, but the results to date are encouraging. March *et al.* (1998) have examined the effectiveness of CBT as a treatment for children and adolescents with PTSD, and found 57% of subjects no longer meeting DSM-IV criteria for the condition immediately after treatment, and at six-month follow-up 96% were free. Two studies have also shown that cognitive-behaviour therapy is effective with sexually abused children (Cohen and Mannarino, 1996 and Deblinger *et al.*, 1996). Goenjian *et al.* (1997) demonstrated that a school-based grief and the trauma-focused cognitive-behaviour therapy intervention effectively decreased symptoms of depression following the earthquake in Armenia. In reviewing these studies Fletcher (1998) adds a cautionary note for practice:

> Directly addressing the trauma is not indicated for all children, however. Insistent focus on talking about the trauma may have adverse consequences for some, especially those who are symptomatic in the first place, or who are embarrassed by the circumstances or in some other way are resistant to discussing the event(s). In this case, more indirect methods of discovering and addressing relevant issues may be more helpful. These include techniques such as art and play therapy, or creative writing of stories, poems or songs.

This echoes the approach described by Meichenbaum in this volume (see Chapters 7 and 9). Though it is important for counsellors to be clear about the theoretical framework they are adopting so that there is a consistency of application, this should not blind them from acknowledging developments with the use of approaches with which they are not familiar, for example, Field *et al.* (1996) have demonstrated that massage therapy can help alleviate symptoms of PTSD among children exposed to a disaster such as Hurricane Andrew.

REFERENCES

Cohen, J.A. and Mannarino, A.P. (1996) A treatment outcome study for sexually abused preschool children: Initial findings. *Journal of the American Academy of Child and Adolescent Psychiatry*, 35, 42–50.

Deblinger, E., Lippman, J. and Steer, R. (1996) Sexually abused children suffering post-traumatic stress symptoms: initial treatment outcome findings. *Child Maltreatment*, 1, 310–21.

Field, T., Seligman, S., Scafedi, F. and Schanberg, S. (1996) Alleviating post-traumatic stress in children following Hurricane Andrew. *Journal of Applied Developmental Psychology*, **17**, 133–45.

Fletcher, K. (1998) Treatment recommendations for children and adolescents suffering from post-traumatic stress. *The Child Survivor of Traumatic Stress*, **3**, 3–6.

Foa, E.B., Rothbaum, B.O., Riggs, D.S. and Murdock, T.B. (1991) Treatment of post-traumatic stress disorder in rape victims: a comparison between cognitive behavioural procedures and counselling. *Journal of Consulting and Clinical Psychology*, **59**, 715–23.

Goenjian, A.K., Karayan, J., Pynoos, R.S., Minassian, D., Najarian, L.M., Steinberg, A.M. and Fairbanks, L.A. (1997) Outcome of psychotherapy among early adolescents after trauma. *American Journal of Psychiatry*, **154**, 536–42.

Kenardy, J.A., Webster, R.A., Lewin, T.J., Carr, V.J., Hazell, P.L. and Carter, G.L. (1996) Stress debriefing and patterns of recovery following a natural disaster. *Journal of Traumatic Stress*, 937–50.

March, J.S., Amaya-Jackson, L., Murray, M.C. and Schulte, A. (1998) Cognitive behaviour psychotherapy for children and adolescents with post-traumatic stress disorder after a single incident stressor. *Journal of the American Academy of Child and Adolescent Psychiatry*, **37**, 585–93.

Mitchell, J.T. and Everly, G.S. (1998) Critical incident stress management: A new era in crisis intervention. *Traumatic Stress Points*, **12**, 6–10.

Rose, S.W. and Bisson, J.A. (1998) Review: a brief psychological intervention (debriefing) is ineffective in preventing post-traumatic stress disorder. *Evidence-Based Mental Health*, **1**, 118.

Scott, M.J. and Stradling, S.G. (1997) Clients' compliance with exposure treatments for posttraumatic stress disorder. *Journal of Traumatic Stress*, **10**, 523–6.

Shapiro, F. (1995) *Eye Movement Desensitization and Reprocessing*. New York: Guilford Press.

Smyth, L. (1994) *Clinician's Manual for the Cognitive-Behavioral Treatment of PTSD*. Baltimore: Red Toad Company.

Van Etten, M.L. and Taylor, S. (1998) Comparative efficacy of treatment for post-traumatic stress disorder: a meta-analysis. *Clinical Psychology and Psychotherapy*, **5**, 126–44.

Wessely, S., Rose, S. and Bisson, J. (1998) Review: A brief psychological intervention (debriefing) is ineffective in preventing post-traumatic stress disorder. *Evidence–based Mental Health*, **1**, 118.

Appendix: Discussion Issues

The following discussion issues relate to the previous chapters. They are included for reflection, discussion or to assist lecturers in setting possible essay titles or course assignments.

Chapter 1

When is PTSD an easy diagnosis to make?
It is important to let the client set the pace of therapy. Discuss.
When might you encounter difficulties maintaining a stance of therapeutic neutrality? Have you ever suffered from 'vicarious traumatization' or 'compassion fatigue'?
False memory syndrome is problematic. Discuss.

Chapter 2

What are the possible advantages and disadvantages of structured interviews for the assessment of PTSD?
Should counsellors and other health professionals who have not received psychiatric training assess clients for PTSD? Discuss.
Do you usually use psychometric tests to assess clients? If not, why not?
The neurochemistry and neuroanatomy of PTSD is different when compared to depressed or stressed individuals. How, if at all, would this affect your choice of interventions?

Chapter 3

What are the main goals of crisis counselling? In what ways do you agree or disagree with them?
During a therapy session therapists and other helping professionals may wish to use realistic labels as opposed to the client's milder terms to describe the client's experience. Is this good therapy? Discuss.
It is beneficial to the client if the therapist expresses reasonable optimism about therapeutic outcome in the immediate aftermath of a trauma. Discuss.

Counsellors normally avoid giving clients advice. Why may this differ during crisis counselling?

Chapter 4

The prevalence rates of PTSD among men and women is relatively high. Discuss.
In what way would your approach to helping Paula be similar or dissimilar to the author's approach?
When considering PTSD, 'relapse reduction' is a more accurate term to use than 'relapse prevention'. Discuss.
What would prevent you from using the 'Yes . . . But' intervention?

Chapter 5

What is a narrative constructivist perspective?
In your opinion, what are the most valuable tools a practitioner can have in the treatment of PTSD?
What are the key differences between a 'here and now' as opposed to a 'there and then' therapeutic approach?
In hindsight, have you had clients who might have benefited from receiving a narrative constructive approach? Discuss.

Chapter 6

What difficulties may be encountered when helping a client suffering from PTSD with a concurrent addiction?
Clients suffering from PTSD are 'not the same person'. Discuss.
What difficulties may be encountered when running groups for PTSD sufferers?
In what ways, if any, would you want to alter the format of the ten-session group programme?

Chapter 7

Why does talking or writing about traumatic stress help?
How can talking or writing strategies and techniques be applied across cultures?
'If therapy is conducted on a group basis such letters can be read to the group.' What would be the indications and contraindications of this intervention?
What difficulties could be encountered when clients write letters to the perpetrator?

Chapter 8

The treatment goals at each phase are realistic. Discuss.
When do you assess the client's strengths?
'The quality of the client–therapist relationship by the third session has been found to be one of the best predictors of treatment outcome for all modes of psychotherapy.' Discuss.

How can counsellors enhance a good working alliance with clients suffering from PTSD or DES?

Chapter 9

'Art is a process of self-healing.' Discuss.
In Croatia more girls than boys report the negative psychological after effects of war. Discuss.
How can imagery be used to help children recover from traumatic stress?
When using metaphorical stories with children what factors would you take into account?

Chapter 10

How can a 'wounded healer' be recognized?
What can cause 'vicarious traumatization'?
What personal and professional interventions can be taken by practitioners to help deal with or manage vicarious traumatization?
Organizations can help their staff avoid vicarious traumatization. Discuss.

Chapter 11

Describe Post-traumatic Therapy.
'I was a victim. I am a survivor.' Discuss.
How is the Counting Method applied in the treatment of trauma and PTSD?
How does the Counting Method work?

Chapter 12

Do you remember the Hillsborough disaster? Do you recall how, when and where you heard about the disaster?
Tragedies become positive turning points for some individuals. Discuss.
Why is it possibly useful to introduce an additional category of a 'sub-threshold level' of PTSD?
What role can social support play in recovery from PTSD?

Chapter 13

This chapter gives an extreme view of the 'Power Therapies'. Discuss.
In what ways do you agree and disagree with the authors of this chapter?
Is the empirical status of the 'Power Therapies' debatable?
'It is fair to compare EMDR with Mesmerism.' Discuss.

Afterword

Are the strategies suggested in this reader a guide to best practice?

A combination of cognitive-behaviour therapy and SSRIs may prove particularly effective in the treatment of PTSD. Discuss.

What are the problems when using techniques at the 'coal-face'?

In the future technical eclecticism will become the most favoured approach when helping clients suffering from PTSD. Discuss.

Index